Forum Italicum
Filibrary Series
No. 25

'Merica

A Conference on the Culture and Literature of Italians in North America

Edited by
Aldo Bove and
Giuseppe Massara

Forum Italicum Publishing
Stony Brook, NY

Library of Congress Cataloging-in-Publication Data

'Merica
A Conference on the Culture and Literature
of Italians in North America

p. cm.
1. Italian emigration. 2. Italian Americans. 3. Italian American literature. 4. Italian Americans - social life and customs
I. Title II. Series

ISBN 1-893127-25-7

FORUM ITALICUM
Center for Italian Studies
State University of New York at Stony Brook
Stony Brook, NY 11794-3358
USA
http:// www.italianstudies.org

Table of Contents

Section III: The Linguistic and Literary Perspective

Section IV: The Shapes of a Culture

INTRODUCTION

'Merica, a conference on the Culture and Literature of Italians in North America, was held in Rome and Cassino in January 2003.

The conference was sponsored by the University of Rome *La Sapienza*, the University of Cassino, the State University of New York at Stony Brook and the *Centro Studi Americani*. This book represents the proceedings of that important cultural event, which we believe marked a change in the general attitude towards this field of studies.

Although in the present format the essays have been arranged in a slightly different order, we have maintained the general framework of the conference. Its interdisciplinary approach is reflected in this book.

Experts in different fields — literature, history, anthropology, linguistics, cinema, geography, fine arts — on both sides of the Atlantic, were invited to discuss crucial developments in Italian American studies. We hope these insights shall be as clear to the reader as they were to conference participants.

There is no doubt that we are living in an age of deep, fast and radical transformations, making cultural adjustments especially difficult, thus bringing to the fore issues regarding roots, ethnicity, identity and even nationality. These categories have been, and still are, largely conflictual; they have political and social implications. For example, Italy is facing the phenomenon of immigration that is influencing Italian culture and life, posing a number of largely unanswered questions. Reflecting on the significance of Italian emigration in the past and on its present consequences encourages reconsideration of some of the concepts crucial for the interpretation of the migratory phenomenology in a dynamic perspective — a view that nowadays is particularly useful.

Underpinning this book is the theoretical interconnection between two different processes: identities in the dialectics of distance and return; and the problematic of identity itself in light of evolving perceptions of the self in societies that have growing multiethnic populations. In this book, we have made an effort to emphasize new approach studies, so it does not have the rigid structure of traditional academic publications.

Interdisciplinarity is particularly relevant and bodes well for the future of research in the field. The conference was particularly forthcoming from this point of view. In fact we regret omitting the interesting contributions of O. Caldiron, R. D'Attilio, F. Marotti, P. Miller, and G. Montaldo, presenters at the Round Table on Sacco and Vanzetti, because they dealt with visual material which could not be shown here in satisfactory detail.

There is one unifying element in the contributions presented here: language, rather than memory, seems to be the real issue at stake. In other words, the processes of expression and communication seem to have been investigated more, or given greater importance, if compared to concepts of identity based on ideas such as heritage, tradition, and family. Which suggests formulating ideas of ethnicity on the basis of actual attitudes of individuals interrelating with specific and limited cultural environments, producing personal, original syntheses. Be it the iconographic and symbolical evidence of Madre Cabrini, or the dramatic perception of Dante's permanence, or the reassuring image of fulfilled dreams in the dialectics of generations, we have the chance to look at the Italian American experience as a potential model of ethnical dynamics in which belonging is less momentous than active consciousness.

It has been well over a century since Italians began their mass migration towards North America, without parallel in Italian history. Consciousness involves a keener sense of appropriation of an objective historical perspective, when current social dynamics may occasionally prove fragmentary and superficial, unable to suggest an identity, or offering distorted identities. In this way consciousness does become an equivalent for meaning. There are an estimated 35 million Italians in North America, many still fighting against the stereotypes that tagged them since emigrating. The Mafia is a case in point. Between 1972 and 2003 more than 260 films have been produced about the Mafia in North America (an average of nearly nine movies a year). Some of these depictions were TV serials which have quite a large following (*The Sopranos*); newspapers and magazine articles often exploit what has become an easy convention, reinforcing an image that is unbalanced, unfair and damaging to the collective reputation of the fifth largest ethnic group in North America.

The role of research is to extract sense and meaning from evidence that appears contradictory and so, at this stage of development, it seems quite natural that issues connected to definitions of Italians in North America are relevant in light of current events and developments in the field of identities. No doubt this book advocates a dynamic approach to the question of identity: we feel that is an important contribution towards reconsidering its theoretical status, given the tragic outcomes and potential dangers of former and easier definitions in terms of static cultural boundaries and heritages.

We are therefore convinced that 'Merica was particularly useful towards that end. We want to take the opportunity to express our wish that the conceptual lines which proved so fruitful at the Conference may be further developed and refined.

We are grateful to the State University of New York at Stony Brook, and to Prof. Mario Mignone, as well as the Center for Italian Studies, for the opportunity to publish these Proceedings.

'Merica was really the result of a joint effort and a positive spirit of cooperation that brought together the University of Rome La Sapienza, the University of Cassino, the Centro Studi Americani in Rome and the State University of New York at Stony Brook. The scientific Committee, chaired by Prof. A. Lombardo, included A. Bove, F. Buffoni, G.G. Castorina, A. D'Alfonso, G. Fasano, L. Ferrarotti, D. Fiorentino, A. Gebbia, G. Massara, F. Marotti, M. Mignone, B. Pisapia, C. Palagiano, F. Pontuale, F. Rosati, R. Severino, M. Vedovelli. We take the opportunity here to express our sadness at the loss of Agostino Lombardo, a great scholar whose belief in this conference and whose support were invaluable. Unfortunately he died before seeing this book published.

We thank all the institutions and people who made the conference a success, in particular the English Department of the University La Sapienza and its staff, and the Department of *Linguistica e Letterature Comparate* of the University of Cassino; the Faculty of *Lettere e Filosofia*, the *Centro Teatro Ateneo* and the Geography Department of *La Sapienza*, which helped in organizing three different exhibitions, one film showing and other visual documents. Special thanks to the *Centro di Eccellenza Osservatorio Linguistico Permanente dell' Italiano Diffuso fra Stranieri e delle Lingue Immigrate in Italia* of the Università per Stranieri at Siena for its dynamic participation in the event. Thanks also to the Dipartimento di Lingue per le Politiche Pubbliche of La Sapienza. Although it is not possible to mention here all the people and institutions who in different ways contributed over a number of months in nearly three years to make the material realization of that event possible, special thanks are due to N. Ceramella, A. Gebbia, F. Mitrano, F. Pontuale, I. Ranzato, C. Scura, and P. Vaglioni. Thanks also to O. Callegaro, C. Carnevale, P. Matteo, I. Platerotі. Among the many sponsoring institutions, those which gave significant support were the United States Embassy in Rome, the Cultural Agency of Quebec in Italy, the *Provincia di Roma*, and Guernica Editions.

A final thanks to Prof. L. Fried and K. M. Crane and to all those individuals who made useful suggestions, provided ideas and contacts, contributed constructively with their comments and criticism, and to the scholars and intellectuals who sacrificed their time to create what can be considered a harmonious outcome.

ALDO BOVE
GIUSEPPE MASSARA

Rome, July 2005

SECTION I

ITALIANS IN HISTORY, POLITICS, AND SOCIETY

MOTHER CABRINI'S HALO AND THE SYMBOLIC ORDER OF THE ITALIAN IMMIGRANT COMMUNITIES

William Boelhower
University of Padua

The Italian-born nun Frances Xavier Cabrini was officially acclaimed America's first citizen-saint by Pope Pius XII on July 7, 1946. Her golden legend and the special quality of her holiness are based above all on her life and work among Italian immigrants in the United States and Central and South America at the end of the 19th and the beginning of the 20th century. Although there are well over six biographies, memoirs, and diaries — not to mention several websites — dealing with this universally acknowledged patroness of immigrants, the current generation of historians and scholars in Italian American studies have largely ignored not only her considerable accomplishments as a founder of schools, hospitals and orphanages but also her abiding presence among those communities where her religious order once brought spiritual solace and material aid. She certainly deserves a place among those truly major figures who helped to shape American urban history at the turn of the last century, and much work still needs to be done at the micro-historical level to clarify the exact nature of her achievement and of her greatness as a person and a mystic.

With the publication of his 1960 biography, *Immigrant Saint, The Life of Mother Cabrini*, Pietro Di Donato, who was once esteemed for his classic novel *Christ in Concrete* (1939) but then quickly forgotten, suddenly found himself a best-selling author. The edition I have of *Immigrant Saint* is a popular Dell paperback reprinted by the Catholic Book Club with the permission of Mc-Graw Hill and prefaced by an appreciative letter to the author from Cardinal Joseph Pizzardo. It is important to note that Di Donato's biography of Cabrini came out the same year as his novel *Three Circles of Light*. Presumably, he was working on both at the same time, perhaps even at the same desk. The latter narrative ends with Annunziata, just widowed, telling her children the following: "Thy father ...left thee hurriedly and without warning, to work on God's mansion, and to construct the foundation of our very true home. He was especially selected and honored by

God, the Master Builder, because thy father is the best of bricklayers. The walls of God's house are to be plumb and level, and each brick in bond" (187). It was with the idea of continuing the work of building God's mansion among the Italian immigrant communities in the Americas that Pope Leo XIII convinced Sister Frances Xavier Cabrini, already the foundress of her own burgeoning religious order, to carry out her mission there instead of in China (Galilea 57-60; Di Donato 54-60). Her achievement on this side of the Atlantic is now a matter of history and legend.

The Golden Legend of Sister Frances Xavier Cabrini

Cabrini arrived in New York on March 31, 1889, and, while living and working in the heart of the Italian ghetto on the Lower East Side, immediately threw herself into the work of finding a home for her apostolate. As a local newspaper noted at the time:

> In these weeks, a group of women, of brunette complexion, dressed like Sisters of Charity, have been seen walking through the streets of Little Italy, climbing up narrow and dark stairs, going down to basements and even risking to enter certain corners where not even the police dare to set foot. They wear a habit and a veil different from those of others. Few speak English. It is an Institute which looks after orphans and all its members are Italian. The five or six sisters who have settled in this city are the pioneers of the congregation in the United States. They are led by Mother Frances Cabrini, a woman with large eyes and an attractive smile. She does not speak English, but she is a woman of firm determination" (quoted in Galilea 68; originally in *The New York Sun*, 30 June 1889).

By the time the saint died in Chicago on December 22, 1917, she had succeeded in turning cities across three continents into a landscape of Christian service, testimony, and miracle. No philanthropic institution or government agency matched her in establishing such a wide network of hospitals, orphanages, schools, and novitiates for the poor, mostly inner-city, immigrant communities in the Americas and in Europe. And although frail and of delicate constitution, Mother Cabrini put up with severe hardships and moved relentlessly from one continent to another before her mortified body finally gave out on her. Pietro Di Donato begins his biography with her birth on July 15, 1850, to a devout peasant family living in the town of

Sant'Angelo Lodigiano in the region of Lombardy, Italy. She was the fourteenth of fifteen children and her mother was already 52 years old when she gave birth to her.

As I have already noted, there is now a small shelf full of books devoted to the first citizen-saint of the United States, but none are written as well as Di Donato's or with as much passion and awareness of what life in America's Little Italies was like at the turn of the 20th century. He writes, so to speak, as an insider. Religion and wrestling with belief are at the very center of Di Donato's fictional preoccupations, and writing about Mother Cabrini was evidently part of his life-long effort to come to terms with them. Thus his narrative is devotional in purpose. He chooses to begin it with the popular legend that when she was born a flock of doves flew over the town, one even flying up to her window the very moment she came into the world, as if to announce her auspicious coming (7-8). Writing in the 1990s, an accomplished Cabrini biographer like Segundo Galilea shuns such a legend as inappropriate, but as Mary Sullivan points out in her biography, narratives of saints' lives are also made of this kind of appreciation.

Hagiography, the highly codified genre about narrating saints' lives, belongs to the history of biography but concerns truths of a higher order than mere history (de Certeau 269-283). The dove at Cabrini's window is worth recounting not for its factual importance, but for its epiphanic value. A professional biographer would simply ignore it or any other legendary event of the kind. But Di Donato recounts the saint's life because it is edifying and exemplary. In short, as her letters and *Pensieri* demonstrate, we have much to learn from her when it comes to commitment, purity of intention, sacrifice, service and, most importantly, the virtues of faith, hope, and charity (1982: 76-86). In the darkest moments of her life, when her very mission seemed on the verge of failing and her adversaries were eager to celebrate her defeat, Mother Cabrini never despaired in the Sacred Heart or in the ultimate success of her missionary activities. As novelist-biographer, Di Donato has no intention to subject Cabrini's holy life to the conventions of modern biography, although he clearly employs its mode of documentary sifting. Significantly, when the National Women's Hall of Fame placed her on its prestigious rolls in 1996, it did so for her humanitarian work, as if she were another Jane Addams. But Cabrini was much more than a humanitarian. She was a saint. And as her *Pensieri* convincingly reveal, she was also a mystic, totally devoted to the Sacred Heart.

Today, we would perhaps want to place Cabrini in the company of a Dorothy Day or a Catherine de Hueck Doherty or even more appropriately in the austere sisterhood of a Simone Weil or an Edith Stein. She is certainly of that stamp. But what distinguishes her so clearly from Weil, for example, is that Cabrini's life is immediately associated with two groups: first, that of the Missionary Order of the Sacred Heart and secondly, that of the various immigrant communities she assisted. Like all saints, she is firmly associated with specific places and these function as so many instances of an extended topology of her founding work — namely that of building God's mansion as mentioned above. Cabrini's life also helps us to distinguish both the time and places of the Italian immigrant colonies in such cities as New York, New Orleans, Denver, Seattle, Chicago and elsewhere. Her founding work both multiplies and connects these places, and her life is rightly celebrated as coextensive with them. All this, however, is insufficient when it comes to appreciating the mystical depths of her spirituality.

Named "Patroness of Immigrants" in 1950 by Pope Pius XII, Mother Cabrini created what we might call a specifically Cabrinian topology within the American urban fabric. Di Donato's biography movingly introduces us to immigrant cityscapes of unacceptable humiliation, of marginal and blighted lives threatened with religious prejudice and violence and racial hostility. It is into such places that Cabrini went to offer her assistance, invariably creating community where previously there were only alienation and resignation. It is no wonder, then, that her founding acts are never less than dramatic, often agonistic, and generally requiring of her exceptional aplomb, courage, perseverance, decisiveness, and *savoir-faire*. As she often counselled her fellow missionaries in her letters, about a thousand of which survive, "Go beyond yourself in all things, you who have wonderful opportunities to make big gains and advance yourself on the way to perfection. Occasionally, offer up the bitter food you eat to the Most Sacred Heart of Jesus for my intentions" (1968: 258-59). And again, "You bear the name that obliges you to be holy in everything and this is what I wish for you" (504). According to hagiographic conventions, her biographers peremptorily order her deeds in a taxonomy of heroic virtues — of "heroicity" *tout court*, if you will. This is what assessing the status of sanctity is all about

(Woodward 50-87, 251-279). The cartography of her foundations and the narrative repetition of her heroic virtues are recounted in her golden legend in order to exemplify how God intervenes in history. Mother Cabrini's reputation ultimately underscores the glory of God. In other words, her life is theophanic.

Thus Cabrini's biographers read the saint's apostolic itinerary providentially — for signs — fully aware, however, that her life also expresses a highly personal economy of salvation. And as we become familiar with the legendary vicissitudes of her story, it inevitably dawns on us that this life is, as the Swiss theologian Hans Urs Von Balthasar would say, theodramatic (106-23). Thus we find her writing in her letters, "The tree that is battered by the wind grows strong; so it is with our Institute which, having grown in the midst of tribulations and often beaten by winds and tempests, is assuming ever widening dimensions" (1968: 488); and in an equally characteristic passage from a late one: "Another (sister) wished that I might encounter many trials and tribulations and that I might see the Institute vehemently contested; which I greatly enjoyed. Pray now with your whole heart that I will be able to face all this with a vivid faith and great generosity, as is proper to a Missionary who bears the name of the Most Sacred Heart of Jesus, who came to earth… for no other reason than to walk in the midst of tribulations, sorrows, torments, agonies, and extreme rebuke" (616).

In truth, in Cabrini's eyes, her world is more theater than mirror. The metaphor of the world as theater best captures the tensions, pace, and abrupt shifts of the saint's constant travels as she crosses the ocean some twenty-two times in not more than twenty-eight years of missionary service abroad. Here the letters — and letter-writing itself — prove to be stunning texts of high spiritual and physical drama. In effect the theodramatic metaphor very closely matches her own apostolic sense of her life and times. "*Vegliare*" (stay alert) and "*slancio*" (drive) are two spiritual watchwords that run through her writings and life. In the letters and *Pensieri* we get an urgent, on-the-scene understanding of her mission in both a public and intimate register. While in Granada, Nicaragua, in 1891, she describes her spiritual state in a way that captures the essence of her dramatic life: "See, oh Jesus, how my little boat must struggle against the immense waves of difficulties and dangers; I pray Thee! Watch over it, oh Jesus, and never let it sink. I feel a great trust in you and, in abandoning myself to your Divine Heart, a deep peace has entered my own heart and comforts me" (1982: 108).

The Gift of Being Called

A good part of the theatrical staging of Mother Cabrini's life derives from the notion of calling or vocation — that is, the act of responding to a Divine summons, commiting oneself to a specific direction, serving God through a mission. I mention this because today we no longer think of what we do with our lives in terms of a calling. Nowadays we have jobs, and we pass from one to the next without too much ado. At the most we have a profession, but a religious calling is significantly different from Max Weber's notion of *Beruf*, based on the idea of a rational scope. Vocation is closer to the notion of *servitium* (service) and goes in tandem with *munus* (burden), which is the root of *communitas* (sharing a common burden). A calling is traditionally considered a gift; it is something we are given. Moreover, everyone has a calling, although we can easily ignore it. As Cabrini's life so dramatically bears out, the idea of *responding* to a call involves her in the burdens of *responsibility*: Will she live up to her mission with her whole heart, mind and soul? Looked at as a gift, the idea of 'being called' also implies a sense of election, of fidelity to it, of nurturing and interpreting it rightly. All this requires a state of constant wakefulness and *slancio*, as Cabrini explains again and again in her letters to her fellow missionaries.

The demands of wakefulness are generated by one's being called and they become manageable and less indeterminate through the instrumentality of prayer and a series of virtues, which are also gifts: hope, trust, prudence, obedience, and so forth. Today the language of virtues is no longer spoken in common, as Alisdair McIntyre in *After Virtue* has famously pointed out. We no longer agree as a community on what a shared list of such virtues might be. For determining who is a saint, however, holiness is still measured by the theological and cardinal virtues, the spiritual and corporal works of mercy, the evangelical counsels, and humility (Crosby 157-264). In this respect, Mother Cabrini's life is more important as a model than as a proper name. As foundress of a religious order, her biography is nothing less than exemplary.

Cabrini's travel-driven life specifically illustrates the effectiveness — the theophanic inscription — of the Sacred Heart in the Americas and in Europe. As Di Donato notes, it was above all Pope Leo XIII who pointed her in this direction and favored her own already fervent attachment to the politics of the Sacred Heart. Here her reading of other mystics deserves further exploration, in particular her penchant for Saint Margaret Mary Alacoque (1968: 257; 1982: 57, 83, 85-86). On the one hand, Cabrini's missionary achievement is articulated in the visible manifestation of some 67 foundations — hospitals, schools, orphanages, novitiates, teacher's schools. And we should not forget that this multiplication of her works took place in a very short time span, from 1889 to 1917, which is a wonder in itself, something truly extraordinary if not miraculous. On the other hand, this foundational work was also accompanied by the multiplication of vocations to the Missionary Order of the Sacred Heart.

This overflowing abundance of vocations, directly related to the exemplary life of Mother Cabrini as superior general of the Order, points necessarily to a symbolic order. In other words, her foundations also alert us to an order of signs alluding to the unleashing or synergy of a tremendous power. If we look at almost any one of the sites or foundations, we immediately see that a mighty agency is embodied in them and a mighty convergence of assistance and participation. Where previously there seemed to be no community, now one springs up — over night, so to speak. And out of the pennies of the poor, sizeable buildings materialize, as if out of God's hat.

Di Donato has us look at each site as an evident manifestation of not only Cabrini's work, but also that of the Italian immigrants and, of course, the Sacred Heart — the three agencies that contribute to the feasibility of each foundation's taking place at all. Cabrini's golden legend represents the synergy of these powers. In truth, the saint's cartography of foundations and, equally, the narrative topology of her life that determines its scale exhibit a theory of what saintliness is as a manifest symbolic order. To be sure, the sequence of places is strung along a recognizable temporal axis. But their symbolic order is projected onto it and cannot be reduced to the temporal axis. This distinction has often caused biographers a good deal of embarrassment. It is this symbolic order linking Cabrini's halo — her holiness — and the Italian immigrant community that deserves further comment now.

For while the topology of scattered sites associated with Mother Cabrini's name responds readily enough to the descriptive order of traditional biography and historiography, the nature of the act of founding does not. Nor for that matter does the programatic activity of her Missionary Order. The nature of this founding act, performed again and again and generating a landscape of repetition, pertains to the prescriptive order embodied in the emblem of the Sacred Heart and the Missionary Order's rule. This prescriptive dimension is apostolic (Cabrini's sense of Mission), ecclesiastical (Pope Leo XIII's mandate), and mystical (the spiritual dedication of each and every sister to the way of perfection). Thus, the naked image of the Sacred Heart embodies a mission, a politics, and an ascetic spirituality.

As evidenced in both her writings and her daily life, Cabrini's Order ideally embodies a mystical sisterhood of saints. The letters and *Pensieri* firmly outline this aspiration and spell out a profoundly ascetic and contemplative mandate. The saint demanded of her sisters whole-hearted commitment, self-detachment, self-abnegation, disciplining of the flesh, humility, simplicity, constant prayer, and obedience. Their life was to be an *imitatio Christi* (an imitation of Christ) and thus lived as a *scientia crucis* (a science of the cross). The Order's apostolate was specifically to assist the Italian immigrants in the Americas and Europe, and this included teaching, catechizing, visiting the sick and the imprisoned, building foundations, and general pastoral care. Cabrini envisioned her vocation as a call to spread the faith and fight the war against materialism, unbridled liberalism, and the secularizing forces of modernism; and even more fundamentally, of course, she sought union with the Sacred Heart.

As evidenced in Mother Cabrini's saintly life, the symbolic order of the Sacred Heart — and here one should keep in mind the encyclicals *Rerum Novarum* (1891) and *Annum Sacrum* (1899), both by Leo XIII — translates into a sequence of places and a multiplicity of foundations which, in turn, illuminate the space of a constancy. And I should add, this constancy is altogether prescriptive. In order to embrace the full synergy of this symbolic dimension, we might place this space of her peculiar wakefulness within a broader interpretive economy. Again and again, Cabrini's biographers recount how at the very last moment money arrived or an unexpected decision was made or some sudden providential coincidence occurred that made a particular foundation possible. What is more, it seems that Cabrini never doubted for a moment that things would eventually work out. She had an incredible confidence and trust in God, people, and things.

The Pure Gift Made Visible

Acts of giving, specific gift occasions, are frequent enough in Cabrini's life to encourage us to read the sequence of foundations as a gift-trail. And this path of gifts not only implies a gift sensibility but something much grander, something having the same paradigm effects as Von Balthasar's theodramatics. Gifting at such a scale of representation as Cabrini's foundational deeds suggests and even demands the positing of a horizon of donation (see Marion 2001a: 1-34). For what perdures at the theodramatic level, that of Cabrini's life, is precisely the agency of giving, of an excess of giving that is phenomenologically evident but is not reducible to a concept or the blinkered forms of secular biography. The French theologian and philosopher Jean-Luc Marion would say that these Cabrinian sites are, in effect, saturated (2001b: 242-246, 277-280).

By moving consciously within this horizon of donation, we put ourselves in a position to capture the movement in Cabrini's life from ordinary to heroic goodness; and from this vantage point we can also watch her clinging in love to a single reference point or, if you will, to the intimate space of a vocational constancy which she shares with the sisters of her Order. And within this same horizon of donation, the legendary space which the saint passes through folds and unfolds in order to display a gift which has become a place, and thus another piece of a specifically Cabrinian topology. This gift-in-place also expresses the taking place of a community (a *koinonia*, if you will), and there can be no community without the horizon of donation to sustain it and bring it into being. Mother Cabrini's foundations, in fact, are nothing if not temples of the Sacred Heart. During her lifetime she often repeated the prayer, "*Omnia possum in Eo qui me confortat*" (1968: 494, 530, 606, 617). She points to the prescriptive nature of this space when she writes in a letter, "the Sacred Heart does not need either me or any of you… rather it is we who need the Sacred Heart of Jesus and it is He who does us a great deed of charity by admitting us among the number of his Missionaries" (1968: 131).

The horizon of donation embraces two extremes, both an economy of salvation and a social order of solidarity, so that the inevitable structural distance between meaning and reference in secular historiography and biography is now overcome by pragmatically blending them in the horizon of donation. The Cabrinian topology of places and acts is in fact eminently pragmatic, but it is also sustained by the pure referentiality of prayer. There is abundant evidence in Cabrini's letters and *Pensieri* of her ascetic giving of self, in imitation of the Sacred Heart. Such is the donnée of her vocation, but this gift of herself, through her apostolate, also reveals a deep recognition of her indebtedness. This is one dimension of the structure of donation that runs through the life of the saint. Christ's giving of self on the cross, the *passio Christi*, leads Cabrini to a science of holiness based on an initial avowal, "Yes, I am nothing, nothing am I worth, but with the help of my most beloved Spouse, I can do everything...for the glory of God, if He wishes" (1982: 183). We have in this declaration the exact opposite of an autarchic perspective that claims, "I don't owe anybody anything."

The other dimension of the structure of donation is that of the *munus* of the Italian immigrant community. The mission of founding schools and orphanages that is prescribed in Cabrini's apostolate and exemplified heroically in her own life mediates gifting among the immigrants. It prompts them to enter the sphere of giving, to own up to the debt they as donors acknowledge in Cabrini's decision to act "in His name." All told, we have a remarkable synergy of donative forces embodied in the Missionary Order's sustaining pragmatics and the mediating figure of Mother Cabrini. As the American theologian John Caputo notes, "A gift is above all something *to do*" (209). Of course, Cabrini, by committing herself totally to her calling, would attribute the gift effect to the mystical economy of the Sacred Heart and then reference it through a liturgical act of praise.

At any rate, what is most evidently manifest in the Cabrinian immigrant topology is an excess of givenness. In the final count Mother Cabrini's saintly life presents us with the fact of an infinite unpayable debt, the dimensions of which can only be construed within the horizon of donation I am suggesting here. Cabrini's own life of giving found its counterpart in the donative sensibilities of the Italian immigrant diaspora, which repeatedly came together as community in order to take on the *munus* of the missionary foundation of the Sacred Heart. What seemed impossible to so many — the building of a hospital or a school out of practically nothing — became possible through the prescriptive agency of Mother Cabrini and her Order. This setting aside of oneself, this *sacrum facere* (making holy), is in the end what saintliness is all about. And to think that Frances Xavier Cabrini considered herself a mere spectator: "it's You who works in me, it's you who does everything, and I am not even a tool in your hands, as the others say.... I am but a spectator of the great and beautiful works that you are capable of performing" (1982: 117). All of her works, we should not forget, were for the most part free.

I have discussed at some length Frances Xavier Cabrini's legendary life because it is so evidently one of the outstanding examples in our country's recent history of the gift economy at work. And it is precisely as an example of a total social fact that we can establish its value because if the gift cannot be successfully defined, at least it can be recounted and appreciated. Cabrini is a case in point. Although historians and literary and cultural studies scholars continue to ignore Cabrini's achievement — with the rare exception of a scholar or two like Richard Sennett (2003: 131-135) — her lesson in charity had no rival in early 20th century America. In addition, through the dedicated agency of her sisterhood of aspiring saints, the very horizon of donation embodied in that apostolate now becomes fully manifest. In other words, the circuit of Cabrini's foundations represents a spectacular instance of Derrida's pure gift made visible (7-33), and it does so by implicating thousands upon thousands of gift-sensitive immigrants who eventually went on to remake and re-compact the nation. Today, as we learn that even the most recent waves of immigrants are also involved in sustaining a fraternal, social and economic ring known as the *hwala*, we realize it is but one more example of the gift principle as it has shaped crucial moments in our cultural history and helped to define us as a traditionally generous people.

Works cited

Cabrini, S. Francesca Saverio. *Lettere*. Milan: Editrice Ancora, 1968.

_______. *Pensieri e propositi*. Rome: Centro cabriniano, 1982.

Caputo, John D. and Michael J. Scanlon, Eds. *God, The Gift, and Postmodernism*. Bloomington and Indianapolis: Indiana UP, 1999.

Crosby, OFM Cap, Michael. Solanus Casey, *The Official Account of a Virtuous American Life*. New York: The Crossroad Publishing Co., 2000.
De Certeau, Michel. *The Writing of History*. Trans. Tom Conley. New York: Columbia UP, 1988.
Derrida, Jacques. *Donare il tempo. La moneta falsa*. Trans. Graziella Berto. Milan: Raffaello Cortina Editore, 1996.
Di Donato, Pietro. *Immigrant Saint. The Life of Mother Cabrini*. New York: Dell Publishing, 1962.
_______. *Three Circles of Light*. New York: Ballantine, 1960.
Galilea, Segundo. *In Weakness, Strength. The Life and Missionary Activity of Saint Frances Xavier Cabrini*. Trans. Colette Joly Dees. Quezon City, Philippines: Claretian Communications, 1996.
Marion, Jean-Luc. *Dato che. Saggio per una fenomenologia della donazione*. Trans. Rosario Caldarone. Turin: Società Editrice Internazionale: 2001a (Published in 1997).
_______. *De Surcroit*. Paris: PUF, 2001b.
Mauss, Marcel. *The Gift: the Form and Reason for Exchange in Archaic Societies*. Trans. W.D. Halls. London: Routledge, 1990 (First published 1925).
Sennett, Richard. *Respect, In a World of Inequality*. New York: W.W. Norton and Co., 2003.
Von Balthasar, Hans Urs. *Introduzione al dramma*. Vol. 1 of *TeoDrammatica*. Trans. Guido Sommavilla. Milano: Jaca Book, 1978.
Woodward, Kenneth L. *Making Saints*. New York: Touchstone, 1996.

AUTOBIOGRAPHICAL WRITINGS AND OFFICIAL HISTORY

Emilio Franzina
Università di Verona

After a prolonged period of silence from Italian academia, for some time now the importance of the migratory phenomenon has also begun to be considered in Italy.[1] Indeed, emigration has been, for our country, rather like the other face (or the interface) of its recent historical evolution, starting at least from the middle of the nineteenth century. It may never have been noted, but if one considers the dates of the progressive growth of migratory flows from Italy (e.g. the 70s and 80s in the nineteenth century), they overlap with the dates of the political unity of the nation and its difficult establishment. If the first fundamental goal of the foundation of a unitary state in 1861 was the beginning of a "new history," it was left to the successive decades to create an effective common national conscience, often imposed from above by the classic means: education, conscription, and so on. It is evident that emigration paralleled the phases of this posthumous achievement: that is to say it took place following the establishment of the political state. In particular, emigration in North America accompanied and supported the difficult formation of that sense of belonging which before unification seemed, and was, rather uncertain and vague all over the peninsula. It is essential, as many experts in *ancien régime* territorial mobility[2] warn us, not to forget that "dispositions" to expatriation existed in Italy before its "borders"were drawn. Crossing them began the phenomenon of emigration abroad in the proper sense of the word in the second half of the nineteenth century. Afterwards the change concerned the links existing between socio-economic dimensions and features and the political and existential aspects of the issue. These very aspects, in the long run, but sometimes even before they came to fruition, ended up characterizing the diaries and even the autobiographies of the emigrants themselves. An enormous mass departure, as we know, doomed to last much longer than others occurring in various parts of Europe in about the same years when our migratory waves chose first the south, and then, between the nineteenth and twentieth centuries, the north of that "Merica" where millions of men and women, unsatisfied or disappointed by their country of origin, pinned their hopeful expectations. However, on crossing the ocean and settling down either temporarily or for good, they brought different cultural heritages with them and made their mark.

In fact, Italians, at least for many decades, did not emigrate from Italy but from its various regions.[3] The specific acquisition of a general sense of belonging to one's national community as that evoked above took place earlier and more easily abroad, while changes towards the "invention" of being "Italians" in their home country proceeded gradually, running into major difficulties.[4]

The latest census carried out in the United States in 2000 recorded the presence of 16 million American citizens of acknowledged Italian descent. Such a sense of being Italian (*italianità*), although sifted through the filter of thousands of crossings, can be certainly claimed with pride, since the social mobility which took place in the meantime allowed the Italian immigrants to place themselves little by little in a very different position from that of their predecessors. As historians and literary people alike know well, respecting chronology is unavoidable. In other words, we need to pay the utmost attention to periodizations. As a matter of fact, we cannot talk about Italian emigration or about Italians abroad as if they were the same thing. The condition of Italian Americans at the end of the nineteenth-century was quite different from that experienced by the early mass of immigrants at the beginning of the twentieth-century; likewise the condition of those Italians who arrived between the two wars was different as was that of the Americans of Italian descent in the second half of the twentieth-century. Moreover, the numerical ratio between the very limited figure of the last post-war emigration and all the preceding ones shows that, in the meantime, Italians as a whole have been pretty successful. In the last phase of this century-long cycle, which ended in about the 1970s, there is a sort of relative *vacuum*.

Indeed, only a few thousands Italians emigrated to the United States after World War II. Perhaps we should compare this data with that of the immigration towards Canada and South America, which, by contrast, had started again at full speed and lasted until the end of the 1950s. This would help us to understand the impact, in memoirs and autobiographies, that the latest generations were going to have on the relationship with the cultural and literal history of the preceding periods.

Halfway through, when emigration to the United States seemed almost over, due in part to the restrictions on entry into the country imposed by the

USA authorities, Carlo Levi in an article published in "Life" in 1947,[5] outlines in an extremely precise and clear way the course of the whole phenomenon in over a century of Italian migration to the New World.

He notes that the peasants, especially those from southern Italy, used to arrive in the United States with their own culture: a rural village culture, which was very much at odds with the idea that American intellectuals had created of Italian culture, which was "high culture." It naturally comes to mind to wonder then[6], what relationship, what probable (or possible) web of links there was between the concrete history of the immigrants (a history of life and work in a context not always welcoming...) their traditions and the great history of Italian culture, and how or when it best reflected itself in the production of memoirs and "ethnic" narrative. The question takes a different value and meaning if the first autobiographer whom we would like to take into consideration belonged, for example, to the early phase of Italian emigration to the United States, the 1820s and 30s. In this case, reference should certainly not be made to any southern peasant, but to famous immigrants including refugees and liberal patriots like Lorenzo Da Ponte. This leading personality, regardless of his fame or ambitions, often experienced many of the problems immigrants had to tackle during his *incognito* wandering for professional reasons.[7] On the other hand, we know what emigration was like at the beginning of the nineteenth century. It was, unquestionably, mainly political,[8] and seems not to have had many links with the successive "popular" emigration, even if a praiseworthy and rather long work, the first volume of *Italoamericana*, an anthology edited by Francesco Durante, has brought to light some autobiographical writings of Italians living in the States in the first half of the nineteenth century. In this book, we feel the sense of this particular presence which, in effect, did not only precede but even conditioned outcomes of the successive mass emigration and even some of its "literary destinies."[9] As we will see, this will be the case, at least from the recollections of autobiographies and memoirs resulting from the reality of the experience of emigration and immigration.

It is appropriate here to underline, from another point of view, how the interest in the development of writings and biographical narrative grew as time passed, roughly around the second half of the 1970s. It must also be said that this phenomenon has emerged because of the research and intense work of experts and intellectuals, mostly of Italian origin, in the United States as well as in the other countries where Italian workers and peasants went (but, as shown by the much wider social spectrum of emigrants, especially in the twentieth-century, they were not the only ones). In fact, it is rarer to find an equal "curiosity" in authors and researchers who have no (or are not proud of) Italian family "roots."[10] This detail also gives foundation to bringing the official history together with the minor history of most biographers and diarists of immigration to America.

In order to address the question which I hold most dear — the proper chronological frequency of emigration — from now on I will proceed by putting together the pieces of a puzzle, based on certain autobiographical sources concerning this social phenomenon. It should also be noted that exceptional social growth in the States allowed Italians to become what they are today: top historians, critics, sociologists, etc., who are, in turn, able to reflect on the group to which they originally belonged. Almost none of the analysts or the experts with an academic background, perhaps because they fear being melodramatic or competing with rhetoric of migrants suffering, have dealt with migration since the topic gained contemporary political salience. Some examples do exist: the real-life stories interwoven with official history and reflected in the autobiographical narratives where the excessive and long-lasting cost paid by many people cannot go unnoticed. This is the very price paid for adaptation and settling, leading to the final integration in America, which, after all, immigrants generally paid, especially those who arrived last. In fact, Italians, up to a certain point and, in any case, until World War One, were among the last of the migrants to the United States; hence, they are the "newest" of the protagonists of the new European emigration. Consequently, as we can infer from most of the available autobiographical evidence, the price they paid was very high, and above all, as time went on and generations changed, it could not possibly condition the doings of those who were about to "become Americans," by also affecting the formation of what is still, and partly remains, a "mixed" identity. One bears only one specific identity, "political" or ethnic — that is unchangeable. Identities are stratified and multiple by definition, unless they are, more often than not, the result of a deliberate choice. Becoming American implies also wishing to be American, perhaps, since it is possible, without giving up one's grandparents' and parents' identity, which represents one more step towards the choice of an identity involving force of character and will. If today, each corner of New York, Boston or San Francisco, where Italian descendants have given birth to children and grandchildren of Italians, means something to those who still live there or that feel it as their own in the way described by Robert Viscusi in his *Astoria*, this has happened or could have happened "at a certain point in time" after it had seemed for a long time that living in America was "naturally" like living in a *no-place*.

On the other hand, this has not always been the case. Thanks to the autobiographical writings of emigrants, immigrants and their early descendants, it is possible to trace and establish a chronology of immigration, indicating its various types and showing the links, or at least throwing light on the intersections between the "official" history, usually dealt with by social or economic historians, and the "minor" history (e.g. not only private or marginal) of average people, and also the dynamics from the ground in which they were involved or which they gave life to with different degrees of awareness. It is certainly very hard to find traces of a direct relationship between migration and high politics, which may fill or clutter up the pages of history books in the autobiographies of the immigrants who had a relationship with powerful men or influential groups. Yet, in my opinion, there are many moments when the history of the weakest and poorest necessarily intercepts official history and helps it to find its bearings.

Without giving grounds to easy populisms, which perhaps is very fashionable nowadays, I believe this is proved by the many biographies that embrace the whole period of the "great emigration."

As certain recent studies on the Great War, Italy and America by D. Rossini, L. Sau and others have shown, the "emigration" variable has had a certain importance in some phases of the history of international relations between our country and the United States, although this relevance changes according to historical moments and the diplomatic, economic or wartime circumstances in different contexts.[12]

I have often wondered about the psychological reaction to the enlistment in the American Army, during the Second World War, of many sons of Italian immigrants to the United States between the beginning of the nineteenth century and the Great Depression. But, on reversing the roles, I have also wondered about the probable parallel bewilderment of the American soldiers who, on moving northwards between 1943-45, met such humble peasants and shepherds in the villages they passed through. These people were able to answer them, perhaps in an approximate, broken English, but which still showed a certain knowledge of the United States and a familiarity with American matters: a situation which was rather unexpected. What was the psychological reaction of the young Italian American soldiers' parents, who remained in the States, while all that was happening in Italy? Perhaps an exhaustive answer to these questions can be found only in the memoirs of some of the protagonists or, in the recollections and experiences of people who went, came back or stayed in America during the great phase of immigration between the middle of the nineteenth and twentieth centuries, which were admittedly sources for some great novelists like Melania Mazzucco in *Vita*.

However, it is worth recalling that, even among historians, most of these themes have only recently been included on the agenda, and that for a long time there was merely an anecdotal or superficial interest instead of the scientific approach required for such studies which was included in historiography mainly towards the end of the 1960s.

Furthermore, it is in this period that the collection and analytical study of the written evidence produced by common people began, at least this was the case in our country, even if it was necessary to wait for about twenty years till this would become a common practice and lead to a systematic, widespread approach.[13] However, the mid-seventies saw a real divide in Italian research, as shown by the first investigations carried out on the subjectivity and real life of the working or lower classes by di Bosio and Montaldi, which were indeed the first archives of common people's writings.[14] But this split represented the beginning, this time in the United States, of a genuine interest in the traditionally "marginalized," in some kind of "ethnic revival" concerning mainly emigrants (without excluding the various minority groups, the youth and women, the marginal or marginalized segments of the population, and so on) and which, after having lasted for a rather long time, perhaps is a bit outdated today. In any case, it is stimulating, and not just for mere concomitant reasons, to see how in about the mid-sixties, among those people who took stock of their lives, there were also individuals who had lived for over fifty years in a migratory "Merica," depicted and described in autobiographies generally hovering between literary narrative (or foolish aspiration) and memory.

This question of autobiographies and their publishing and "literary" links initially disregarded some other noteworthy facts emphasized in their stories. If the awareness of being about to give historical evidence is heartfelt by the immigrants who write or, like Rosa Cavalleri, are willing to give interviews,[15] their awareness must be linked to the background events and the implications of the "emigratory/immigratory epos." And, mind you, one could begin from very far indeed. In fact, other levels of the relationship between Italy and America are mirrored in the management of literary production in publishing ever since the dawn of mass emigration. The first draft of the book, *Un italiano in America* by Adolfo Rossi, which was written in Terni in 1884, soon after the author's return home, was published under the almost incredible title, *Nacociù. La Venere americana. Avventure degli emigranti al nuovo mondo!* by the "popular" bookseller Perino in Italy in 1889. This was a favourite book with the readership but, paradoxically, before meeting with success, its title and, above all, its publisher had to be changed. It would become the best known account of *Un italiano in America*,[16] bearing, like all the other autobiographical evidence of the time, the signs of and, in a sense, the reasons for many repressions in the near future. In some successful autobiographies there was already a patent undertone of embarrassment and shame for the appalling living conditions of many Italian e migrants w ho ha d no choice a nd c ontinued no t t o ha ve o ne, b ut dragged out a wretched existence which became an inevitable object of contempt, and every now and then, of ill-treatment and xenophobic harassment by the natives and even by many of those, among their own compatriots, who had overcome the status of being immigrant and had put down roots in the local society becoming completely assimilated.

Pompeo Coppini, a Mantuan sculptor who would spend the rest of his life in Texas, after emigrating to the United States in 1896, described the first impact the late nineteenth century Little Italy of New York had on him in writing his memoirs, *From Dawn to Sunset (dall'alba al tramonto)* in 1849.[17] He remarked that what he saw followed a prescient and disheartening conversation with the famous General, Luigi Palma di Cesnola, at the Metropolitan Museum. The officer had left his casual acquaintance and, being quite rightly convinced that he could not understand, commented on that meeting in English, "These people arrive in America thinking they can find gold along the streets!"

> I leave it with you readers to imagine what a lush I received that day...
> My dear companion took me to the old Bowery on a streetcar still drawn by horses. We stopped by "Five Points" and turned into Mulberry Street, the heart of the Italian colony. "These are poor people!" he exclaimed, "and Americans think all Italians are like them." Not even in

> the wildest and most inland parts of Medieval Sicily, where I was a few months before, not even in the dirtiest places of the dirtiest streets in Naples' port, I saw so many dirty and stinking men, women and children; each of them spoke a different dialect, I could not catch a single word of Italian. They gesticulated, screamed, quarreled around the market stalls full of fruit, vegetables and what not, along the sides of the street. Some policemen, brandishing their blackjacks, hanged out in the middle of that bustle trying to keep order; looking like horse-breakers, ready to intervene at the slightest provocation. "My God!" I said to my companion, "Are they all Italians? But is there any real Italian here?" "Oh, sure," he said, "But they don't live here." I felt humiliated: went back to my hotel and, when I was in my room, I began to cry like a child. If I had known such things before leaving! What could I do in a hostile land, among people I could not even speak with, and whose criticism I could not defend myself from? If I only could have gone back, but how? Moreover, I had sworn that I would have gone back home only when I had succeeded and that I would have never asked for my parents' help…" (P. Coppini, 26)

When we take into consideration auto-biographers like Coppini, who showed his talent early, or others who became journalists, writers, free-lance journalists, and so on, but only as time went by, it must not be forgotten that they had made their way in America fighting and working all the time. In other words, ever since the second half of the nineteenth century, there have been auto-biographers and literary people who have patiently dedicated themselves to work, held back in some kind of working / existential waiting room, which was vital to get them into the new world. However, this by no means meant that their writings did not retain traces of the past or the most remote and "atavistic" ethnic legacy in a mixture of invincible mental oppositions, but they also bore projections already soaring and boldly reaching up towards the future.

Camillo Cianfarra's *Diario di un emigrato* appeared in 1904 when autobiographers like Pietro Greco, who, by not mere chance, would tell the story of his life sixty years later, and other future authors with a certain cultural background, namely Pascal D'Angelo and Emmanuel Carnevali, arrived in the United States.[18] Cianfarra draws an overall picture of his American experience which is both brief as limited to a few years; nevertheless what he relates represents many thousands of personal experiences expressing the typical reality of an enormous and chaotic immigratory stream.

Before he became, during the Great War, Francesco Saverio Nitti's right-hand man in the United States, his name, linked to the Italian American subversion, rapidly was absorbed into the higher circles of our ethnic communities at the end of the century. Yet, there is room for annotations in his work, showing a higher awareness and an intelligence, which besides being lively, is capable of looking beyond the self-perception of the conditions imposed by America on the average immigrant, and can go beyond a generic horizon of mere material expectations by interpreting it with the future in mind. The objective is the same as that which supported the plot of many contemporary stories and songs ripened in the Little Italies where, Greco remarks:

> poets and musicians composed poems and music, without forgetting the popular tradition and taste. Novelty was not rejected... it was listened to and taken into consideration, according to its merit, but it had to be grafted on the tradition, which without neglecting the present, had to take into account the past and bear it in mind to project oneself into the future... (P. Greco, 108)

For example, the emancipation of the immigrant through social climbing and the Americanization of his sons and grandchildren:

> Today they call us "dagoes," today they reproach us for our scant cleanliness, the frequent use of knives... But we'll be a fraction of this whole tomorrow and will begin to make them feel our value, the value of a healthy and strong race, in whose blood have been flowing for countless generations the tendencies and dispositions which made it great and now make it likeable...One day, the hundreds of dollars saved by fumbling in trunks, or by making shoeshiner chairs, or selling fruit on a pushcart, will be needed to educate our children, set them up in this American world, where we'll never enter because we got here too late. (M. Marazzi, 31)

We often find, in the autobiographies, the ambivalent signs of this sorrowful conscience of an almost unavoidable destiny. But, at the same time, there are also the proud traces of a realistic hope for themselves and their children which has become a stubborn will to make it, an almost dogged project to realize the specific "American dream" of the emigrants who went to the New World to settle. In brief, this is the subject-matter which swarms of sociologists and historians would work on later, while the tangible figures of the emigrants and their mental world, if not the relational one, have often a certain difficulty, sometimes even today, to appear, to filter, in short, to work their way, in their books. However, the road is not always uphill in the literal sense of the word, although an upward course is expected as a rule; there are sometimes lucky outcomes and prospects, and, generally speaking a satisfactory development and improvement. Notwithstanding the fact that the context has changed, sometimes the road is still uphill, since the hardest part of the migratory experience can repeat itself generation after generation. Lots of Italians were already full members of the American establishment — when in 1947, the year Carlo Levi gave *Life* an interview, Tommaso Bordonaro, an emigrant from the Palermo province, arrived in the United States already an elderly gentleman. It was thanks to his novels published in the previous decade that a trend of Italian American fictional literature enjoyed a fair reputation.[20] Yet, the memory of his autobiography is still marked by the same thematic and narrative elements which we found more or less in all the previous autobiographies. Above all, for example, the wearing and continuous work of the immigrant.

> 5th April 1947, eight days after my arrival, I began to do my first country job in America, in the Jewish cemetery at Lodaio, pruning trees, planting flowers, straightening up tombs, working with a wheelbarrow, burying bodies, digging some graves and always these rather heavy jobs, doing road maintenance, in brief always outdoor work. At the time I was still young, and even if I worked like a dog passing from job to job: working for the City on Saturdays and Sundays digging sewers, waterworks for drinking water, during the week at the cemetery, in the evening sometimes for three or four hours at La Perla pasta factory, and I could never make enough [money] to keep my family decently, and many times being humiliated by very ignorant people who offended you: — Why do you like having kids? Listen [you listened to] Mussolini and now you can't make up a living — These superficial words were like the nails used when they crucified Christ on the cross...
> (T. Bordonaro, 54-55)

The example offered by Bordonaro, in terms of what has been said so far, could expose itself to some criticism from the "serious" historians of official history, for the late date of his contribution or for the lack of a visible plot. But this was a deliberate example, if for no other reason, because it duly proves by documents the persistence of some structural aspects of emigration autobiographical writing in connection with social and existential problems and linguistic and stylistic questions and content. It would be worthwhile to ponder over one of them, let's say the linguistic question, whether for Italian, English or any other languages of the receiving countries, but this is not the place for such a digression and, what's more, at the end of a fragmentary incursion into the territory of biographies, which has proved to be wider and wider, and consequently worthy of being analysed with the utmost thoroughness. We could associate, for comparative purposes, the American journey, starting from the sea voyage where appropriate, from the above-mentioned Adolfo Rossi to Joseph Tusiani and in between Panunzio or Jerre Mangione, to the recounted journeys to Latin America or various other immigrant destinations by other Italians, absorbed in recalling and putting down in writing "in their own hand"[21] the meaning of an experience which, today, is acknowledged as being the hub of many crucial changes in the contemporary world.

Lately, after World War II, for instance, there has been a strong renewal of interest in the autobiographical writing of Italian emigrants to another America, Canada and Australia.[22] From an analysis emerge all the difficulties related to the command of the host country's language and the desire not to lose the knowledge even of one's native accent and dialect, which is shown by the language emigrants chose to write in. Pietro Greco among other auto-biographers, besides taking English classes, also took Italian, which confirms some emigrants' intention to improve or rather acquire a true competence of their "mother tongues" abroad, to be used for literary aims. This seems contrary to what would happen to the great majority of the children and the descendants of the immigrants of the whole English-speaking area where Italian is today more or less an unknown language and virtually incognito, except the more or less traditional song and musical repertoires of a controversial melodic tradition.

I have recently written a short essay about the so-called songs of emigration and you are kindly referred to it to dispel any doubts and avoid any misunderstandings concerning this topic.[23] But it is undoubtedly an area bordering on the literary and theatrical fields whose mark can be found in diaries and autobiographies which often stream with musical notes and abound in literary quotations from opera pieces, political chants and anthems, songs, and so on. To this day, ethnic drama production is also extremely lively in its relationship with literature and music that bears an Italian background. In America, the typical Italian, according to the negative stereotype, is fond of lazing about and every once in a while plays the concertina, the guitar, or the mandolin. Excluding the patent slander of indolence and reluctance to work, perhaps all that is true judging by what many immigrant autobiographers write about themselves and their compatriots in America. I would emphasize that it is true, but not in an inferior sense, because the bent for singing has no negative connotation in itself, as shown by various quotations from the autobiography by Carmine Biagio Jannace, *La scoperta dell'America*, another book dating back to that crucial circumstance of the 60s[24] I made reference to above. Even pay homage to all of you in such a way as to contextualize and challenge the worst common places — above all, the anti-Southern ones — which have been piled up and befallen on the Italians and their descendants in America for over a century. This has occurred only because the only things that were known about them and their way of being was just what came out in an irregular and deformed way (but it must be stressed that the same thing was happening in Italy too). Meanwhile, many voices made a major effort, from within that American world of immigration and gradual settlement, to put into writing the witnessing of a life destined to be rediscovered only later on by critics and historians who now admit their true value for even the most sophisticated and complex reconstructions of our common past.

Translated by Nick Ceramella, Università degli Studi di Roma, La Sapienza

[1] Sanfilippo M., *Problemi di storiografia dell'emigrazione italiana*. Viterbo: Settecittà, 2002, 21-48.

[2] Pizzorusso G., 'Le radici d'*ancien régime* delle migrazioni contemporanee: un quadro regional,' in *Giornale di storia contemporanea*, IV, 1, 2001, 162-183.

[3] Franzina E., *La storia altrove. Casi nazionali e casi regionali nelle moderne migrazioni di massa*.Verona: Cierre 1998.

[4] Bartocci E., Cotesta V. Eds, *L'identità italiana: emigrazione,immigrazione, conflitti etnici*, Roma: Edizioni Lavoro, 1999.

[5] Levi C., 'Il mito dell'America,' in *Idem, Le molte patrie. Uomini, fatti, paesi d'Italia*. Ed. G. Di Donato and Intro. by L. M. Lombardi Satriani. Roma: Donzelli Editore, 2000, 5-20.

[6] Bertelli L., *Cultura di élite e cultura di massa nell'emigrazione italiana negli Stati Uniti*, in Aa.Vv., *Gli italiani negli Stati Uniti. L'emigrazione e l'opera degli*

italiani negli Stati Uniti d'America. Procedings of the Third Symposium of American Studies (Firenze, May 27-29, 1969), Istituto di Studi Americani, Università degli Studi di Firenze, 1972, 45-109.

[7] Lanapoppi A., *Lorenzo Da Ponte. Realtà e leggenda nella vita del librettista di Mozart.* Venezia: Marsilio, 1992.

[8] E. Franzina, *Gli italiani al nuovo mondo. L'emigrazione italiana in America,1492-1942.* Milano: Mondadori 1995, 87-140; and Gabaccia D. R., *Emigranti. Le diaspore degli italiani dal Medioevo a oggi.* Torino: Einaudi, 2003, 33-60.

[9] Durante F., *Italoamericana. Storia e letteratura degli italiani negli Stati Uniti,1776-1880.* Milano: Mondadori, 2001.

[10] Even if one of the seminal studies in our key theme, *Immigrant Autobiography in the United States. Four Versions of the Italian American Self.* (Verona: Essedue Edizioni 1982), which lays great emphasis on the autobiographical writings by some of our immigrants, has been written by B. Boelhower, an American researcher who teaches at the University of Verona, and who has written many books for Italian publishers.

[11] Martellini A., "Zone d'ombra e nuove frontiere della storia dell'emigrazione." Aa.Vv., *Quale futuro per lo studio dell'emigrazione? L'attività dei Centri di Ricerca: bilanci e prospettive.* Ed. by N. Ugolini. Atti del Convegno di Studio omonimo, 4/5 ottobre 2002. San Marino: Guardigli Editore, 2003, 36-37.

[12] Rossini D., *Il mito americano nell'Italia della Grande Guerra.* Roma, Bari: Laterza 20 02, a nd S au L ., *S tati Uniti e Italia nella Grande Guerra, 1914-1918.* Firenze: Leo S. Olschki Editore, 2003.

[13] I would like to mention the pioneer initiatives of the research group from Rovereto, contributing to the journal *Materiali di lavoro* where the proceedings of as many as eight conferences on popular writing held between 1987-1998 appeared. Then I would like to cite the activity of the "Archivio diaristico nazionale," founded by Severino Tutino in Pieve Santo Stefano di Arezzo, and whose 20th anniversary will be celebrated this year. For anything concerning all the above cf. *Per iscritto. Antropologia delle scritture quotidiane.* Ed. D. Fabre. Lecce: Argo, 1998., and *Archivio diaristico nazionale. Inventario, Introduzione.* Ed. L.Ricci. Roma: Ministero per i Beni e le Attività Culturali — Direzione Generale per gli Archivi (Pubblicazioni degli Archivi di Stato, Strumenti CLIX), 2 vols., I, XI-XXII.

[14] A. Iuso, "Archivi autobiografici in Europa. Un primo itinerario" *Archivio trentino di storia contemporanea*, XLIV, 2, 1996,121-135; and *Vite di carta.* Ed. Eadem and Q. Antonelli. Napoli: L'Ancora del Mediterraneo, 2000.

[15] Cf. Hall M. Ets, *Rosa, vita di una emigrata italiana.* Ecoistituto della Valle del Ticino 2003 (1st Ed. Minneapolis: University of Minnesota Press, 1970). For a proper placing of emigration writings still missing even in praiseworthy works like *Scritture di donne. Uno sguardo europeo*, Ed. A. Iuso. "Quaderni della Biblioteca Città di Arezzo." Arezzo: Protagon Editori Toscani, 1999, I take the liberty of referring to E. Franzina, *Immagini al femminile.* Idem, *L'immaginario degli emigranti. Miti e raffigura-*

zioni dell'esperienza italiana fra due secoli. Paese (Treviso): Pagus Edizioni, 1992, 159-182.

[16] For a reconstruction of the whole publishing story cf. Franzina, *L'immaginario degli emigranti*, op. cit. 221-24. A recent reprint of Rossi's production has appeared in a Trevisian edition, edited by "Associazione Polesani nel Mondo," Rovigo: 1995.

[17] Coppini, P. *From Dawn to Sunset.* San Antonio,Texas: The Naylor Company. 1949. Now there is a translation subsidized by Comune di Moglia — Assessorato alla Cultura. Suzzara: Arti Grafiche Bottazzi. 1997. (My quotation from this book is from p. 26).

[18] Greco, P. *I Ricordi d'un immigrato. Autobiografia.* New York: Gaus'Sons 1964, p. 108.

[19] Cianfarra, C. *Il Diario di un Emigrato.* New York: Tipografia dell'Araldo Italiano 1904, pp. 99-100. (For convenience, I have quoted from the latest book by Martino Marazzi, *Misteri di Little Italy. Storie e testi della letteratura italoamericana.* [Milano: Franco Angeli 2001. p. 31], which dedicates an interesting paragraph of his valuable work (29-35) to the "memoir writing and commitment" of the Italians in the USA at the beginning of the twentieth century.

[20] Bordonaro, T. *La spartenza.* Preface by Natalia Ginzburg. Torino: Einaudi 1991, p. 54-55.

[21] Cf. C .Cattarulla, *Di proprio pugno. Autobiografie di emigranti italiani in Argentina e in Brasile.* Reggio Emilia: Diabasis. 2003.

An excellent study on Argentina and refers also to some old studies of mine on Brazil (see *Scritti autobiografici di emigranti italiani in America Latina*, in *Materiali di lavoro* 1990, n.1-2, 15-222, and *Autobiografie e diari dell'emigrazione: esperienza e memoria nelle scritture autobiografiche di emigranti e immigrati in America tra otto e novecento*, in Ed. M. R.Ostuni. *Studi sull'emigrazione. Un'analisi comparata.* Milano: Electa 1991, pp. 221-241, which I do not consider completely outdated, even from the purely documentary viewpoint, and which have been collected in E. Franzina, *L'immaginario degli emigranti*, op.cit. pp. 183-241.

[22] Rosoli, G.F. "From the Inside: Popular Autobiography by Italian Immigrants in Canada," in Eds G. E. Pozzetta and B. Ramirez. *The Italian Diaspora. Migration across the Globe.* Toronto Multicultural History Society of Ontario. 1992. 175-192.

[23] Franzina, E. "Le canzoni dell'emigrazione." Eds P.Bevilacqua, A.De Clementi e E.Franzina , *Storia dell'emigrazione italiana.* Vol. I. *Partenze.* Roma: Donzelli Editore 2001. 537-562.

[24] Iannace, C.B. *The Discovery of America — La scoperta dell'America — An Autobiography — Un'autobiografia.* A Bilingual Edition translated by William Boelhower, West Lafayette: Indiana Bordighera Press, 1999. Cittadella (Padova): 1st Ed. Bino Rebellato Editore, 1971.

Italy and America Over a Span of Three Italian American Generations: First Results of a Research Project

Marcello Saija
Università di Messina

When we planned to carry out a research on fascism and the identity of Italian communities in America[1] we did not intend to limit the sample of interviewees to immigrants coming from predetermined Italian geographic areas or regions. However, after finishing the interviews, we realized that, as we expected, over 60% of the interviewees were indeed third generation Italian Americans, grandchildren and great-grandchildren of Italian emigrants of Sicilian origin. This result, partly due to the fact that — according to recent estimates — almost 4/5 of Italian emigration to America comes from southern Italy while 2/5 of the emigration to the Tri-state area originates in Sicily,[2] was determined also by our deliberate decision to let the order "Sons of Italy" provide us with the entire sample. The lodge masters, on saying where we came from when they introduced us, catalyzed the attention of those members who were somehow related to Sicily.[3]

The marked homogeneity of the origins of the interviewees, naturally, induced us to concentrate in particular on the analysis of Sicilian emigration and the history of the communities derived thereof. It goes without saying that it is impossible to give here an account of all the results of the research which will be published in a book later. Nevertheless, we believe it is useful to illustrate the interpretative methods that have allowed us to analyze the Sicilian-American communities of the Tri-state area through the experience of three generations.

• The first segment of emigrants we dealt with left Sicily between the end of the 19th century and the beginning of the 20th. This is a generation who was actively working during the first three decades of the 20th century;

• The second segment was made up by American-born men who were working between the 1920s and the 1950s;

• The third segment was represented by 369 interviewees of Sicilian origin (a little more than 60% of the whole sample, consisting of 600 interviewees), all ages between 55 and 92, the grandchildren of the early immigrants who, by the end of the 20th century, had either already concluded their own work experiences or were just going to. These people told us their family stories as they recalled them from their fathers and grandfathers.

In order to retrace a unitary explanatory line, we concentrated on one element of analysis only for each of the generations examined. We let ourselves be guided in taking our decision by the judgment of the New York State Democratic Congressman Tom Di Napoli who, during the interview, summarized the interpretative paradigm that we intend to propose. He said, "my grandfather had a problem: how to survive here in America; my father had a problem: how to hide his Italian identity because of general ethnic discrimination against Italians. My problem is how to have my own Italian identity back. I don't speak Italian at all but I would like to feel myself as Italian."[4]

Thus, on following this framework, we focused our attention on the processes of social and economic integration with regard to the first generation, and on the reasons that caused a rift between communities and parents' homeland with regard to the second.

As for the third generation, we tried to explain why almost all of our interviewees, by now entirely Americanized, at times revealed particularly intense sentiments showing their wish to get back their Italian identity.

Once the field of analysis was limited to Sicilian emigration, and the data entry phase was completed, the first thing we did was to unify the earliest emigrants by geographic sub-areas. In this way, we were able to distinguish a coastal, predominantly eastern Sicily, with valuable crops, characterized by small and average sized farmland, from a western inland Sicily, deeply marked by extensive corn cultivation large landed estates.

It did not take us long to realize there was a noticeable difference between the two areas: The so-called Mutual Aid Societies, particularly popular among the communities coming from the eastern coast of Sicily and the areas with small and average size farms, were virtually absent among the communities originating from the inland large landed estates. Indeed, in this latter area, it was difficult to come upon any form of aggregation, with the exception of those put in place by the Catholic Church that gathered men and women without the geographical distinctions usually raised by the Mutual Aid Lay Societies.

But why was there such a marked difference? The reason needs most likely be looked for in the very socio-economic conditions of people's place of origin.

Coastal Sicily, the eastern side in particular, characterized by the small and average sized estates (I am speaking about the *Ragusano*, the *Catanese*, but also about the *Messinese*), represented an integrated society, where the class differences were vaguer and certain forms of limited social mobility, which have nurtured the farmers' hopes of economic growth, have existed for centuries. Here, one can notice evident signs that attest to a life of relations and an important internal communication on the level of effective culture, art and popular literature. I am thinking of storytellers, cart craftsmen, carpenters from Catania who created a furniture style in the 18th and 19th centuries, which antiquarians are particularly interested in today. But I am also thinking about the grafters and experimenter botanists, who were very popular all over the eastern coast of Sicily. In truth, there was certainly not much of that in western inland Sicily, where the large noble landed estates represented a dichotomous society, in which 1% of the population owned 99% of the land, conversely, the small and average size property was assigned to only 1% of the resident population. This is a Sicily which never changed through centuries, where the only class layer different from the aristocracy and the land proletariat was represented by the *gabelloti*, tenants of the large landed estates, and the *mazzieri* ("dealers"), who managed the market of the farm laborers by using various forms of mafia violence.

On continuing to use, as a discriminating factor, the division into two Sicilies — although this time we applied it to the official emigration statistics — we found ourselves face to face with another substantial difference. While the emigration from the large landed estate areas had been hemorrhagic since the 1880s, the flows coming from the coast had been slower. In particular, in the areas where the small and average size farmland was the norm (see the *Ragusano*), the migrant flows were reaching high levels only around the time of World War One. The difference is most significant, bearing in mind also that the salary of a large landed estate was more than double of that in the Iblean area.[5]

In short, it is as if the large landed estate farm laborers wanted to escape from a cruel and disrupted society which was the result of an unfair social balance stratified in inland Sicily through centuries.

As soon as the culture of emigration spread out in these areas, the peasants, also owing to the the good job done by immigration agents, did not think twice and left, without even knowing what was really expecting them overseas.

On the contrary, the more culturally integrated eastern Sicilian society, despite its not prosperous economic condition, succeeded in keeping its residents from leaving for a longer time. Although enticed by the American dream, men and women found it harder to abandon the little certainties of a peasant world which was even familiar with a limited process of social mobility. It is evident that the myth of the American fortune was spread there too by immigration agents and by a communication system comparatively more efficient than that in inland Sicily; but initially it allured just those who were after an adventure and only a few of those who, however things might develop, had still an alternative in their native land.

If we then go and see what was happening on the opposite shores of the Atlantic, we realize that these two different realities project their original culture onto their country of adoption. The eastern communities quickly found the way to the Mutual Aid Societies. These associations were established between the 1880s and the 1920s and had a strong local characterization because they tended to gather only the emigrants coming from villages, or, at most, from a very limited area located where they originally came from.

The founding conditions, the statutes, and the finalities were those inherited from the Savoy Piedmont and had already been experimented in Italy since the Unification.[6] Sometimes, in fact, as in the cases of *Modica* and *Salina*, the statutes were those of the societies operating in their places of origin, allowing the odd addition. It is, however, interesting to note that in America, these associations were normally established on the initiative of whomever, once on the other side of the Atlantic, succeeded in investing the money that he had brought from home, which allowed him to fit into the hosting society at an acceptable level. This is the case of the Mutual Aid Society, "Isola di Salina" (but many other examples of *Catanese* and *Ragusano* communities can be cited) founded by a hundred New York greengrocers, mainly former sea captains, who had abandoned the Aeolian Islands right after the phylloxera infection of 1889. These people, thanks to mutual aid, created the conditions to receive their fellow countrymen, and so saved them from the abuses and the harassment of the bossing and mafia system of hiring farm laborers at very low wages.[7]

But the immigrants from inland Sicily could not escape this very lot. They experienced the early form of integration in America characterised by an exaggerated individualism. They were hired for humble if not servile jobs for a long time. In most cases, we are talking about unskilled labors on construction sites and railways, or dockers and unloaders at wholesale food markets.

The family memory — gathered by their grandchildren — passes on that the link to get these jobs were sometimes the Catholic parishes. Most of them, however, have a clearer memory of the bosses' role, and at times acknowledge with a certain shame the humiliations their grandparents suffered on asking the mafia to be employed as dockers and labors. According to the research carried out by Daniela Irrera, and financed by the Nara Department of Justice,[8] this was bound to happen mainly to the men who came from inland western Sicily.

The Italians put down in the police records as petty criminals in the first two decades of the 19th century, came in most cases from Agrigento, Caltanissetta, and Palermo, where the prevalence of large landed estates was much higher than in the other provinces.[9]

This data, to some extent already known or at least perceived by historiography,[10] was not however due, as it was said, to the *mafioso* culture widely present in those areas. In our opinion, it was the lack of any chance that forced so many wretched people to get hooked by the mafia from which they had tried to escape back home. This different early stage of the immigatory experience of the Sicilian communities was bound to have a varied impact on the following generations, both with respect to the varying speed of social mobility and repatriation. But we cannot deal with this issue here because the indicator that we have selected is another one, that is the split with Italy.

Now we need to reckon with the way the communities have perceived fascist Italy from overseas. It is widely believed Italian Americans not only had a clear perception of fascism but were emotionally involved in the events of that regime. According to certain scholars, in fact, fascism contributed a lot to give them national identity that their fathers, coming from all over Italy during the 1800s, could not have. This very sensation emerges rather clearly from the reading of some remarkable books such as those by

Duff, Diggins, Cannistraro, and more recently Luconi, to name just a few of the most famous scholars.[11] In these works, one can read about Mussolini's feelings towards Italian Americans, Fascist fervor, the various Little Italies, the strategy adopted by ambassadors and consuls to use the community as a means of a "parallel diplomacy," the services rendered to Roosevelt and Mussolini by Generoso Pope and *Il Progresso Italoamericano*.

Everyone speaks about Italian American communities in an indistinct way, and this generalization emerges also from the essays included in the recent volume edited by Bevilacqua, De Clementi, and Franzina.[12] The reader is certainly brought to believe that the narrated events end up involving all the Italian Americans. It is clear, at this point, that we are surely speaking about a high level historiographic production, where events and opinions are strictly documented and demonstrated. Yet, we think that as far as the involvement of the community goes, or rather, the blame for this behavior or just for a sense of belonging, things are different from what they appear in current generalizations.

The well-known opinion of Salvemini, quoted also by Vecoli, for example, underlines how only 5% Italian Americans regarded themselves as fascists, another 35% was generically pro-fascist, 10% were antifascist, and the remaining 50% was made up of individuals "*interested only in their own business*."[13]

If we analyze critically the data on the political participation of Italian Americans and on the circulation of newspapers in Italian, and then pay due attention to the valuable indications that come from the innumerable memoirs written by immigrants, we can realize that the behavior and feelings of participation the fascist consuls and ambassadors relied on to support Italians' interests were, in effect, those of a small portion of the community. Certainly, there is no doubt this community overlapped with that social area Generoso Pope and other prominent figures counted on. Yet, at a closer look, they were less than a few thousand people, which is not a small figure, but is nothing compared with the 6,000,000 Italian Americans resident in the US during the 1930s. Consequently, it is within such a framework that the indications we gathered from the encoding of our data acquired a meaning they would not otherwise have.

In any case, it must be stressed that out of 369 interviewees only 1.8% remembered their fathers having the odd discussion about Fascist Italy. Another question shows that in all of these cases immigrants could still speak Italian. The remaining 92% did not remember either hearing their fathers expressing their opinions on Fascism, or missing their homeland. For as many as 37.8%, instead, Italy was a country they had never known and represented only their ancestors' poverty from which they had tried to free themselves.

On the whole, according to our statistics — and this too is a significant statistic — only 20% of the second generation families still here speaking Italian (or rather, Sicilian), during the period between the two World Wars. In the other cases, the language of the ancestors disappeared when the grandfather died, and, usually, only a few words of common usage, almost always related to food, survived in the family lexicon.

Now, we find ourselves facing the first general indicators of the split that arises between the communities and Italy during the era of the second generation. Naturally, in the answers to the questionnaires, it is possible to point out a few more specific examples; but rather than insist on the demonstration of the event, perhaps it is preferable to try to understand the causes which, from our point of view, started to pile up from the early 1920s.

As Philip Cannistraro himself points out, some Fascist groups, operating predominantly in the various American Little Italies, despite the disagreeing opinions of the ambassadors and consuls, and the early substantial ambiguity of Mussolini, pushed with a certain insistence to impede the naturalization process of many Italian Americans.[14]

It is evident that in the 1920s the Italian American community was different from that stratified in the first 30 years of emigration. During the whole of the 19th century, and at least until World War One, most immigrants intended to return to Italy with the money they earned, therefore, only a few of them aimed to be naturalized. After the enforcement of certain restrictive laws, however, more and more people preferred to settle down for good and call over their families. It is easy to understand then why the fascist claim against naturalization seemed unjust and irritating. Little wonder if we found significant traces of this irritation in our questionnaires.

A pensioner from Glen Cove told us how his father used to tell the story of his anger, which he openly showed to whomever, wearing a black shirt, maintained that one had to choose between the loyalty to Italy and naturalization: "I had struggled so much to be granted the citizenship — said the elderly emigrant — and when I was ready to get it the Fascists told me that becoming American meant betraying my homeland. I said to them:

'Well, go to hell, along with Italy, Mussolini and the poverty that we left behind us!'"

We realized from our interviews that cases like this did neither concern antifascists nor individuals with a particular political affiliation. They were common people who, as stated by Salvemini, thought only about improving their social positions and settling down in America. On the other hand there was an area of consent to the Fascists and our studies demonstrate it, but let's try to quantify it. According to the most recent data, 800,000 Italians arrived to America between 1876 and 1900, and in the following period, until the restrictive laws were enforced between 1920-24, just a little less than 5,000,000 more Italians reached the American territory. Even if we take into account a repatriation rate of 40% and without considering the not negligible number of Italians arriving to the United States from Canada and South America, who, however, compensate the number of those who died, we can conclude that in the period between the two wars, there were at least 3,000,000 first generation Italians and as many second generation in the United States. After taking into due account every element we have at our disposal, everything allows us to believe that the Fascist militants or sympathizers were just about 10% in the 1920s, which is clearly a rate that does not justify the triumphant statements of those who say that the Italian community was permeated by Fascism. It is true, though, that during the 1930s, things changed. Due to the good relationship between Roosevelt and Mussolini, the strategy adopted by Italian consuls and ambassadors, but above all by prominent members of the community and associations to use the community as an instrument of pressure to defend Italian interests[15] — or perhaps, in the case of leading figures only to look after their own business[16] — consensus to fascism conveyed by Pope, with the *Progresso Italoamericano*, and by the order "Sons of Italy," with the first massive diffusion of lodges, increased. But by how much?

To start with, we have to exclude almost entirely the second generation of Italian Americans who did not speak Italian, were educated in a school system marked by the principals of the philosopher and pedagogist Dewey, accepted and shared the rules and the philosophy of the American productive world. Moreover, they voted either Democratic or Republican, according to the interests of their employers, and hurried to modify their own family name to hide their origins. They represent, as we have already said, a percentage as high as 50%.

The pro-fascist journalists addressed the remaining 50%. But how many copies did they sell? According to Vecoli's estimate, "*Progresso Italoamericano*," definitely the most popular paper of the time, reached, at its best, a circulation of 175,000 copies,[17] helped to form opinions, stimulated thousands of Italian Americans to express their indignation and become fully aware of the events of Italian fascism, flaunt the grandeur of a distant homeland confronted with daily discrimination, send postcards with iron and wedding rings for the war in Ethiopia. But how many were they? It is difficult to say. Nevertheless, we think they were a loud group, but far from the majority. But that is not all. Moreover, it is necessary to consider also the quality and depth of this emotional involvement.

Historiography, this time agrees unanimously in maintaining that the Italian American support to fascism partly broke up after the famous speech about the stab in the back of Roosevelt (reported with great emphasis by the *Progresso Italoamericano*) and, definitely, with the declaration of war on the United States. Hence, it is not difficult to hypothesize that the force behind these sentiments were neither fascism nor Italianism, as one might assume, but the strategy of people like Pope and of those associations which, above all, cared about their political position in America.

The prominent members of the Italian community had remained afloat by "serving two masters," which was possible until this attitude had been compatible with Roosevelt mood. Then, when the hard times came, they coherently opted in favor of the American interests.[18] It is this very passage which makes the answers to our questionnaires comprehensible: 44% of the interviewees told us, for example, that their fathers, when America entered the war, simply felt Americans and believed it was just right to go and fight against Italy, considered an enemy just like Germany and Japan; 26%, of course, recall their fathers' disappointment to be enlisted to fight against Italy, but they observed that Mussolini was wrong in forming an alliance with Hitler, so it was right to go and fight Nazi-fascism which wanted to dominate the world through a dictatorship.

Moreover, the data we gathered on the opposite side is equally significant: only 4% spoke of generic feelings of aversion shown by those Italian Americans called to war against Italians, while 15% avoid responding, claiming that they don't remember anything about their fathers' beliefs.

In such a well defined outline, it is then possible to maintain that the moving apart of these communities from Italy is not determined by the

Great War. Yet, the war is, however, the litmus test paper of a split that had gradually developed over the preceding twenty years. Besides, it makes any analysis, meant to emphasize the role of fascism in the creation of a national consciousness on the other side of the Atlantic, risky. Instead, the dynamics of the Italian American identity must be interpreted over a long period of time, especially in the light of the generational events that we tried to outline. In order to be clear and concise, even if we may run the risk of generalizing, we are trying to borrow the concept of the opposition couple of mother and wet nurse from psychoanalytical analysis and transfer it into the experience of the three generations of Italian Americans.

It is evident that the conflict between mother and wet nurse arises only for the first generation of emigrants who are painfully rushed into choosing. Most of them sustain the conflict by keeping their original ethnicity, but some others have begun to give in.

On the contrary, the second generation Italian Americans mostly choose what had been presented to them as a wet nurse by their fathers, although they gradually identify her as their mother, giving definitely up their Italian identity and resolving in this way their ethnic conflict.

Finally, as far as the third generation is concerned, the conflict does not exist because both mother and wet nurse identify with America right from the beginning.

However, despite feeling more American than their fathers and grandfathers, they generally seek to enrich their own identity with the fundamental values of Italian American culture. Yet, there is no desire for a new naturalization in this option. Now, the acceptance of the Italian identity suggests only an ethical belonging, no longer able to create a conflict. They feel American, but in a special way, with a culture and values that distinguish them from others. In this sense, the response that we got from our sample appears most significant when we gave them a multiple choice questionnaire, asking if they felt:

1. American,
2. Italian American,
3. American of Italian Origin,
4. American of Italian Origin and Culture,
5. Italian.

76%, without hesitation, chose the fourth option.

[1] This paper shows the results attained by the research unit at the University of Messina, working in the inter-university project (Atenei di Messina, Bologna, Roma 3, Orientale di Napoli), promoted by the Department of International and Community Studies, English and Anglo-American, directed by the writer and financed by MIUR in 2000 with 40% of the funds.

[2] S. Bugiardini, *L'Associazionismo negli USA*, in B. Bevilacqua, A. DE Clementi, E. Franzina (Edited by), *Storia dell'emigrazione italiana*, Donzelli, Roma, 2003, p. 560.

[3] We must express our overwhelming gratitude to Professor Mario Mignone, Director of the Center for Italian Studies of the SUNY Stony Brook, who has personally welcomed us at his center and has helped in our research in every possible way.

[4] Our interview with the honorable Thomas Di Napoli, recorded the 27th of January, 2002, New York State Assembly Representative of Albany.

[5] For a more in-depth analysis of these aspects, see M. Saija, *Una Sicilia non bella a prima vista*, in "*Gazzetta del Sud*," special monographic number, January 1 2000, pp. 96-97.

[6] For a more in-depth study on the Italian *Mutuo Soccorso* societies of the 1800's, see Ghezzi, Fabbri, *Solidarismo in Italia tra XIX e XX secolo*, Torino, 1996.

[7] Writers of Aeolian emigration have a study in progress that is proceeding at the same rate with the documentation stratification that, from 1999, is being collected in the *Museo Eoliano dell'Emigrazione* site in Malfa, on the island of Salina.

[8] The publishing of the essay is underway in the *Atti del II Convegno* on transoceanic Italian emigration between the 1800's and the 1900's and the history of the derived communities, taken place in Salina from the 30th of August to the 2nd of September 2002.

[9] M. Saija, *Una Sicilia non bella a prima vista*, ...cited.

[10] S. Lupo, *Cose Nostre: Mafia Siciliana e Mafia Americana*, in B. Bevilacqua, A. De Clementi, E. Franzina (Edited by), Storia dell'Emigrazione Italiana, gli Arrivi, cited pp. 245 and SS.

[11] J. B. Duff, *The Italians* in J.P. O'Grady (Edited by), *The Immigrants Influence on Wilsons' Peace Policies*, University Press of Kentucky, Lexington, 1966; J. Diggins, *Mussolini and the Fascism. The View from America*, University Press Princeton, 1972; Id. *L'America, Mussolini e il Fascismo*, Laterza, Bari, 1982; P.V. Cannistraro, *Generoso Pope and the Rise of Italia-American Politics 1925-36*, in L. Tomasi (a cura di), *Italian Americans. New perspectives in Italian Immigration and Ethnicity*, Center for Migration Studies, New York, 1985; Id. *Per una storia dei fasci negli Stati Uniti (1921-1929)*, in "Storia contemporanea" XXVI, 6/95; Id. *Blackshirts in Little Italy. Italian-Americans and the Fascism, 1921-29*, Bordighera Press, Lafayette, 1999; S. Luconi, *La "Diplomazia Parallela." il regime fascista e la mobilitazione politica degli Italoamericani*, Franco Angeli Editori, Milano, 2000.

[12] B. Bevilacqua, A. De Clementi, E. Franzina (Edited by), *Storia dell'Emigrazione Italiana, gli Arrivi*, Donzelli, Roma, 2003, found, in particolar, in the essays of Rudolph Vecoli, Stefano Luconi, and Sergio Bugiardini.

[13] G. Salvemini, *Italian Fascist Activities in the United States*, Center for Migration Studies, New York, 1977; see also R. J. Vecoli, *Negli Stati Uniti*, in B. Bevilacqua, A. De Clementi, E. Franzina (Edited by), *Storia dell'Emigrazione Italiana, gli Arrivi*, cited., p. 74.

[14] P. Cannistraro, Blackshirts in Little Italy,... cited.

[15] S. Luconi, *La Diplomazia Parallela*...cit.

[16] S. Vaccara, *Generoso Pope al servizio di due padroni, Mussolini e Roosevelt.* The essay is about to be published in the *Atti del II Convegno* on transoceanic Italian emigration between the 1800's and the 1900's and the history of the derived communities, held in Salina from the 30th of August to the 2nd of September 2002.

[17] R. Vecoli, Negli Stati Uniti, in B. Bevilacqua, A. De Clementi, E. Franzina (Edited by), *Storia dell'emigrazione italiana, gli Arrivi*, ...cited p. 66.

[18] S. Vaccara, *Generoso Pope al servizio di due padroni, Mussolini e Roosevelt*, ...cited.

Italian Immigration to North America as a Clash of Cultures

Frank Sturino
York University

The focus of my paper as revealed in its title has to do with the clash that occurred between Italian immigrants to North America and the Anglo-Saxon-based culture that awaited them in the period of mass immigration at the turn of the twentieth-century. The theme itself, of course, is not new since almost all the work done on Italian immigration to North America has, in fact, stressed the theme of conflict. This conflict has been cast as one between a traditional, peasant culture and urban, industrial society; a struggle between newly proletarianized workers and industrial capitalism; and as an ethnic battle between immigrant foreigners from the Mediterranean and established Northern Europeans of the American mainstream. Although the conflict has been seen in terms of class or ethnicity, gender has also recently emerged as a major category.

My purpose today, however, is not to dwell on this literature, but to extend the discussion of conflict by focusing on one element that has always been part and parcel of the discussion on the Italian immigrant experience, but has essentially remained in the background. This has to do with the question of literacy, and my purpose today is to highlight this element as a fundamental basis for cultural clash between Italian immigrants and North American society.

It is well known that Italians coming from the peasant south of Italy had one of the highest rates of illiteracy during the Great Migration that washed on American shores between 1880 and World War I. In the first decade of the twentieth-century the U.S. Congressional Immigration Commission placed the illiteracy of southern Italian immigrants at almost 68%, surpassed only by Eastern Europeans. This was well-recognized by nativists such as Senator Henry Cabot Lodge who, working with the Immigration Restrictionist League, were able to finally capitalize on nationalist zeal during the first World War to finally convince Congress of strict controls over immigration with the introduction of a Literacy Test in 1917, a measure adopted by Canada two years later. The aim of the Literacy Test legislation was simple:

Keep out the illiterate immigrant and America would be protected from "undesiderables" from Southern and Eastern Europe who were threatening North American values and institutions. Illiteracy was at least associated with, if not seen as *the* cause of a long list of problems that beset America at the turn of the twentieth-century. Crime, vice, slums, disease, political radicalism and, for eugenicists, even racial degradation, were all tied up with heavily-pre-literate "New Immigration" from the supposedly inferior cultures outside the preferred sources of Northwestern Europe.

Italians were singled out not only for their high illiteracy rates but also for the extremely high rates of return migration. The Italian government estimated a return rate from the United States of 63% between 1902 and 1923 and, although the figure may vary by regional group, this was certainly the rate of return for Southern Italians, who made up 80% of the total immigrant population from Italy. The return rate from Canada was even higher still. Ironically this movement back across the Atlantic often offended native-born Americans since it seemed to show ingratitude for the blessing of opportunity they were sure the New World offered those willing to assimilate. While the pattern of Italian illiteracy and return cannot be disputed, its meaning has not always been clearly appreciated. What I wish to do today is to provide some suggestions of how the fact of illiteracy can be seen as pivotal in the cultural clash between Italian immigrants and North American society.

The inspiration for my comments comes from the work of Marshall McLuhan and the Toronto School of communications and cultural studies which has emerged around McLuhan and the earlier work of economic historian Harold Innis, both of the University of Toronto. In writing this paper I could not help but think back to my time in the 1970s as a graduate student at the same University where, on the campus of St. Michael's College I was working out of the Multicultural History Society of Ontario founded by the late Robert F. Harney, the first scholar to seriously study the Italian experience in Canada. Adjacent to the Society was the Centre for the Study of Technology and Culture founded by Marshall McLuhan about a decade earlier. In hindsight, I realized that although the two research centers were next door to each other there was no communication between them. In my many years of working with Robert Harney I never once heard him talk of McLuhan. And yet, it is clear that they both had visions that presciently pointed toward the 21st century, and that the work of the two men and their centers was at the very least complementary.

Both the history professor and the English scholar were concerned with society as a cultural mosaic. The defining feature of the twentieth-century was the emergence of a new world that would break open the neatly constructed forms of the eighteenth and nineteenth centuries — rationalism, nationalism and scientific materialism — and replace these with a mosaic of sensitivities and identities. It is interesting to note that the journal of the Multicultural History Society was entitled *Polyphony*, a term also used with fondness by McLuhan. Polyphony is a term that deals with variety in sound, either counterpoint in music or phonetic value in speech. Sound, of course, involves the ear and oral sensibility. The ear is the main sense organ of an oral or pre-literate society. And this brings me to the particular elements of cultural clash between Italian immigrants and North American society which I here wish to stress: the uncompromising differences between oral and literate societies which clashed head-long in the mass migration of Italians to North America in the late 19th and early 20th centuries.

Harney mentions that for the peasant immigrants of this period, literacy was popularly referred to as "white magic" and indeed it was the key that could open up the promised riches of the New World, its cities and factories. But I would suggest that for many this white magic also has its darker side and it was beheld both with anticipation and anxiety. The *contadini*, as well as knowing that literacy represented opportunity in the new machine age that confronted them, also perceived that it would mean an end to their traditional way of life. Literacy would mean an end to the family as the focus of both social and economic activity; it would mean the end of the respect and honor owed to parents by their children; and it would mean the desacralization of life in a world where the market ruled supreme.

In the decades of mass migration, every autumn young sojourners in North America would rush away from dehumanizing jobs on the railroads, mines and constructions sites to return back to their families, farms and villages throughout the Italian peninsula. These sojourners wished for economic stability in local peasant communities that were being shaken by incorporation into the Italian nation-state and international trade. They were also, however, trying to preserve a way of life that revolved around an oral sensibility increasingly threatened with the standardization and individualism of literate society. Something of this was recognized a decade ago by Mark Wyman, one of the few American scholars to examine the immigrants' return to Europe. His book *Round Trip to America* contains a suggestive chapter titled "Leaving the Land of Bosses and Clocks," but the oral-literate conflict encountered in North America remains undeveloped. In the United States numerous reports by educators and social workers attested to the reluctance of Italian parents to have their children educated in the public school system. The Immigration Commission in 1910 reported that less than 1% of the children of Italian immigrants were in high school compared to 6% from Northwest European origin. As late as the 1940s Leonard Covello, in his classic study of Italian American schoolchildren, was lamenting the value differences between the Southern Italians in New York and the American school system. Covello, who was a principal of a high school, reported how parents expected the school to make their children "ben educato," that is, to reinforce values of respect toward elders, traditional sex roles, and responsibility towards the family. What they got instead, of course, was an education that instilled loyalty to the nation-state, individualism, and an egalitarian ethos that dissolved distinctions between generations and genders. In short, both the high rates of return migration by Italians and the low rates of school attendance for the families who stayed (as well as other indices such as the low rate of naturalization) are illustrative of the deep cultural clash that separated an oral people from a literate nation-state.

Just how deep this clash was for a very many Italian emigrants can be appreciated by referring to Marshall McLuhan's *The Gutenberg Galaxy* published in 1962 and sub-titled, *The Making of the Typographic Man*. On p. 68 he writes, "there can be no greater clash in human cultures than those representing the eye and the ear ...." This work that does so much to probe the constellation of changes (or galaxy) that took place in man and society after the advent of print technology has virtually been ignored by social historians and, curiously, even by students of culture. This is unfortunate for in this great text McLuhan provides us both with an insightful history of literacy and a useful analysis is of the effects of the Gutenberg print revolution on all aspects of western development ranging from individual psychological effects to cultural influences to changes wrought upon the economy and polity of the West.

To understand McLuhan's analysis we must start with his position that all technology is an extension of man and that any technological innovation will have a feed-back effect on the human person. Technology alters sense perception which, in turn, has an effect on a society's collective life, whether this be economic, political, or cultural. For McLuhan there are two moments in human history that are fundamental: the establishment of the printing press during the fifteenth-century, which gave rise to mass print literacy and a visual or modern mode of organizing the world, and the harnessing of electricity in the late nineteenth-century, which gave rise to electric mass media and a tactile or post-modern way of perceiving. This second transition was the subject of McLuhan's best-known book *Understanding Media: The Extensions of Man*, published two years after the *Gutenberg Galaxy*. In any case, just as print literacy gradually displaced the oral cultures of Europe after 1500, so too did electric mass media begin to displace literate culture around 1900.

The replacement of the oral man with the typographic man was gradual but inexorable throughout the Renaissance, Reformation and Enlightenment. Luther's theology of salvation though faith alone acted as a catalyst for mass literacy throughout Northern Europe and thence to its North American colonies. But only with difficulty did literacy make inroads in Latin Europe, where oral local cultures survived well into the mid-20th century. Throughout the entire West mass literacy was indispensable for the spread of individualism and nationalism and the concomitant industrial revolution, both of which could only happen if oral man was cut loose from ties of kin or clan — the main function of literacy.

All this is familiar territory to which McLuhan provides insightful glosses but does not himself invent. More important is his analysis of the effect of print literacy on the psyche and sensibility of the human being. First, he outrightly acknowledges his preference for the oral man. In oral cultures the centrality of the ear gives rise to a sensibility which is open-ended, multi-directional and abstract. It is 360 degrees around like the sense of hearing itself. Moreover, all the senses together are in fair equilibrium and interplay, giving rise to a rich, tactile sensibility or experience of the world. The ratio of the senses is essentially wholesome giving rise to true rationality, which is holistic.

Contrary, for McLuhan, the typographic man replaces an eye for an ear. Print gives rise to a visual mode in Western man which privileges perspective, a fixed point of view, and chronological order or cause and effect. Unlike the oral mode with its interplay of sense and thereby, of emotions, print gives rise to the isolation of sight from the other senses and hence the isolation of the emotions. Through the tyranny of sight over the other senses, man becomes mesmerized by the printed word, as becomes clear after Luther when the written Bible upstages the word of the Holy Roman Catholic Church. The trance created by print leads to the internalization of print technology and the visual, sequential, uniform and lineal become privileged within both the Western psyche and society. The printing press itself, as the first mechanization of a handicraft, becomes the template for applied knowledge. Take any manufacturing process whatsoever, reduce it to its segmented, homogeneous, repeatable components, and the process can be mechanized. This too is internalized in creating typographic man.

But what does this mean in concrete terms for the study of Italian immigration to North America? How do McLuhan's insights play out in the daily lives of immigrants? Let me give some illustrations while steering away from some of the more obvious examples of an oral culture, such as familism, *campanilismo*, and patronage. We mentioned earlier that Italian peasants at the turn of the last century often viewed literacy as white magic since it could gain them entry into the wider world. But within their own communities they also considered the oral word as magical. McLuhan notes how in pre-literate societies there is no separation between a verbal thought and action. Thoughts are dynamic and can have direct consequences. The separation between thought and action can only take place with literacy when words are written down. They then become part of the visual world and something static; they become controllable rather than having a power of their own. But in peasant societies we note a confluence of thought and action. We can readily note here the mechanism of the *malocchio*, that is, that evil thoughts can spell bad consequences which, in turn, can be lifted through the ritual recitation of prayers by a folk healer. Hence, we have the power of words among Italian immigrants. We can better understand the power of oaths and oral agreements and the immigrant's recourse to these rather than to legal contracts. Hence, too we can better understand the immigrant's often violent reaction to insults and curses. For the Italian immigrant, the North American schoolyard rhyme, "sticks and stones will break my bones / but names will never hurt me" had absolutely no meaning.

For the literate North American, on the other hand, verbal thoughts are private, individual and no one else's business. Words, even when spoken, are really not real until they are written down (something North American Indians discovered with a vengeance). Hence the prevalence of lawyers and dictionaries. It is easy to see how such radically different views of the status and legitimacy of the spoken word between the oral peasant-immigrant and typographic man of North America could lead not only to cultural misunderstanding, but to outright clash.

Related to differences in the perception of the word, whether thought or spoken, are differences in the perception of the sacred. The whole field of

Italian popular piety is infused with sensibilities which are oral and tactile rather than literate and visual. That is to say, Italian peasant religiosity is noted by its pervasiveness and its sensuality. There is no distinction between the sacred and the profane, and the sacred can be touched as with a saint's statue, a candle or a relic. Gutenberg and Luther, on the other hand, separated the sacred from the profane, and both religion and vision were turned inward to be reprocessed as personal, individualized faith and point of view. Nothing could be more chilling to the Italian immigrant's sense of the sensuous sacred than the austere protestant morality of North America with its simply designed churches, puritanical laws, and the sacred reserved for one day a week. Perhaps nowhere did these differences become clearer than in the numerous arguments that broke our wherever Italians settled in North America over the practice of the *feste di paese* saints. The noise, banners, statuary, food and drink that accompanied these saints' day feasts struck North Americans as gaudy, pagan, superstitious affairs that had no place in a civilized democracy. For the immigrants they reflected an oral /tactile way of relating to the sacred, that even today is a marker of Italian ethnicity.

Another area that illustrates the division between oral and literate societies is that of human sexuality. Germain Greer in her 1984 book *Sex and Destiny* relates how during her visit to Calabria in the late '60s she was surprised at the matter-of-fact nature with which young virgins spoke of the human body and matters of sex. Sexuality was seen as completely natural and organic. "Sexuality was not a resource of the individual personality in this part of Magna Grecia" she wrote, "it was a universal power palpable in the air itself."

In many ways the peasant women were much less inhibited than the supposedly more liberated woman of North America who, reflecting the society about her, often isolated sexuality so that it was experienced as tantalizing, illicit or political rather than as part of the fabric of life. A particularly glaring instance of this could be seen in North American attitudes towards breast-feeding in public places. Young Italian mothers looked upon baring their breast to feed their infants in public as natural and wholesome. North Americans, however, were scandalized by an act they regarded as indecent, if not outright illegal. The North American, accustomed by a liter-ate mind to pigeon-hole everything, could not conceive of the female breast as both profane (it provided pleasure) and sacred (it sustained life), and was determined to rid himself of confusion by codifying both.

These are only a few of the examples of the cultural clash that occurred between Italian immigrants and North Americans. The list could be augmented indefinitely to include almost all the attitudes and behaviors commented upon by learned observers such as Edward Banfield and Herbert Gans — almost always negatively — as characteristically Italian. A deep difference in attitudes towards wine-making and alcohol lead to Prohibition and ethnic crime in the 1920s; differences in the conception and objective of human commitment led to the pernicious literature of "amoral familism"; differences in the definitions of neighborhood led to the wholesale gutting of Little Italies across the United States under the euphemism of "urban renewal." And the list of issues reflecting cultural clash could go on and we could mention deep misunderstandings around gender roles, child-labor, strike-breaking, status symbols and even backyard gardens.

These and other topics that make up the scholarship and commentary concerning Italians in North America have to date been discussed as conflicts between peasant and city, immigrant and native, or worker and employer. All these interpretations add to our store of knowledge about the Italian immigrant experience in *Merica*. However, McLuhan's work suggests that fundamentally what lies behind the conflicts between oral-oriented immigrants and highly literate North Americans is a difference in sensibilities and perceptions resulting from the extensions or inventions of man. McLuhan's famous aphorism "the medium is the message" refers to his conviction that the significance of any medium or extension of human communication lies not in the content of the medium, but with its form. As the professor related to the famous Canadian photographer Yousef Karsh, "What I study is not the content but the effect of the instrument itself on whole situations."

After 1500, human extension was foremostly invested in the printing press, which democratized literacy and led to a wide range of effects including a modern mentality characterized by visual stress in perception, linear/-sequential thinking, and the homogenization of social life. But in Southern and Eastern Europe, much of the older, more holistic characteristics of an oral-based society survived well into the last century. On p. 229 of *Understanding Media*, McLuhan made specific reference to Italy in the aftermath of World War II:

> "After the Second World War," he wrote, "an ad-conscious American army officer in Italy noted with misgiving that Italians could tell you the names of cabinet ministers, but not the names of commodities preferred

> by Italian celebrities. Furthermore, he said, the wall space of Italian cities was given to political, rather than commercial, slogans. He predicted that there was small hope that Italians would ever achieve any sort of domestic prosperity or calm until they began to worry about the rival claims of corn flakes or cigarettes, rather than the capacities of public men. In fact, he went so far as to say that democratic freedom very largely consists in ignoring politics and worrying, instead, about the threat of scaly scalp, hairy legs, sluggish bowels, [etc.]...

Then McLuhan gave his own evaluations of the observations by the American:

> "The army officer was probably right. Any community that wants to expedite and maximize the exchange of goods and services has simply got to homogenize its social life. The decision to homogenize come easily to the highly literate population of the English speaking world. Yet it is hard for oral cultures to agree on this program of homogenization, ..."

I would suggest that a great many Italian immigrants understood very well the North American project of homogenization, though this understanding was probably more visceral than intellectual. They resisted individualization and held on to corporate structures of family, kinship and community because they realized that only such cohesion, like the fingers of a hand, could give them the strength to resist the pull of the American leviathan. It was to resist the modern homogenization implicit in a highly literate society that peasant-immigrants returned to their villages from America's worksites and cities whenever possible, and that settled immigrants refused assimilation by a myriad of strategies ranging from anarchist radicalism to forming *paese* clubs to making tomato sauce.

For Italian immigrants, then, it can be said that upon arrival to North America among all the challenges, it was the clash of oral ways and sensibilities against literal methods and logic that was the most "shocking" and difficult to absorb. Obviously, for the moment, this appraisal can only be offered as a working hypothesis since no one has yet bothered to delve into it. While we must leave assessing the ultimate nature of the conflict experienced by pre-War Italians in the U.S. for a future date, I am convinced McLuhan's work, especially his *Gutenberg Galaxy*, provides us with valuable insights for such an assessment.

Let me turn at this junction to some observations about Italian immigration to my own country of Canada. First, it should be noted that viewing the movement in its general contours one is struck not by similarities to Italian immigration to the United States, but by several contrasts. Obviously the major contrast is that the movement to Canada was predominantly a post-World-War II influx, but even before this, differences existed between the contemporaneous, pre-War American and Canadian experiences. Early immigration to Canada was even more temporary than that to the U.S.; regions of origin carried different weights, with the Calabresi and Friulians, for example, being relatively more common in Canada compared to Sicilians and Neapolitans in the U.S.; and furthermore the political cultures of the U.S. and Canada produced significantly different ethnicities. Such differences, however, are secondary when the heavy post-War Italian immigration to Canada is compared to the pre-War influx to the U.S.

There can be little doubt the more recent Italian immigrants to Canada who were predominantly permanent settlers have been much more upwardly mobile socially, economically and politically than their American counterparts. Italians in Canada have accomplished in one generation what it has taken their counterparts in the U.S. at least twice as long to achieve. Moreover, this mobility in Canada has been accompanied by Italians' more comprehensive preservation of identity. There are several reasons for the generally smoother adjustment of Canada's Italians, including that they now emigrated as settlers rather than sojourners, the absence of a Great Depression in the post-War Keynsian era and, after 1970, Canada's adoption of an official state policy of multiculturalism in contrast to the American melting pot. But once again, using a McLuhanesque analysis I would like to suggest another scenario for the greater vibrancy of the Italian presence in Canada.

While the Italian immigrants after World War II were no longer illiterate as had been their fathers or grandfathers, only a small minority had more than the basic three or four years of elementary schooling, especially the majority from the South whose background was essentially a rural peasant one. Print literacy had not been around long enough to destroy oral sensibilities. The mentality of the post-war immigrants to Canada (as well as Australia) was essentially the same as those at the turn of the twentieth-century. But in contrast to the earlier influx into the United States, Italian immigrants in Canada found a society that was no longer under the visual hypnosis of print. Starting in the mid-nineteenth-century with the advent of the telegraph, the typographic man was increasingly challenged by the new electric media, which ultimately led to a full-fledged change in sensibilities with the establishment of television in the 1950s. What McLuhan calls the electric man was coming into his own as Italians entered post-war Canada, and a global village was being formed, held together not by print, machines and easy travel, but by the instantaneous relay of information through electricity. The telephone, radio, television and then computers were increasingly encircling the globe to instantaneously link anyone with everyone, anywhere.

What is critical for McLuhan, however, is that the electric age in which he was writing would increasingly come to cultivate in human kind patterns of perception, emotion and thought which had a greater affinity with the oral man than the typographic one. Electric media, rather than reinforcing a linear perspective fostered by print, was reversing the Gutenberg Revolution by fostering a sensibility that was 360° sensitive to total fields of information. These perceptional fields were mosaic in form and involved all the senses at once in wholesome ratio. The tyranny of a print-based visual point of view was over, to be replaced by the multiple perspectives fostered by electric media. As already mentioned, McLuhan cared not a whit about the content of the media. It was the media's form that mattered and that impacted on the total human being: "the medium is the message."

What all this meant for Italian immigrants going to Canada after World War II was that they encountered a society that, in fact, was increasingly moving towards oral/tactile sensibilities which were inclusive, organic and multi-varied. These sensibilities were being unconsciously absorbed through the very form of the electric extensions of man. Pre-War one-way assimilation characteristic of print technology gave way more quickly than anyone thought possible to multiculturalism, multiculturalism being merely the outcome of the mosaic sensibilities cultivated by electric media. Thus, by the 1970s, in Canada the Italian immigrant from an oral culture could more than at any other time in North America, feel quite at home in an environment where electricity was increasingly illuminating the mind and emotions as well as the physical space. The oral world of the Italian immigrant found no wall of incomprehension as earlier occurred in the early twentieth-century. It could well be that the remarkable upward mobility and integration experienced by Italians in Canada in the second half of the twentieth-century owes more to this confluence of the oral with the post-modern that occurred after 1950 than any other factor.

Moreover, within the world of culture, the post-War Italians in Canada soon found themselves in tune with the new artistic expressions being engendered by electric media. Joseph Pivato, who has almost single-handedly put Italian-Canadian literature on the road map of scholarship, has noted in his book *Echo: Essays on Other Literatures* that Italian-Canadian writing is grounded in the oral traditions of Italian immigrants and he perceptively notes how many Italian-Canadian writers were influenced not only by home and neighbourhood, but also by Italian-language radio, records, television and movies. Nowhere is the oral/tactile sensibility of Italian-Canadian writing better illustrated than in the poetry of Antonino Mazza, where this interplay of the senses is linked to memory (memory of course being synonymous with the oral). The title of his famous poem "Our House is a Cosmic Ear" is instructive for it suggests the entire human sensorium being open, like an ear, to the whole world around it. Set in his boyhood Calabria and stretching back to Ulysses, the poem is offered as a gift to the reader. Nothing could be further from the single-mindedness of print, and indeed Mazza went on to extend his orally-rooted art even further by turning directly to the sound of the spoken word in his LP *The Way I remember It*, a performance of the poems, songs and stories from the experience of immigration.

McLuhan, as professor of English, believed passionately that artists and writers are the antennae of society picking up and registering cultural currents long before they are recognized by the masses. Such art can point toward the future. Similarly, Italian-Canadian artists, by drawing upon their oral cultural inheritance, are simultaneously expressing sensibilities characteristic of the post-modern era in which we live. In this sense they, like Italian-Canadians generally, have become part of an uprooted mainstream seeking new paradigms and meanings in the Electric Age.

At the beginning of the twentieth-century the Italian experience in the New World was marked by intense cultural clash between oral and literate interpretations of reality; at the end of the century, however, as cultures are imploded by electric media and once again the ear replaces the eye, Italians in North America are perhaps in a position to act, if they so chose, as guides to the new global village taking shape around us.

Section II

✦

Towards a Definition of Italian Identity in North America

THE ITALIANS AND THE 'MERICANS: MYTHS AND METAPHORS OF BECOMING AMERICAN

Fred Gardaphé
Stony Brook University

In *The New Science*, eighteenth century philosopher Giambattista Vico identified what he called the mythic stage of history as developing after families and social institutions were established. During this stage an aristocracy would develop against which the common people stage a revolt that should enable them to gain greater control of their lives. Out of this struggle would rise heroic figures who replace the divinities of the previous age as models for human behavior. Vico notes that this shift occurred when man moved away from an agrarian culture and into an urban culture, from a theology based on fear of the gods to one in which man would begin to struggle with the gods. Vico theorized that men rewrote the stories of gods as divine creatures in myths that gave the gods human qualities. The key to understanding this mythic mode lies in Vico's suggestion that "poets do not make ethnic myths; they simply record in allegorical poetic form the histories of their people" (Bidney 274). Myths then are recorded realities that over the years become stories that change as the need for change arises in each generation.

I use Vico not as a guide to reading Italian American histories, but as a way of envisioning the myths that result from the histories that have been fashioned out of the experiences recorded by Americans of Italian descent. In many respects, Italian Americans are just beginning to create their own histories in writing. For a long time, much of what we have come to call Italian American history was passed on from one generation to the next by word of mouth. And in this system of oral tradition what doesn't get spoken, doesn't get remembered. In cultures and communities that function primarily in the oral modes, silence becomes an organizing principle by which some realities can be entirely eliminated from cultural memory. Silence can erase a legacy of shame, can teach the lesson of shut up and assimilate. Few Italian Americans conditioned by oral traditions, especially in the Roman Catholic Church, ever incorporated the stories of historical figures such as Sacco and Vanzetti into their consciousness as they shifted from becoming to being Americans. Figures such as Sacco and Vanzetti simply did not represent acceptable ways for Italians to be or to become Americans. No one knew this better than the Italians themselves, especially those who were brave enough to testify at the famous trial only to see their testimony ignored, not believed, and ultimately dismissed. Although Sacco and Vanzetti have not made it into the consciousness of most Italian Americans, there is today a strong trend in the writing of Italian Americans to reclaim the history of Sacco and Vanzetti, perhaps precisely because their story has safely become mythic.

The seventy-fifth anniversary of the execution of Sacco and Vanzetti, passed without much attention, especially in the Italian American community where fictions of gangsters like Tony Soprano have become more real than its own history, especially to those who call themselves advocates of Italian American culture. Because stories of Sacco and Vanzetti were not useful in helping Italians become Americans, they would be repressed for at least one generation until Italian immigrants to the United States could feel safely enough as Americans to revisit gaps in its history. This will help us understand why there is so little recognition of stories that surround such historical figures as Sacco and Vanzetti in today's Americans of Italian descent. This essay comes from a much more involved investigation I have been making into the way Italian Americans process their personal histories in relation to the public histories into which they are born and indoctrinated through the Americanization process.

I

Inventing Italian America

America was an idea long before it became a place, and as an idea it enveloped all hopes of complete freedom, real equality, absence of persecution and unlimited potential for living life to its fullest. As Djelal Kadir glossed the word in his *Columbus and the Ends of the Earth*, America just might mean "nowhereland" a place that can only exist as an idea. Once that idea took residence in a land called the United States, it fell victim to the wiles of reality that make the perfect practice of theory impossible. I turn now to a personal anecdote that I believe will help us see what happens when Italians become Americans.

Two years ago my family was to travel to Italy to visit, together for the first time, our ancestral homeland — the birthplace of my grandparents. The terrorist attacks on the World Trade Center on September 11, 2001 scared most of my relatives and so the trip was cancelled. In our discussions, one of my uncles commented on Italy's response to President Bush's call for help. "Those damned dagoes. Can you believe they had the *coglioni* to say they weren't going to send any troops. Who do they think they are? I'm ashamed to say we came from there. And after we saved them in two wars and kept them from becoming communist. What kind of way is that to respond?" This response indicates the failure of American education and points to the success of the United States institutions in assimilating Italian immigrants and their offspring. My uncle's response, couched later in religious fluff, shows not only his own ignorance about the reality of Italy's relationship to the United States in two wars, but also the success of the master narrative of history mediated by the power brokers of the United States.

A second instance comes from an Editorial that appeared in the October 7th (2002) issue of the *St. Augustine Record.* Author Hansen Alexander writes: "Tomorrow's Columbus Day Celebration will go forth undeterred by the fact that the Genoese mariner helped Spain, not Italy stake a claim to the Americas." Then begins his lament, "The holiday has come to celebrate that which is Italian, or more specifically, that which is southern Italian." Having made this distinction is interesting, but why is another story. Alexander characterizes southern Italy as an area more impoverished than the rest of Italy, and the birthplace of "tomato based foods like thin pizza, the notorious Mafia, and poor fishermen like Joe DiMaggio's father." He complains that we do not celebrate northern Italian traditions like "the industrial might of Milan, the intellectual heritage of its great universities at Bologna and Padua," or the genius of da Vinci, Michelangelo, Galileo, Dante and Bocaccio. "No," he continues, "tomorrow will be about cheap wine and stereotypical visions of Italians as a congregation of vigilantes."

Unlike my uncle, whom I know well enough to realize there is almost always a bit of irony in what he says, I continued reading the editorial hoping that this was someone's idea of a joke. But it only got worse from there. While the publisher of the paper later apologized for the publication of this editorial and it has been pulled from its online archives it represents little more than the ignorance of one man. Both my uncle and Alexander suffer from the same affliction which are both traceable to the difficulty in interpreting the various metaphors that have come to be associated with the United States of America.

To the Italian immigrant America first existed as a metaphor and there was virtually no distinction between North and South America. America meant going west across the ocean where there was work. One needed to compare the American experience to what a fellow Italian could understand. So those who had been to America and returned to their native homelands necessarily employed metaphors when relating their experiences to their paesani. Far too often exaggerated accounts of their successes and failures were created so that through story the myth of America was created and through metaphor the myth was communicated. Like any good metaphor, America has always been subject to many interpretations; the struggle for identification with America was one of the immigrant's first battles. Even at the entry to America, immigrants were immediately aware of their difference, their un-Americaness.

Now whether the metaphor came to one through song, letters or conversation it communicated a variety of messages. Much of the metaphor centered around ideas such as freedom, boundless opportunity and golden streets. A typical Italian immigrant was lured to America by this myth and its promise that life is greener on the other side of the ocean. In Pietro Corsi's novel, *La Giobba*, the real myth was dispelled when the immigrant came to the realization that 1. the streets were not paved with gold; 2. few if any of the streets had been paved at all; and 3. the Italians were expected to pave them. In fact, a contemporary and chauvinistic Italian American t-shirt reads: "America, We discovered it. We named it. We built it."

The early Italian American literature focuses on this dream/reality dichotomy and the coming to terms with the dispelling of the myths and metaphors that lured the immigrant to America. To the Italian American, even those born in the United States, America immediately became a metaphor through such myths, and as such it stood for something to strive for. First it was a metaphor of separation: there are those things which are and are not American. This notion is reflected upon in much of the early Italian

American literature. Jerre Mangione's *Mt. Allegro* for example opens with the exploration of this issue.

> "When I grow up I want to be an American," Giustina said.
> We looked at our sister; it was something none of us had ever said.
> "Me too," Maria echoed.
> "Aw you don't even know what an American is," Joe scoffed.
> "I do so," Giustina said.
> It was more than the rest of us knew.
> "We're Americans right now," I said. "Miss Zimmerman says if you're born here you're an American."
> "Aw she's nuts," Joe said. He had no use for most teachers.
> "We're Italians. If y'don't believe me ask Pop."
> But my father wasn't very helpful. "Your children will be 'Americani.' But you, my son, are half-and-half. Now stop asking me questions. You should know those things from going to school. What do you learn in school, anyway?"

This confusion over what was and was not American carried over into the next generation.

I believed that my maternal grandfather, an immigrant from Southern Italy, was not American. I was convinced that the good immigrants were those who struggled to be American with the knowledge that the past contained much of what was not considered to be American. At least, I thought, the good immigrant realized the need to disguise or better yet erase all traces of un-Americanness: stop speaking one's native language, rid one's self of accented American English; start dressing in the latest American fashions, and spurn Italian restaurants and eating Italian food in public. However, I would find that all these material things were easier to dispose of than the spiritual. When it came to things like the family, dignity and self respect, my grandparents' *Italianità* could not be smothered. In terms of such Italian values they revealed *Italianità* in spite of conscious attempts to control or mask it.

To Italian Americans, America as a metaphor communicated denial. It wasn't a problem of knowing what being American was, rather the problem came in trying to avoid everything that common knowledge said being American wasn't. As a kid, I thoroughly despised any mark of *Italianità* and did my best to rid myself of such evidence as darker skin (I wouldn't go shirtless in the summer). Once relatives from Italy visited us and I ignored them. I told my non-Italian American friends (the ones who had pointed them out in my yard as though they were some circus oddity) that those "wops" were strangers who had missed a plane and my family was putting them up until the next plane left for Italy.

It was difficult, even for those of us who had been educated in American schools, to hide the more instinctual aspects of *Italianità* that had somehow survived our parents' conscious renunciations. Being American meant talking without using hands. Once a speech teacher wrapped string around us so we wouldn't gesticulate during a speech presentation. Without hands, the job of communicating through kinetics was taken over by shoulder shrugging, facial twitching, and waist turning. Some aspects of *Italianità* were destined to betray my Americaness in spite of all I could do. To be American, was to be what others were and so we modeled ourselves after those that the media gave their attention to. We made heroes out of others — astronauts, sports figures, media stars and assassinated Presidents. Italian American literature is filled with this desire to be the "other," as the following selection from John Fante's *Wait Until Spring, Bandini* novel demonstrates: "His name was Arturo, but he hated it and wanted to be called John. His last name was Bandini, and he wanted to be called Jones. His mother and father were Italians, but he wanted to be an American. His father was a bricklayer, but he wanted to be a pitcher for the Chicago Cubs." In order to be American, to be the "other," we needed to defy our parents, and our grandparents and anyone or thing else that reminded us of our non-American ancestry. We needed to turn our backs on what was our past, to melt the mold of our heritage and hope that it was ice: melt and evaporate without a trace.

Italians learned about America through television, schools, newspapers and through Irish American administrated religion and politics. Those media portrayed America as sleek, fashionable, material, present and future oriented. History played a minor (if any at all) role in the life of the average American. History was facts, figures and military victories in which the losers were always the non-Americans. Those victories represented the conquering of enemies that were inhuman or cowards, especially we learned, that Italians were cowardly soldiers. Italy was fine until Rome fell, but then again it was the Roman empire that killed Christ; after that it was all down hill.

Even England, the basis of much of America's early development was viewed as a quaint land of cottages and castles, a place more romantic than realistic. All that were not Americans were weak and needed American assistance to stand up to enemies. Nothing was complete unless America had had a hand in developing it. America was the metaphor of glory; and as such its antithesis, Russia, necessarily became the metaphor of doom. As we grew older we realized America was a mis-read metaphor, but there had been clues all along: Foreigners never fared well in the novels taught in schools and Italians, if they had written any American novels at all didn't count; boy scout uniforms didn't fit the peasant stock frames that we of Mediterranean ancestry were issued at birth that needed grandma's magic needle work to make us presentable and that needle often embellished the interiors of the uniforms with stitched crucifixes and crocheted symbols that would protect us from "malocchio," the evil eye.

America's imperialistic commercial and military ventures forced an increased awareness of other cultures: first, those who were aided in the battles against Nazism and fascism; then those who were threatened by the iron curtain; then when they started blacklisting our artists who associated with foreign elements it became obvious that many people were confused about what was and wasn't American. The House Committee on Un-American activities scared everyone whose name fell short of Anglo-Saxon simplicity. By the time the sixties came along the spotlight revealed the un-American activities that were being perpetrated by America: attempts to assassinate Castro, and meddling in the affairs of smaller countries.

As Guido D'Agostino's novel *Olives on the Apple Tree* warned, there was nothing to be done about not fitting into America. How can you expect an olive to grow from the apple tree. But the culture of the 1960s changed such immigrant fatalistic attitudes. It was as though life in America had been a masquerade party in which everyone in attendance had been wearing American costumes. And in the sixties came the unmasking, and many of us found that most were not really Americans at all. A once strong American identity was found to be a fragile facade, a surface, like ice strong and reflective until the heat comes upon it. And the heat of the sixties proved to be too much. Breaking the surface we find, like the analysis of any metaphor will prove, that its origins were much more complex than we had thought. The early metaphor was a primitive reaction between self and other. We would soon find out that Indians were the real Americans, the first Americans and so they would be renamed Native Americans--this carried over to Black Americans, Jewish Americans, until it seemed the hyphenation craze would never end. But this still wasn't quite what we were hoping for. Although we were now better connected by a bridge of punctuation to the word and thus to the metaphor we were still without accounts of us in history. What we had learned in history classes was not the real us, but the us that others saw and depicted. So many of us fell for those portrayals that when something like Mario Puzo's *The Godfather* came along in 1969, we were forming "Godfather clubs" so we didn't think we mattered, what mattered was what was historical and that meant it had to be red, white and blue.

More than a few who were brave thinkers didn't fall for such nonsense, and realized they had always been in involved in history, and so started documenting their participation in it. Now there are many books about Italians in the United States, novels, plays, and poetry that shows the creation of the metaphor, the interpretations of the metaphor and the alternatives to the metaphor. The United States is experiencing a cultural renaissance that has come from the reawakening, the researching and recasting of its ancestors' roles in the development of this land called America.

It was typical of America to take the past, rename it, hide its origins and make us think it was so brand new, but the same education that was hoodwinking many of us, enlightened enough of us to begin learning for ourselves. Metaphor was responsible for identity crisis of the children of immigrants, and the search though the metaphor for the real basis of the American signs. Once the immigrant lost the original idea of America, and the dispelling of some of its early metaphorical associations took place, Italians needed to replace it with another ideal — and that's where the notion of the "old country" came to life.

Italy became a metaphor for the post-immigrant generations, though stories told by immigrant relatives, the images began building. With that image in mind we went off to find that place called "bell'Italia." But it was nowhere to be found. Italy had changed, the metaphors of the past no longer could be found in the present reality. So that they could live on, writers captured them in literature. So the metaphor, becomes the map, and once that map is used the metaphor is no longer useful to the few who used it to control. America was not a foreign language, yet the answer to what America is was always right there in front of our eyes, in the very name. The process by which America was named should have told us that American had its roots in foreign countries. So those who learned to use the language of the land that imperialized, colonized us, were also learning to use other languages that gave new words, new meanings new dimensions to the American metaphor and with all this came new interpretations of the metaphor. The irony is that America was built by metaphor, and the American myth is destined to be dismantled by the very language that created its metaphor. When we began to learn Italian, we began to see America in a new way.

History is catching up quickly with America. As soon as the idea became a place, it was eventually doomed to succumb to the realities of every other place in the world. And those who fell prey to the myth and metaphor, once they had become a part of the place, realized that it wasn't all it was cracked up to be. It was not the utopia they had hoped for. And once they became a part of the place, they began losing the original idea of the place. That is the threat that we face today: the loss of the original idea of the United States of America. As long as we refuse to face histories we are destined to continue denial of rights and freedoms to minorities. It is up to individuals, brave creative individuals to be different, to stand up and refuse to turn on each other and feed our greed and selfishness on the weaknesses of others.

This is how we can work with the myth, to use it to study the history of America in the context of the history of the world. To study the idea of America in the context of the ideas of the worlds. A history of the metamorphosis of America as metaphor needs to be written, to be studied and to be acted upon. That history is there, somewhere in our culture and it needs to be identified and examined for truths to extract and use toward the rebuilding of the metaphor. The tension between the metaphor of Italy and the metaphor of America is at the foundation of this study. Through that tension Italian America was created.

II

For many years, Italian American culture has been preserved in the Little Italy neighborhoods, and over the years, more likely than not, in the basement of those homes, where grandpa made wine, where grandma had a second kitchen, and now material legacies and memories are stored. Outside celebrations such as religious *feste* became the most important public presentation of Italian American culture, but these annual events were never frequent enough to protect Italian American culture from the regular mass media bombardment of negative stereotypes.

Where Italian Americans have never organized as a cultural group is in the mainstream institutions of education. The public programs that might have taught Italian Americans the value of their own culture and subsequently fortified future generations, the public programs that would have challenged media-made impressions, were never created. Italian Americans have kept their heads in their basements, in what they fondly refer to as the "basciuments," where Italian American culture is safe inside family celebrations.

Now is the time to move beyond the basements of yesterday and out into the streets of today. The romance and tragedy of early twentieth-century immigration can no longer serve as models for identity. The key to creating a meaningful sense of Italian American culture that means something to today's youth is to first insure that they have access to histories, of their families and of their communities. They need to be exposed to historical and contemporary models in the areas of arts, business, and education that they can study, emulate and transcend. The Little Italys that once served as the source and haven of Italian American identity, where Robert Orsi's notion of "the domus" in his important study *The Madonna of 115th Street*, was nurtured and enacted, have become little more than cultural theme parks in gentrified land. With the move to the suburbs, Italian Americans have created scholarships for higher education, but have done little to help those applicants understand what it means to be Italian American once they enter those institutions.

While the great body of work that makes up Italian American studies began in earnest after the Second World War, it would not be until the reformation of the American literary canon, in the 1970s and 90s, that Italian/American literature was posited as a serious field of inquiry. A pioneer in the field, Rose Basile Green, presented an extensive survey of the novels written by American writers of Italian descent in *The Italian-American Novel* (1974). That same year Richard Gambino's *Blood of My Blood: The Dilemma of Italian Americans*, explored the psychological impact of the ethnic identity of America's Italians. Gambino's notion of creative ethnicity as an alternative to ethnic chauvinism laid the groundwork for criticism of myths created by and about Italian/American culture. Along with anthologies such as Helen Barolini's *The Dream Book* (1985), Ferdinando Alfonsi's *Dictionary of Italian-American Poets* (1989) and Anthony J. Tamburri's et al. *From the Margin* (1991), Gambino's and Green's studies have enabled a distinct cultural tradition to be identified and maintained.

When Frank Lentricchia located the origins of Italian/American fiction in Luigi Ventura's 1886 collection of short stories *Misfits and Remnants*, he made us realize that it took nearly one hundred years for the identification and appreciation of a literary tradition within Italian/American culture. Now that this discovery is being expanded upon and revised by young scholars and journalists such as Martino Marazzi and Francesco Durante, it is important for us to understand the process by which Italian immigrants became 'Mericans.

Most immigrants from Italy came to America with the idea of earning a livelihood and then returning to Italy. These immigrants were hesitant to adapt too quickly to American ways. Their goal was simply to do whatever was necessary to improve their lives in this new land. Early twentieth-century immigrants from Italy to the United States did not immediately refer to themselves as Americans. Most of the early immigrants were sojourners or "birds of passage," primarily men who crossed the ocean to find work, make money, and return home. This experience is well presented in books such as Michael La Sorte's *La Merica: Images of Italian Greenhorn Experience* (1985). In addition to language barriers, these immigrants often faced difficult living conditions and encountered racism. In *Wop! A Documentary History of Anti-Italian Discrimination* (1999), Salvatore La Gumina gathers evidence of this racism from late nineteenth- and twentieth-century American journalism appearing in the *New York Times* and other major publications.

In response to this mistreatment, many of the Italians referred to Americans as "Merdicani" short for "Merde di cane" (dog shit). The word was also used as a derogatory reference by Italians to those who assimilated too quickly and readily into American culture. My grandfather would refer to me as a "Merican" whenever I made a mistake or did something foolish. He used the word as a way of punishing me whenever I did something of which he did not approve. For those immigrants who intended not to return to Italy, the experience of the transition might become the basis for the creation of art, but it would be most likely the children of the immigrants who would begin using that experience to create art. And when they did, it was never their intention to be perceived as Italian American artists. Rather, influenced by the literature encountered in schools, in libraries, and in bookstores, such writers saw themselves as American writers and so from the beginning they didn't want to see themselves as Italian. Most novels published prior to World War II depicted this vexed immigrant experience of adjustment in America: Louis Forgione's *The River Between* (1924), Garibaldi La Polla's *The Grand Gennaro* (1935), Valenti Angelo's *Golden Gate* (1938), Guido D'Agostino's *Olives on the Apple Tree* (1940), Mari Tomasi's *Deep Grow the Roots* (1940), and Jo Pagano's *Golden Wedding* (1943).

In spite of a substantial presence in literature, other than the romantic exotic types epitomized by Rudolph Valentino and the criminals encountered in the gangster films Italian Americans had little visibility in American popular culture. Norman Rockwell paintings and illustrations, considered in the 1930s and 1940s to be typically American, never included images of Italians. Even the works of Italian/American artists themselves were conspicuously void of direct references to the immigrant experience. Filmmaker Frank Capra, who emigrated from Sicily with his family in 1903, managed to include the Martini family in *It's a Wonderful Life* (1946) as a marginal reference to the poor helped by George Bailey. In the literary arts, becoming an American is the focus of much of the early artists such as John Fante, whose "The Odyssey of a Wop," appeared in H.L. Mencken's *American Mercury*, a popular magazine of the 1930s and 1940s. Fante, a self-proclaimed protégée of Mencken, wrote novels and became a Hollywood screenwriter. His *Full of Life* (1957), a mainstream Hollywood comedy starring Richard Conte and Judy Holiday, was based on his novel of the same title which helped bring this experience into the American mainstream.

Immigrant struggles, beyond trying to make a living and feed self and family recounted in such novels as Pietro di Donato's *Christ in Concrete* (1939), John Fante's *Wait Until Spring, Bandini* (1938), Mari Tomasi's *Like Lesser Gods* (1949), Julia Savarese's *The Weak and the Strong* (1952) and autobiographies as Jerre Mangione's *Mount Allegro* (1943), included coping with the prejudice and discrimination which reached extremes in the 1891 mob lynching of innocent Italians who were accused and acquitted of the murder of New Orleans' police chief, and the trial and 1927 execution of Sacco and Vanzetti. The literature produced during this period provides great insights into the shaping of American identities and into the obstacles that these immigrants faced in pursuing their versions of the American dream.

The rise of Fascism in Italy during 1920s-40s would have a tremendous effect on the identity and behavior of Americans of Italian descent. This effect would become a prime subject in their literature. Jerre Mangione captured this experience in his memoirs, *Mount Allegro* (1943) and *An Ethnic At Large* (1978):

> In my years of becoming an American I had come to understand the evil of Fascism and hate it with all my soul. One or two of my relatives argued with me on the subject because they had a great love for their native land and, like some men in love, they could see nothing wrong. Fascism was only a word to them; Mussolini a patriotic Italian putting his country on its feet. Why did I insist on finding fault with Fascism, they asked, when all the American newspapers were admitting Mussolini was a great man who made the trains run on time? (*Mount Allegro* 239-40)

Trapped between two countries (their parents' homeland and their own), Italian/American writers tended to stay aloof of the international political situation of their time. It wouldn't be until after the fall of Mussolini that Italian Americans would, in any significant way, address fascism in their fiction and poetry. The earliest anti-fascist writings dared to contradict the pro-fascist posture assumed by the American government and such leading figures of the American literary scene as Wallace Stevens, Ezra Pound and T.S. Eliot, who as proponents of modernism were also, interestingly enough, if not outright pro-fascist, at least sympathetic to Mussolini's fascism (Diggins 245). Those Italian/Americans who opposed Mussolini from the beginning did so at the risk of being attacked or labeled as communists by the larger American public as well as their own pro-Mussolini countrymen.

One of the earliest Italian Americans to voice his opinion of Italian fascism in his poetry was Arturo Giovannitti, who, with Joseph Ettor, organized the famous 1912 Lawrence Mill Strike. In his poem "To Mussolini" he accuses the Father of Italian Fascism of winning "fame with lies." And he tells *il Duce* that "No man is great who does not find/ A poet who will hail him as he is/ With an almighty song that will unbind/ Through his exploits eternal silences./ Duce, where is your bard? In all mankind/ The only poem you inspired is this." In "Italia Speaks," Giovannitti depicts America as a child of Italy who can rescue its mother from "The twin ogres in black and brown [who] have polluted my gardens." Giovannitti composed poems that echo Walt Whitman's patriotic odes during the Civil War. In his "Battle Hymn of the New Italy" we find a synthesis of Giosue Carducci and Whitman, as Giovannitti calls for the Italian people to rise up against Mussolini and Hitler.

Along with Giovannitti, those most prominent anti-fascists whose writing appeared most frequently in American publications were the "fuorusciti," those Italian intellectuals who left Italy and found refuge, more often than not, in American universities: Gaetano Salvemini at Harvard, Max Ascoli at the New School for Social Research, Giuseppe Borgese at the University of Chicago, and Lionello Venturi at Johns Hopkins (Diggins 140). These "fuorusciti" were responsible for a number of influential anti-fascist publications. Their presence made "the universities one of the few anti-Fascist ramparts in America" (Diggins 261).

Similar anti-fascist sentiments are found in the fiction of Jerre Mangione. Mangione's interactions with activist Carlo Tresca became the material upon which he would build his second novel, *Night Search* (1965). Based on Tresca's assassination, *Night Search* dramatizes the experience of Michael Mallory, the illegitimate son of an anti-fascist labor organizer and newspaper publisher by the name of Paolo Polizzi, a character based on Carlo Tresca. Through an investigation of his father's murder, Mallory learns to take action, and in doing so, comes to an understanding of contemporary politics. Mallory very much resembles Stiano Argento, the main protagonist in Mangione's earlier and more strongly anti-fascist novel, *The*

Ship and the Flame (1948). Based on his European experiences of the late 1930s, this novel presents a more sophisticated overview of the effects of fascism by creating an allegory for the sorry state of political affairs in Europe prior to America's entry into the Second World War. Argento is one of a number of characters fleeing Fascist and Nazi powers who were smuggled aboard a Portuguese ship carrying other refugees. The ship, run by a Fascist sympathizing Captain, is denied entry into Mexico and heads for Nazi controlled Casablanca. A liberal Catholic, Argento realizes that the prayers his wife urges him to make won't be enough; he risks his life to take control of the situation. His decision to act comes from the guilt he feels about having let the flame ignite the fascist power that virtually destroyed his Sicilian homeland. Mangione, aware of the dilemma of the liberal and the fate of the revolutionary in the pre-World War II period, suggests that while the struggle against fascism can be won through heroic action, there still remains intolerance and persecution of those who think and act differently.

While immigration to the U.S. from Italy slowed between the 1920s and 1940s due to political maneuvers such as the U.S. quota restrictions of 1924, a number of Italian intellectuals were allowed to immigrate to the United States in flight from fascism. Most prominent among those included scientists such as Enrico Fermi, who has come to be called father of the atom bomb and writers Arturo Vivante, P.M. Pasinetti, and Nicolo Tucci. Vivante, a physician, contributed frequently to such major publications as the *New Yorker*. His fiction includes a collection of short stories *The French Girls of Killini* (1967), and three novels: *A Goodly Babe* (1966), *Doctor Giovanni* (1969) and *Run to the Waterfall* (1965). Pasinetti came to study in the United States in 1935 from Venice and first published fiction in *The Southern Review*. He earned a Ph.D. at Yale in 1949 and went on to teach at UCLA. Pasinetti published three novels, *Venetian Red* (1960), *The Smile on the Face of the Lion* (1965) and *From the Academy Bridge* (1970); his work earned him an award from the National Institute of Arts and Letters in 1965. Tucci, who first came as a student, published two autobiographical novels using European settings to depict a liberation from the history that the emigrant experiences (*Before My Time* (1962) and *Unfinished Funeral* (1964)). For these writers, their sense of the literary was significantly shaped by the prominence in 1930s Italy of *Americanisti* such as Elio Vittorini and Cesare Pavese, both translators and influential editors who helped introduce American literature to Italian culture.

Prior to the U.S. entry to World War II Congress passed the Alien Registration Act (the Smith Act) that required all noncitizens over 14 to be fingerprinted and registered at their local post office. At the outset of the war the FBI identified many Italian Americans as dangerous enemy aliens. Due to political pressure, some of the restrictions were removed on Columbus Day, 1942. In all, 10,000 Italian-Americans were restricted to certain areas or held in 46 detention camps in Texas, California, Washington, Montana, North Dakota, Oklahoma, New York and New Jersey. The father of baseball great, Joe DiMaggio, had his fishing boats and radios confiscated by the government. While such violations were not as severe or pervasive as those enacted against the Japanese Americans, they did significantly disrupt the lives of those imprisoned. A traveling exhibit entitled *Una Storia Segreta* (A Secret Story) has revealed that many Italian Americans suffered civil rights violations that seriously affected their lives and livelihoods. This collection of oral histories, photographs letters and papers documenting the evacuation and internment of Italian "enemy aliens," was compiled at the lead of Lawrence DiStasi and has been touring the country as a public display since 1994. This revision of history and the giving of voice to those who had suffered in silence place significant pressure for a political response. In 1999, the U.S. House of Representatives passed Resolution 2442 that acknowledged government violations of civil liberties, and in 2000 with the signature of President Bill Clinton, the Wartime Violation of Italian American Civil Liberties Act became Public Law 106-451 that acknowledged the government's misdeeds.

At the outset of the war, Italian immigrants were the largest foreign born group in the U.S. One way of proving unquestionable loyalty to the new country was performing military service during World War II. Estimates of the number of Italian Americans serving in the armed forces run from upwards of a half million to a million, numbers in excess of their percentage of the population at the time. Poet Felix Stefanile captures the motivation of the young Italian American in "The Dance at Saint Gabriel's": "In those hag-ridden and race conscious times/ we wanted to be known as anti-fascists,/ and thus get over our Italian names." The films of Frank Capra during this period celebrated American democratic ideals. *Mr.*

Deeds Goes to Town (1936) and *Meet John Doe* (1941) established a reputation for Capra that would equal Norman Rockwell's for making art that typified American life of the times. From 1935-1941 Capra served as president of the Academy of Motion Picture Arts and Sciences. During the war he produced a series of documentary films with the Signal Service Photographic Detachment entitled "Why We Fight" (1942-1945). Because of Italy's alliance with the Axis powers, World War II was not a time to assert one's Italian ancestry. If it did one thing, the war turned Italians into Americans. As Ben Morreale recounts in his autobiographical novel, *Sicily: The Hallowed Land* (2000): "The army, the war, was the final assimilation...for the second generation Sicilian. It was the good war to which they all willingly sacrificed themselves and it became the source of passionate patriotism for many of the second generation. America, after all, had asked them to serve 'their' country."

Through their participation at home and on the front lines, Italian immigrants had proven they could be good Americans and the post-war period saw the rise of those new Americans in action. Italians continued to play a major role in what historian Reed Ueda has so aptly called "the cycle of national creation and re-creation through immigration" (*Postwar Immigrant America* 4). After the war, Italians were among the larger groups of foreign or mixed parentage were the Italian with 3.3 million. Like other children of immigrants, Italian American artists reflected the major themes expressed in post-war literature, such as the soldier's return, the generation gap, the sexual revolution, the focus on education, the struggle for civil rights, interest in jazz, the rise of Catholicism, the creation of suburban culture, and the rise of mass culture and the consumer society. As Ueda notes: "Encouraging the individualist pursuit of pleasure and novel sensation, [American] consumerist mass culture was at odds with certain aspects of their [foreign-born parents] tradition that emphasized moralistic and ascetic values, the stoical acceptance of self-denial and abstention for the sake of family propriety.... Mass culture became a part of their developing a sense of self as 'ethnic' Americans" (Ueda 108). And after World War II the Italians shifted from becoming to being Americans. Implicit in this move of assimilation was that Italians became Americans when they learned to pronounce the "A" in America, forgot the history of their ancestors and no longer smelled the stench of the merde-cani.

Works Cited

Alexander, Hansen. Editorial. *St. Augustine Record.* (October 7, 2002): 1.

Alfonsi, Ferdinando. *Dictionary of Italian-American Poets*. New York: Peter Lang Publishing, 1989.

Barolini, Helen, Ed. *The Dream Book. Writings by Italian American Women*. New York: Schocken, 1985.

Bidney, David. "Vico's New Science of Myth." *Giambattista Vico, An International Symposium*. Ed. Giorgio Tagliacozzo. Baltimore: Johns Hopkins Press, 1969. (259-67).

Corsi, Pietro. *La Giobba*. Reprinted as: Winter in Montreal. Toronto: Guernica Editions, 2000.

D'Agostino, Guido. *Olives on the Apple Tree*. New York: Doubleday, Doran & Company, 1940.

Diggins, John P. *Mussolini and Fascism: The View from America*. Princeton: Princeton UP, 1972.

Fante, John. *Wait Until Spring, Bandini!* 1938. Santa Barbara, CA: Black Sparrow, 1983.

Gambino, Richard. *Blood of My Blood.* 1973. New York: Anchor, 1975.

Giovannitti, Arturo. *The Collected Poems of Arturo Giovannitti.* Intr. Norman Thomas. Chicago: E. Clemente and Sons, 1962. Rep. New York: Arno Press, 1975.

Green, Rose Basile. *The Italian-American Novel.* Cranbury, NJ: Associated UP, 1974.

Kadir, Djelal. *Columbus and the Ends of the Earth: Europe's Prophetic Rhetoric as Conquering Ideology*. Berkeley: University of California Press, 1992.

LaGumina, Salvatore J. *Wop!, A Documentary History of Anti-Italian Discrimination in the United States*. San Francisco: Straight Arrow Books, 1973.

La Sorte, Michael. *La Merica: Images of Italian Greenhorn Experience*. Philadelphia: Temple UP, 1985.

Lentricchia, Frank. "Luigi Ventura and the Origins of Italian-American Fiction." *Italian Americana*. 1.2 (1974) 189-95.

Mangione, Jerre. *Mount Allegro*. 1943. New York: Columbia UP, 1972.

_______. *Night Search*. New York: Crown Publishers, 1965.

Morreale, Ben. *Sicily: The Hallowed Land.* New York: Legas Books, 2000.

Orsi, Robert Anthony. *The Madonna of 115th Street: Faith and Community in Italian Harlem, 1880-1950*. New Haven: Yale UP, 1985.

Tamburri, Anthony Julian, Paolo A. Giordano and Fred L. Gardaphe, Eds. *From the Margin: Writings in Italian Americana*. West Lafayette, IN: Purdue UP, 1991.

Stefanile, Felix. *The Dance at St. Gabriel's*. Brownsville, OR: Story Line Press, 1995.

Ueda, Reed. *Post War Immigrant America: A Social History*. Boston: Bedford/St. Martin's, 1994.

Joseph Tusiani: A Multilingual Profile

Cosma Siani
Università di Cassino

Joseph Tusiani's work is multifaceted. The aspect of it I intend to consider in this presentation is its multilingualism. Tusiani is the author of creative writing, mainly poetry, in four languages: English, Italian, Latin and his Gargano dialect. How have such languages arisen in his experience and developed into means of literary expression? As with all bilingual or multilingual speakers, the answer to such a question is embedded in the user's own life history. Let us therefore briefly look at that.

Joseph Tusiani was born to poor parents in a small town on the Gargano Mount, San Marco in Lamis, in the province of Foggia. His mother was a seamstress, and his father, a shoemaker who left for North America six months before his only child was born and never came back. Tusiani's native language, and the language of the single-parent family where he was brought up, was in fact the dialect of poor people in a faraway, backward land during the interwar years. The local dialect was Tusiani's true mother-tongue, and it remained so throughout his stay in America: it was the basic means of communication between mother and son until old *signora Maria* died in 1998. Tusiani has derived much of the language in his dialect poetry exactly from such domestic use.

Italian came later into Joseph Tusiani's life. As a child, he may have perceived it as the language of more formal communication in the letters between his mother and father. Then it became the tongue of his course of education: primary school in his native town, then five year's *ginnasio* in Combonian seminaries at Troia (Foggia) and in Northern Italy, at Brescia; then the three-year course of *liceo classico*, back in his native places, when he gave up his vocation to the priesthood; finally, the university of Naples, wherefrom he graduated in *lettere* in 1947. Tusiani's primary-school teacher, Luigi Martino, was also a locally-known poet and a polished user of the Italian language. Such a teacher may have instilled the idea of literary expression into the boy's mind. In fact, it was not long before Italian was used by the young man as the means of elevated expression in his first poetic exertions. After his emigration to America, Tusiani never totally abandoned Italian, but he used it very little. However, when a long time later he decided to write an autobiographical narrative, he took up the Italian language; and significantly so, just as later in his life he has consistently taken to writing numerous poems in his native dialect.

The use of English was the consequence of Tusiani's migration. Whereas English had only been a school subject for the young Tusiani (he wrote his graduation thesis on the poetry of William Wordsworth), it became the medium of his adult and professional life once in the United States. Tusiani and his mother arrived in New York, and the family was reunited, in 1947. There the young man began to make his way into the academic world, and developed his teaching career, mainly in the College of Mount Saint Vincent, in the Bronx, and then at the Herbert H. Lehman College of the City University of New York, until 1983, when he retired. His literary aspirations drove him to master English not only for everyday communicative needs, but for creative purposes as well. He wanted to be "an American poet," just like Emanuel Carnevali and Pascal D'Angelo and successful or unsuccessful others before him. He wrote poetry in English, and his literary ambition even pushed him to take up the translation of Italian poetry into English.

The fourth language which Tusiani uses is Latin. This means of expression, too, first emerged as a school subject dating back to his course of education in Italy. But it was in America that his Latin output was refined and grew to volume size. Prolific as he is in everything he sets out to write, Tusiani has composed an enormous amount of Latin verse. He is an accepted author in the transnational community of neo-Latin poets, though perhaps a controversial one, for he contaminates the purity of classical measure with experiments in form and pattern that are unusual in Latin – the *ottava rima*, for example, and even the sonnet form.

*

In this brief presentation there is little scope for examples from the whole range of Joseph Tusiani's output. I shall therefore focus on Tusiani's outstanding achievements in the language that is dominant in his experience, the English language.

The reputation of Tusiani as an author rests in the first place on his activity as a translator of Italian poetry into English, and precisely on the quantity and the quality of it. A glance at the bibliography at the end of this article will give an idea of the amount of works he has translated. The list includes all major poets from Dante to D'Annunzio, either in selections or even entire works. Felix Stefanile has jokingly called Tusiani's activity as a translator "A veritable one-man industry."[1] As for the quality of his translations, Tusiani sticks to a lofty idea of poetic translation as opposed to prose translation. In his construction, rhythm and musicality, rhyme-schemes and metrical patterns, have to be reproduced as far as possible, along with surface meanings and deeper meanings, in a balanced amalgam of outward structure and partial fidelity to linguistic sense. A couple of examples will suffice to illustrate the point and show the extent to which the translator manages to render some basic features of the original into English.

Consider the very first line of the most famous lyric of Italian poetry, Leopardi's "L'infinito," where I have marked out the sequence of unstressed/ stressed syllables:

x x /x x / x / x /x
Sempre caro mi fu quest'ermo colle

A literal rendition, that has actually been adopted by some translators, would run as follows:

x / x / x / x / x /
This lonely hill was always dear to me

As a matter of fact, accuracy here does not include rhythm and musicality. A scanning of the translated line brings out a regular iambic pentameter, and correctly so, since an English pentameter is the equivalent of the Italian hendecasyllable. However, an ear attuned to Italian prosody soon detects that the regular iambic beat, and especially the strong masculine ending of the line, is extraneous to the original. By saying:

/ x x /x x x / x /
Fond I was ever of this lonely hill[2]

Tusiani softens the whole line into a mellower sound and sense. He does so by varying the iambic pattern of his pentameter with an opening trochee and an unstressed foot, a pyrrhic, in the very middle of the line. This prosodic sequence makes the masculine ending of the line sound less strong, and it also seems to help convey a sense of open space coming up as an image in the reader's mind later in the poem. Such a sense is reinforced by the use of *ever* in mid-position. (*Always* would have left the rhythm unaltered, but not as effectively conveyed a sense of spatiality.) All this is obtained at the cost of an inversion in the word order that may not sound natural to an English ear.

The relative faithfulness (or indeed 'controlled unfaithfulness') that is Tusiani's basic criterion in his translating art is perhaps better shown in his rendering of the well-known 'ottava di bisticci' from *Morgante* (which indeed calls for a Tuscan-Italian "translation"):

> La *casa* parea *cosa bretta* e *brutta*,
> *vinta* dal *vento*, e la *natta* e la *notte*
> *stilla* le *stelle*, ch'a *tetto* era *tutta*;
> del *pane* ap*pena* ne *détte* ta' *dotte*;
> *pere* avea *pure* e qualche *fratta frutta*,
> e *svina*, e *svena* di *botto* una *botte*;
> *poscia* per *pesci lasche* prese al*l'esca*;
> ma il *letto* al*lotta* alla *frasca* fu *fresca*.
> (Pulci, *Morgante*, XXIII, 47)

["La casa pareva cosa sordida e brutta, / battuta dal vento, e il canniccio [di copertura] e la notte / lasciano filtrare il lume delle stelle, perché [la casa] aveva quel solo tetto; / del pane [il romito] appena ne diede talvolta; / pere aveva soltanto, e un po' di frutta frantumata, / e spilla ed esaurisce subito una botte [*i.e.* era quasi vuota]; / poi [per offrire] pesci prese delle lasche con l'esca; / ma allora [*i.e.* dopo mangiato] il letto fu di frasche fresche"].

The translator here is faced with technicalities. Each line of the original includes two couples of paronomasias, that added to the effort of conveying the rhyme-scheme, make it extremely hard to find a way with the translating task. Tusiani achieves such results as the following:

The house to *oglers ugly seemed*, and *seedy*,
wind-worn; and the reed's rattle and the night
distilled the stars down through the gaping roof;
the hermit with a crust and crumb of bread
had *pairs* of *pears* and some leftover fruit;
he *tipped* and *tapped* a barrel most bartenderly,
and then for *fish* some *fishy* scales he caught:
but, ho, not *bad*, the *bed* with shoots was wrought.[3]

The translator uses a blank-verse stanza that only keeps the rhyme in its final couplet. He can reproduce six paronomasias (*oglers/ugly*, *seemed/-seedy*, *pairs/pears*, *tipped/tapped*, *fish/fishy*, *bad/bed*) and makes up for the others by using alliterations and assonances (*wind/worn*, *reed's/rattle*, *dis-tilled /stars*, *crust/crumb*, *barrel/bartenderly*). Those who expect a substantial degree of literalness will perhaps object to the inclusion of fillers (*to oglers*, *rattle*, *most bartenderly*), or point out some mismatches (*a tetto era tutta/ through the gaping roof, pere avea pure / pairs of pears*, *fratta frutta/leftover fruit*, *lasche/fishy scales*) and some missing items (*fresca*, l. 8, and the Past Tense-Present Tense variation). However, the global rendition will probably be appreciated by the monolingual reader; and, on a comparative scrutiny, it may appear to capture the quality of the original to a reasonable extent.

As an English poet, Joseph Tusiani had his golden days during the Sixties, when his first two collections of poems appeared — *Rind and All* and *The Fifth Season* — and he was accepted in two associations based in New York, the Poetry Society of America and the Catholic Poetry Society of America. The quality of his poetry has been described as:

> "[...] idea poetry. You will find little in the way of picture painting or character sketching: it is reflective poetry, a controlled rhetoric of problems and deep feelings [...] a searching after the solution to the profound [...] enigma of identity: one's inner world and the world all around — what is the relation between them? what am I? how far does the world's reality depend on my reaction and perception?"[4]

Such a reflective mood often results in long monologues after the Browning model (one of the major influences on Tusiani's poetry). In the Seventies, when Italian American ethnical consciousness and studies developed in the US, and courses were started in universities, such a mood was applied to an ethnical kind of production, and the collection *Gente Mia and Other Poems* was published. The often-quoted lines describing a migrant's plight: "Two languages, two lands, perhaps two souls... / Am I a man or two strange halves of one?" are found in a long poem from this collection, "Song of the Bicentennial."

Tusiani's work is popular among the Italian American community of scholars and readers. On a wider scale in the United States, one may find that his English poetry does not attract much attention nowadays, and one of the reasons may be its steady sticking to traditional forms. As a matter of fact Tusiani has never been prone to modernistic experiment. He has never written free verse, nor has he ever translated modern poets after Marinetti.

By way of a conclusion to my paper, I would like to touch on the fact that Tusiani has conceptualised his entire life and work as being the *metaphor* of translation. One of his poem "*incipits*" sounds as follows:

> To comprehend my life, I think of it
> As a translation from a flowing past
> Into a flowing present, from a birth
> Utterly unintelligible, to
> An altogether signifying sound
> Which I call language, life and love of it.[5]

This is what Tusiani says in well-balanced metrical lines. Below is what has been said not by men-of-letters or literary critics but by geographers investigating the activity of writing connected with migration:

> ...once a migration takes place, the migrant may never be quite sure where home is, ever again. What ensues is a permanent mobility of the mind, if not the body, a constant dual or multiple perspective on place... For those who come from elsewhere, and cannot go back, perhaps writing becomes a place to live.[6]

On the one hand we have an analysis by the objective social scientist; on the other, the agonizing quest for identity by the emotional poet. Let me leave it to the reader the task of assessing how close to each other such different conceptions and points of view are.

---

[1] Felix Stefanile, "Introduction" to Joseph Tusiani, *If Gold Should Rust. A play in verse*, in Paolo A. Giordano, ed., *Joseph Tusiani Poet Translator Humanist. An International Homage* (West Lafayette, IN: Bordighera, 1994), p. 267.

[2] *Leopardi's Canti*. Trans. Joseph Tusiani. Intro. Pietro Magno. Pref. Franco Foschi (Fasano, Br: Schena, 1998), p. 57.

[3] Luigi Pulci, *Morgante*. Trans. Joseph Tusiani. Intro. and notes Edoardo A. Lèbano (Bloomington and Indianapolis: Indiana UP, 1998), p. 538.

[4] John Duffy, review of Joseph Tusiani's *The Fifth Season*, *Spirit: A Magazine of Poetry* 21, No. 6 (January 1965), 176-78.

[5] Joseph Tusiani, "Heritage," *La Parola del Popolo* 65, No. 116 (March-April 1973), 71.

[6] Russel King, John Connel, and Paul White, eds. *Writing across Worlds. Literature and Migration* (London and NY: Routledge, 1995), pp. xiv, xv.

Select Bibliography

I. JOSEPH TUSIANI'S MAIN WORKS

English poetry

Rind and All. Fifty Poems. New York: The Monastine Press, 1962.

The Fifth Season. Poems. New York: Obolensky, 1964.

Gente Mia and Other Poems. Stone Park, Ill.: Italian Cultural Center, 1978.

Ethnicity. Selected Poems. Edited with Two Essays by Paolo Giordano. Lafayette, In: Bordighera, 2000.

Dialect poetry

Làcreme e sciure. Pref. Tommaso Nardella. Foggia: Cappetta, 1955. (2nd edition: ed. Antonio Motta. San Marco in Lamis, Fg: Quaderni del Sud, 2000.)

Tìreca tàreca. Poesie in vernacolo garganico. Ed. Antonio Motta, Tommaso Nardella and Cosma Siani. Illus. Franco Troiano. San Marco in Lamis, Fg: Quaderni del Sud, 1978.

Bronx, America. Poesie in dialetto garganico. Italian trans. Tommaso Nardella. Manduria, Ta: Lacaita, 1991.

Annemale parlante. Italian trans. Tommaso Nardella. San Marco in Lamis, Fg: Quaderni del Sud, 1994.

La poceide. Poemetto in dieci canti in dialetto garganico. Italian trans. Anna Siani. San Marco in Lamis, Fg: Quaderni del Sud, 1996.

Na vota è 'mpise Cola [Una volta sola s'impicca Cola]. Favola in dieci canti in dialetto garganico. Italian trans. Anna Siani. Afterword by Cosma Siani. San Marco in Lamis, Fg: Quaderni del Sud, 1997.

Li quatte staggione e poesie ritrovate. Italian trans. Anna Siani. San Marco in Lamis, Fg: Quaderni del Sud, 1998.

Lu deddù. Poemetto in ottava rima in dialetto garganico. Ed. Anna Siani. San Marco in Lamis, Fg: Quaderni del Sud, 1999.

Maste Peppe cantarine. Favola in sette canti in dialetto garganico. Ed. Anna Siani. San Marco in Lamis, Fg: Quaderni del Sud, 2000.

Lu ponte de sòla. Melodramma in dieci canti in dialetto garganico. Ed. Anna Siani. San Marco in Lamis, Fg: Quaderni del Sud, 2001.

L'ore de Gesù Bambine. Favola natalizia in dialetto garganico. Ed. Antonio Motta. San Marco in Lamis, Fg: Quaderni del Sud, 2002.

La prima cumpagnia. Ed. Anna Siani. San Marco in Lamis, Fg: Quaderni del Sud, 2002.

Lu cunte de Pasqua. Ed. Antonio Motta. San Marco in Lamis, Fg: Quaderni del Sud, 2003.

La tomba de Padre Pi'. Ed. Anna Siani. San Marco in Lamis, Fg: Quaderni del Sud, 2003.

Latin poetry

Melos Cordis. New York: The Venetian Press, 1955.

Rosa rosarum. Carmina latina. n.p. [Oxford, Ohio]: American Classical League, n.d. [1984].

In exilio rerum. Carmina latina. Ed. Dirk Sacré. Avignone: Aubanel, 1985.

Confinia lucis et umbrae. Carmina latina. Ed. Dirk Sacré. Lovanio: Peeters, 1989.

Carmina latina. Ed. & intr. Emilio Bandiera. Fasano, Br: Schena, 1994.

Carmina latina II. Ed. & intr. Emilio Bandiera. Galatina, Le: Congedo, 1998.

Radìcitus (Ritorno alle radici). Poesie latine. Ed. & intr. Emilio Bandiera. S. Eustachio di Mercato di Sanseverino, Sa: Il Grappolo, 2000.

Italian poetry

Amedeo di Savoia. Poemetto in isciolti. Pref. Ciro Soccio. Sant'Agata di Puglia, Fg: Tip. Casa del Sacro Cuore, 1943.

Flora o primi fiori di poesia. n.p. [New York]: n.p. [Prompt Press], n.d. [1946].

Amore e morte o sogni delle quattro stagioni. Liriche. San Marco in Lamis, Fg: Tip. Giovanni Caputo, 1946.

Petali sull'onda. Poesie. New York: Euclid Publishing Co., 1948.

Peccato e luce. Pref. Cesare Foligno. New York: The Venetian Press, 1949.

Lo speco celeste. Siracusa-Milano: Ciranna, 1956.

Odi sacre. Pref. Alfredo Galletti. Siracusa-Milano: Ciranna, 1957.

Il ritorno. Liriche italiane. Pref. Pietro Magno. Fasano, Br: Schena, 1992.

Fiction

Dante in licenza. Romanzo. Verona: Nigrizia, 1952.

Envoy from Heaven. A Novel. New York: Obolensky, 1965.

La parola difficile. Autobiografia di un italo-americano. Fasano, Br: Schena, 1988.

La parola nuova. Autobiografia di un italo-americano (Parte II). Pref. Angelo Di Summa. Fasano, Br: Schena, 1991.

La parola antica. Autobiografia di un italo-americano (Parte III). Pref. Angelo Di Summa. Fasano, Br: Schena, 1992.

Critical essays

La poesia amorosa di Emily Dickinson. New York: The Venetian Press, 1950.

Two Critical Essays on Emily Dickinson. New York: The Venetian Press, 1951.

Poesia missionaria in Inghilterra e in America. Storia critica e antologica. Verona: Nigrizia, 1953.

Sonettisti americani. Intro. Frances Winwar. Chicago: Division Typesetting Company, 1954.

"The Translating of Poetry," *Thought* 38, No. 150 (Autumn 1963), pp 376-390.

Influenza cristiana nella poesia negro-americana. Bologna: Editrice Nigrizia, 1971.

Dante's Divine Comedy. *As Told for Young People*. New York-Ottawa-Toronto: Legas, 2001.

Translations

The Complete Poems of Michelangelo. Trans., notes & Intro. Joseph Tusiani. New York: Noonday Press, 1960.

Lust and Liberty. The Poems of Machiavelli. Trans., notes & Intro. JT. New York: Obolensky, 1963.

Torquato Tasso's Jerusalem Delivered. Trans.& Intro. JT. Rutherford-Madison-Teaneck: Fairleigh Dickinson UP, 1970.

Giovanni's Boccaccio's Nymphs of Fiesole. Trans.& Intro. JT. Rutherford-Madison-Teaneck: Fairleigh Dickinson UP, 1971.

Italian Poets of the Renaissance. Trans.& Intro. JT. New York: Baroque Press, 1971.

The Age of Dante. An Anthology of Early Italian Poetry. Trans.& Intro. JT. New York: Baroque Press, 1974.

From Marino to Marinetti. An Anthology of Forty Italian Poets. Trans.& Intro. JT. New York: Baroque Press, 1974.

America the Free. Five Odes by Vittorio Alfieri. Trans.& Intro. JT. New York: Italian-American Center for Urban Affairs, 1975.

"Ugo Foscolo, *Le Grazie*. Trans. JT." *Canadian Journal of Italian Studies*: "Hymn One. *Venus*," Vol. 5, No. 1-2 (Fall-Winter 1981-1982), pp. 101-8; "Hymn

Two. *Vesta*," Vol. 5, No. 3 (Spring 1982), pp. 211-21; "Hymn Three. *Pallas*," Vol. 6, No. 4/Vol. 7, No. 1 (1983), pp. 183-88.

Torquato Tasso, *Creation of the World*. Trans.& Intro. JT. Annotations by Gaetano Cipolla. Binghamton, NY: Center for Medieval & Renaissance Studies, 1982.

"Manzoni's *Inni sacri* and "Il Cinque Maggio." A Translation," *Annali d'Italianistica* 3, (1985), pp. 6-43.

"T. Tasso's *The Amorous Pyre*. Trans. JT," *Forum Italicum* 21, No. 2 (Fall 1987), pp. 353-75.

Dante's Lyric Poems, Trans. JT. Intro. & notes Giuseppe C. Di Scipio. New York: Legas, 1992 [revised ed., 1999].

Luigi Pulci, *Morgante*, Trans. JT. Intro. & notes Edoardo A. Lèbano. Bloomington and Indianapolis: Indiana UP, 1998.

Leopardi's Canti, Trans. JT. Intro. & notes Pietro Magno. Pref. Franco Foschi. Fasano, Br: Schena, 1998.

II. SELECTED CRITICISM

Cosma Siani. *La terra garganica nella poesia di Joseph Tusiani*. Foggia: Amministrazione Provinciale, 1975.

Gaetano Cipolla, ed. "Omaggio a Joseph Tusiani." *La Parola del Popolo* 71, No. 150 (Nov.-Dic. 1979), pp. S/1-40.

Lucia Petracco Sovran. *Joseph Tusiani poeta e traduttore*. Pref. Pasquale Tuscano. Perugia: Sigla Tre, 1984.

Paolo A. Giordano, ed. *Joseph Tusiani Poet Translator Humanist. An International Homage*. West Lafayette, IN: Bordighera, 1994.

Cosma Siani. *L'io diviso. Joseph Tusiani fra emigrazione e letteratura*. Roma: Cofine, 1999.

Cosma Siani, ed. *"Two Languages, Two Lands." L'opera letteraria di Joseph Tusiani. Atti della giornata di studi, San Marco in Lamis, 15 maggio 1999*. San Marco in Lamis: Quaderni del Sud, 2000.

Cosma Siani. "Bibliografia di/su Joseph Tusiani." In Siani, ed. 2000: pp. 153-72. Updated in *Frontiere* (San Marco in Lamis, Fg), Vol 1, No. 2 (Dec. 2000), pp. 23-25; Vol. 2, No. 3 (June 2001), pp. 28-31; Vol. 2, No. 4, (Dec. 2001), pp. 26-29; Vol. 3, No. 6 (Dec. 2002), pp.43-46.

Cosma Siani. *Manhattan Log. Geografia e storia di Tusiani*. Pref. Furio Colombo, n.p. [Foggia]: Protagonisti, 2000.

Cosma Siani, ed. *In quattro lingue. Antologia di Joseph Tusiani*. Roma: Cofine, 2001.

ITALIAN AMERICANS AND RACE: TO BE OR NOT TO BE WHITE

Rudolph J. Vecoli
University of Minnesota

Race has been and remains one of the major themes of American history. Ever since the first Europeans ("whites") encountered the indigenous peoples ("redskins") and enslaved Africans ("blacks"), skin color has been a marker of one's identity and status in North America.[1] For three centuries, European Americans "removed" or exterminated American Indians and kept African-Americans in bondage or subject to Jim Crow. "White privilege," i.e., the dominance of European Americans, has been a constant in both the colonial and national periods of the United States. We need only cite the Naturalization Act of 1790 which restricted access to citizenship to "free white persons" as an early expression of this principle. Yet while subordinate "racial" groups, e.g., as distinguished by skin color, have long been the objects of extensive study, "whiteness" as such has been taken for granted.[2]

Race, we now all agree, is not a biological fact. Like "black," "red," "brown," and "yellow," the category "white" does not exist as a genetic reality; rather the idea of race is the product of historical processes which in turn become a force in history, and thus its study falls within the purview of the historian. To assert that "races" exist as social constructions is not to deny that racial beliefs have powerfully affected human thought and behavior. While the role of "blackness" or "redness" in American history has been well understood, it has been only within the last decade that have we begun to interrogate "whiteness": What exactly has it meant to be "white" — and who decides who is and who is not "white?" What have been the advantages of "whiteness?" Can a "non-white" group become "white?" Such questions have spawned a burgeoning literature of "whiteness" studies.[3]

While race may be a fiction, its institutionalization as expressions of racism (prejudice and discrimination based on presumed racial differences) and racialism (theories of racial superiority and inferiority) have had a powerful impact on all aspects of American life. The racial hierarchy which had been established by the early nineteenth century with Anglo-Saxons ruling over lesser "breeds" was challenged by the arrival of masses of immigrants from Europe. Among these, the racial ideology readily accommodated the British as close cousins, while the Scandinavians and Germans were regarded as distant cousins. However, the "whiteness" of the Irish, because of their alleged brutal, vicious, uncouth "nature," and Roman Catholic religion, came into question. They were the first of many subsequent immigrant arrivals whose place in the racial hierarchy was initially indeterminate. David Roediger and Noel Ignatiev have argued that the Irish in time acquired the privileges of whiteness by embracing anti-black racism.[4]

Theological and political formulations of racial thinking were replaced in the late nineteenth century by scientific racialism stemming from the theories of Charles Darwin, Frances Galton, and others. Racialists now maintained that nature rather than nurture, heredity rather than environment, determined the mental, moral, and physical qualities of persons. This paradigm shift coincided with the mass migrations of Eastern and Southern Europeans to the United States. Where these newcomers belonged in the racial hierarchy became a matter of dispute, with the placement of the Italians being particularly problematic.[5] Robert Harney has described the longstanding "Italophobia" of the English-speaking world. On one hand was the Italy of the Roman Empire and the Renaissance; on the other, contemporary Italy depicted in travel writings as primitive, dirty, and dangerous. Americans viewed the immigrants through the colored lenses of such literary sources or personal visits to Italy. Sensational accounts in the yellow press of "Little Italies," of *lazzaroni,* brutal *padrones*, little slaves of the harp, and knifings, confirmed their worst expectations. The "Mafia" episode of 1891 in New Orleans which resulted in the lynching of eleven Sicilians ironically hardened the perception that Italians were a lot of bloodthirsty cutthroats. From such negative stereotypes it was but a short step to the conclusion that such a breed was unassimilable and a danger to the republic.[6]

But were Italians "white?" Americans learned early on to distinguish between north Italians and south Italians. As Peter D'Agostino demonstrates in a recent article, racial theorists in the United States were strongly influenced by the works of Cesare Lombroso and his followers which attributed the poverty, backwardness, and lawlessness of southern Italy to the racial deficiencies of its inhabitants.[7] William Z. Ripley in his influential work, *The Races of Europe* (1900), synthesized the research findings of these and other scholars. Europeans, he concluded, could be divided into three distinct races: the Nordic, the Alpine, and the Mediterranean.[8] Within this scheme, northern Italians (restricted to the regions of Piedmont, Lombardy, and Veneto) were Alpines while southern Italians (including Genoese) were Mediterraneans. While Ripley was restrained in making evaluative judgments regarding these "races," others were not. The sociologist, E.A. Ross, was only the most blatantly racist in his characterizations of the south Italians.[9] These categories of "north" and "south" Italians were espoused by educated Americans and incorporated in the gathering of statistical data on immigration and population. This invidious distinction percolated through American society via popular magazines and public discourse. Immigrants from the northern regions contributed to this pejorative view, asserting that southerners were not Italians at all, but rather Arabs. "Africa begins just south of Rome," was their common observation. Perversely Italian immigrants contributed to their own racialization by transporting racist prejudices and behaviors (e.g., northerners frequently segregated themselves in their residential areas and organizations from southerners) from Italy to America. The immigration act of 1924, which established a quota system severely limiting the number of immigrants from Italy, did not make a distinction between northerners and southerners in its allocation of Italy's quota.[10]

In their writings, Robert Orsi, David Roediger, and James Barrett have used the term "In-Between Peoples" with respect to the Italians.[11] This seems to be an apt description of their placement within the racial hierarchy, somewhere between whites and blacks. On the chromatic scale, the adjective most commonly used for the Italians was "swarthy." Epithets hurled at the immigrants had racial connotations: "Guinea" was applied to antebellum slaves who had been kidnapped from that region of Africa, while "Dago" originated from the Spanish Diego.[12]

The majority of the Italian immigrants were *contadini,* the so-called *cafoni* (rustics, which itself conjured up racist images), from southern Italy. For decades, most were consigned to dirty, hard, dangerous jobs, which were defined as "nigger work." Both economics and prejudice confined them to the cheapest and poorest housing. Ignorant of American racial mores, the immigrants often worked with and lived as neighbors with African Americans, mingling with them socially and, on occasion, intermarrying with them. In schools, Italian children were often regarded as mentally retarded and troublesome. When intelligence tests came into use, they confirmed the prejudices of the educators. The IQ tests administered to recruits during World War I established the sub-normal mentality of Italians, roughly equal to that of African Americans. Indicative of the ambiguity of their racial status, Italians were lynched, and not only in the South, in greater numbers than any other European nationality.[13] In the 1920s and 30s, social distance measures, i.e., degree of social acceptability, found Italians ranked near the bottom with Asians, Mexicans, and blacks. In 1942 a public opinion poll asked respondents: "Taking into account all the qualities possessed by the different people or races of the world, how would you rate the people listed below, in comparison with the people of the United States?" Of the seventeen groups listed (African Americans were not included!), Italians ranked near the bottom, slightly above Mexicans and Japanese, on the measure "as good as we are in all important respects [14 per cent];" somewhat above those groups on the scale "definitely inferior [36 per cent];" but below them on the question *"Not quite as good in major respects [43 per cent]."*[14]

The date of this Gallup poll indicates that racial prejudices afflicted the second generation as well as the immigrants. Oral histories confirm that being identified as being "Italian," influenced adversely one's ability to secure desirable employment, move to better housing (restrictive covenants in some areas specified Italians, along with blacks and Jews), and date and marry "Americans." Not a few Italian Americans anglicized their names and repressed their "Italian" lifestyle in order to pass as "white," just as did many light skinned African Americans. While this hostile treatment of Italians reflected in part their low working class status, the perception of them as "not-quite-white" was perhaps a more important factor.[15]

Matthew Frye Jacobson has argued that the racial terminology of the early twentieth century encompassed many different *Shades of Whiteness*. Hence while relegated to the Mediterranean branch of the Caucasian race, south Italians were still "white." In a recent book, entitled *White on Arrival*, Thomas Guglielmo has developed this thesis at length in a case study of Italians in Chicago. Noting that while official US statistics used racial designations for north Italians and south Italians, in the color column, they were all listed as white. Also he notes that their eligibility for naturalization as "free white persons" was not challenged. Guglielmo places great emphasis on this distinction between the categories of race and color.[16] While acknowledging that Italians experienced various forms of racial prejudice, he maintains that their "whiteness" entitled them to privileges denied to African Americans, Asian Americans, and Hispanic Americans. I would not contest that as an overall generalization. However, I question Guglielmo's sharp distinction between race and color. Those categories blended easily in common practice and discourse. One encounters many instances in which the whiteness of Italians was questioned or denied. An employer in response to the question: "Is an Italian a white man?" replied, "No sir, he is a Dago." A railroad superintendent wired his labor agent: "Dagoes only men who will work. Send more dagoes and shut off off white men." An Irish woman upon learning that a young lady married an Italian, commented: "And why didn't she marry a white man?" My friend, Giovanna D'Agostino, daughter of Calabrian immigrants, recalls how eighty years ago, her schoolmates called her "nigger." Many other examples could be cited of the hateful language of color being used to denigrate Italian Americans.[17]

How did Italian immigrants and their children themselves understand the racial order of the United States and how did they adapt themselves to it? Did they like the Irish and Jews become "white" and, if so, what was the process by which that was accomplished? As a Mediterranean people, Italians had long known, associated, and interbred with persons of various "shades of blackness." A dark skinned uncle of mine in Tuscany was known as *"Il Moro,"* a woman in the *paese* was called "*La Scarcena*." These nicknames recalled the Moorish invasion and occupation of much of the peninsula and islands which have been memorialized in Italian opera and Sicilian puppetry. In the late nineteenth century, thousands of Italian soldiers and colonists (some of whom subsequently immigrated to the United States) knew Libya, Ethiopia, Somalia, and Eritrea at first hand. From accounts and photographs, their *paesani* learned about dark skinned peoples of Africa. My mother recited the following *barzelletta* which she had learned as a child in the 1890s in Camaiore (Lucca): "*La signora Taitu, Menelik, non lo vol più, ha sposato Baratieri, fa figlioli bianchi e neri*."[18] Most Italians were obviously familiar with "shades of blackness" among human beings. Robert Orsi's anecdote about the Italian immigrant who, seeing a black person for the first time, could not resist the urge to rub his face to see if the blackness would come off, is at best improbable. What value did Italians attach to skin color? Racialism as a component of imperialist ideology was characteristic of the Italian upper and middle classes. However, among the common folk, the peasants and artisans, race does not appear to have been a significant source of self-identification. They were more likely to distinguish themselves from the Other, not by asserting "*noi siamo bianchi* [we are white]," but by declaring "*noi siamo cristiani, non siamo turchi* [we are Christians, not Turks]."[19]

As noted above, Italians lived, worked, socialized, and inter-married with African Americans. Vincenza Scarpaci has documented these relationships in her studies of Sicilians in Louisiana. In fact, their failure to observe the "color line" called into question their "whiteness," and exposed them to violence customarily reserved for blacks. In Madison, Wisconsin, in an area called "The Marsh," Italo-Albanians and Lombards resided on neighborly terms with African Americans. Women exchanged recipes, children played and went to school together, and men drank a glass of wine under the grape arbor. Such interrelations occurred in many communities. However, given the power of *campanilismo* which kept even immigrants from different *paesi* at arm's length from each other, the degree of intimacy between Italian Americans and African Americans should not be exaggerated. Still the *modus vivendi* between them, particularly when compared to the Negrophobia of Irish immigrants, was unusual in twentieth century America.[20]

Toni Morrison, the African American writer, has asserted that the first English word learned by the immigrant was "nigger." For the Italians at least, this was not the case. Certainly they used the term, *neri*, and heard racist epithets from white workers. An anarchist writing to his comrades in Italy reported that blacks, known as "*cuns*" [coons], were badly treated by white w orkers. I talians de vised t heir o wn *s oprannomi* (nicknames) for blacks. One was *melanzana* (eggplant), another was *tizzone* (charcoal), terms still used by Italian Americans in their corrupted form as "mellonjohns." and "tutsun." Racial epithets? Of course, but lacking the historical and ideological burden of "*nigger*."[21]

Relations between Italians and African Americans were not always amicable. Economic competition, rather than race per se, appeared to have provoked hostilities between them. Rivals for common labor jobs, they came into conflict, particularly when employers pitted one against the other as strikebreakers. A major conflict did occur in 1896 in the mining town of Spring Valley, Illinois, when blacks imported by mine owners were violently driven out of town by Italians and other Europeans.[22] The infamous Chicago race riot of 1919 testifies to the relative lack of hostility between Italians and blacks. Those parts of the city where they lived in close proximity were largely free of the violence and mayhem which characterized other areas. The commission investigating the causes of the riot noted the peaceful calm that prevailed in most Italian neighborhoods. The brutal murder of a black by a gang of Italian youths on the city's Near West Side proved to be the exception. Having assembled a group of Italian leaders, Jane Addams asked how such a horrible act could be committed by Italians who were noted for their racial tolerance. The reply was: "They are being Americanized."[23]

Did Americanization entail becoming a racist? Sad to say, for most of the twentieth century, it did. Behind the facade of the Declaration of Independence and the Constitution existed the ugly reality of racism. The children of immigrants assimilated racist stereotypes and language from their textbooks and teachers as well as from popular culture. Old timers on Minnesota's Iron Range, where blacks were rare, remembered seeing David Griffith's *The Birth of a Nation* which glorified the Klu Klux Klan and beastialized African Americans. As "in-between people" and themselves the object of racial prejudice, they hungered to shed their "wopness" and be accepted as true Americans (which meant as "whites"). However, negative feelings towards Italians on the part of white Americans were intensified in the 1920s. Prohibition provided opportunities which Italian Americans along with others seized. While their role in organized crime brought wealth and notoriety, e.g. Al Capone, it also reinforced the racial stereotype of the Italian as criminal. "Scarface" and "Little Caesar," first of the genre of Mob/Mafia films, established the Italian gangster as a racial icon which has persisted to this day (viz., "The Sopranos").[24]

Between World War I and World War II, while Italian Americans experienced limited economic mobility and social acceptance, they fashioned an ethnicity in response to the corrosive influences of urban, industrial, multiethnic modernity. As Simone Cinotto maintains in his *Una famiglia che mangia insieme* (A Family which Eats Together), at the center of Italian American ethnicity was "*la famiglia*" (the family) which found its quintessential expression in food and the rituals of eating. Immigrant wives and mothers through their culinary skills created a "domestic ethnicity" to hold the family together. Cinotto also argues that food culture became one of the basic forms by which Italian Americans differentiated themselves from the African Americans and Puerto Ricans. "*They* don't eat together," "*they* eat beans; we eat meat," affirmed the "white" status of Italians Americans vis-a-vis "people of color."[25]

The Ethiopian War (1935-1936) was an important turning point in the racial views of Italian Americans and of their relationship with African Americans. The great majority of the immigrants, and even of the second generation, hailed the rise to power of the Fascists as a rebirth of Italy and Mussolini as her savior. This ethnic nationalism was itself a response to their marginal position and sense of inferiority. Il Duce's imperial aspirations were greeted with wild enthusiasm as Italian Americans followed Italian victories through a Fascist-dominated press and radio. At rallies, they lustily sang the Fascist hymn, *Faccetta Nera* (Litttle Black Face), which portrayed Italy's imperialist aggression as a civilizing mission. African Americans, for their part, were enraged by this invasion of the last independent state in Africa. They boycotted Italian merchants and clashed with pro-fascist Italian Americans on the streets of Newark, Boston, and New York. A war thousands of miles away engendered a lasting hostility between these two populations which had previously enjoyed relatively peaceful relations.[26]

Following its conquest of Ethiopia, the Fascism regime, which here-to-fore had not espoused racial doctrines, established a separation of races in many spheres in its new colony. Mussolini denounced the mingling of blood between blacks and whites as resulting in "mixed bastards, offspring of perverted primitivism." Following the formation of the Axis with Hitler's Germany, Italy's racial policy was codified in the *Manifesto della razza* of July 14, 1938 which declared that biologically distinct races exist, that there is a pure Italian race, and that it is an Aryan race. The Ethiopian War and Fascist racial policies profoundly influenced Italian Americans' racial attitudes, particularly with respect to African Americans and Jews. The theme of racial purity found its echo in the Italian American press, stridently in Domenico Trombetta's *Il Grido della Stripe* (The Cry of the Race), muted in Generoso Pope's *Il Progresso Italo-Americano. L'Italia* of San Francisco justified Mussolini's racial policies by citing the United States' history of slavery and segregation.[27]

To what extent did such views penetrate into the consciousness of Italian Americans? While it is difficult to quantify an answer, there is reason to believe that Vincenzo Frazzetta, a factory worker in Bridgeport, Connecticut, was articulating the thought of many in an interview of 1939:

> What Mussolini done in Ethiopia, I think that he done a good thing because that country belonged to him, and he want to make the people there civilized like they should be. He is making schools for these people and he is making them like Christians....Sometimes I pass by the black people's house, and then I hear them laugh and make all kinds of

> noise just like they be in Africa. Well, some day Mussolini will fix them up, and maybe they get to be like people some day, and not like animals.[28]

World War II profoundly altered the status and self-concept of Italian Americans. Although Italy and the United States were at war, they suffered mildly from wartime hostility. Italian Americans were not imprisoned in concentration camps as were Japanese Americans, nor were they placed in segregated military units as were African Americans. I would venture that the negative attitudes reported in the Gallup poll of 1942 improved substantially by 1945. Wartime patriotism demonstrated by Italian Americans contributed to a greater acceptance, as did their breakthrough in popular culture, to mention only Joe Dimaggio and Frank Sinatra. US government propaganda which stressed the theme "Americans All" (restricted however to those of European ancestry) brought them within the magic circle of "whiteness." Wartime black migration from the South and their employment in war industries resulted in heightened racial tensions. As Nadia Venturini has reported, Italian Americans were active participants in race riots in Detroit and elsewhere.[29]

Following World War II, second generation Italian Americans enjoyed increased socio-economic mobility as indicated by higher educational achievement, movement up the occupational ladder, and increased income levels. Migration from Little Italies to lily-white suburbs followed. This exodus was hastened by public housing and highway construction projects which destroyed many of the old neighborhoods — and by the influx of African Americans. The "black revolution" of the sixties inspired fears among those Italian Americans who remained in the central cities. Some joined the "white flight" to the suburbs; others armed themselves. Anthony Imperiali organized a militia in Newark to "protect" the Italian neighborhood. Jonathan Reider's study of Canarsie (in Brooklyn) analyzed the siege mentality of Italians and Jews. Italian Americans were conspicuous in acts of protest and violence against "invasion" by African Americans. Most notorious was the verbal and physical aggression vented against the "open housing" march of Martin Luther King and his followers through Cicero, Illinois. Lumped together with other European Americans as "white ethnics," Italian Americans were labeled "fascist racists" by liberals and radicals.[30]

In recent decades, as they have risen into the middle and upper classes, Italian Americans have increasingly espoused a conservative political ideology with a resulting shift to the Republican Party. Polling data indicate that by the 1990s a higher percentage of Italian Americans as compared with other Americans opposed increased spending on blacks, on welfare, and on government help for the poor. More unexpectedly, seventy per cent of Italian Americans favored admitting fewer immigrants (only the British at seventy two per cent felt more strongly about this), but most surprising is that 66 per cent thought immigrants were demanding too many rights and 81 per cent believed that immigrants reduced national unity! Italian Americans ranked the highest on both of these issues. The fact that contemporary immigration has been predominantly Asian and Hispanic no doubt affected the responses. That so many of the grandchildren and great-grandchildren of the *contadini* hold such views reflects both their repression and distortion of family histories and an embracing of American racist ideology.[31]

David A. J. Richards (Ricciardelli), in his book, *Italian American: The Racializing of an Ethnic Identity* (1999) has argued that Italian Americans made a "Faustian bargain" by which they accepted the benefits of white privilege (and racism) and silenced their protests against injustices suffered both by themselves and others. In so doing, they suppressed memories of struggles, denying knowledge of the heritage of wrongs they had suffered to future generations. Italian American identity thus was privatized and led to the acceptance of white racism.[32]

Richards' thesis, however, neglects the countervailing tradition of those Italian Americans who rejected the Faustian bargain and who over the course of generations protested injustices, whether to themselves or others. Among anarchists and socialists, who believed in the solidarity of the working class across ethnic and racial lines, racism and particularly the lynching of blacks were vociferously denounced. This radical tradition was manifested by Italian American participation in organizations which crossed racial boundaries such as the Industrial Workers of the World, the Congress of Industrial Organizations, and the International Workers' Order. Others inspired by the social justice teachings of the Roman Catholic Church have been activists in peace and human rights movements.[33]

Reflecting the ambiguity of their own racial status, Italian Americans have had ambivalent relationships with African Americans in the cultural sphere. Three murders of blacks in New York Italian neighborhoods in recent years reveal the persistence of racial fears and hatreds among younger generations. Paradoxically, hip-hop "black culture" has provided models for teenage Italian Americans in language, music (rap), and dress. As Lou De Caro, Jr., has commented, Italian Americans have "a certain affinity to African American culture that they cannot escape." However, in the complex "black/Italian crossover," influences have run both ways. While Frank Sinatra became, in the words of John Gennari, "a gangster rap icon," he in turn acknowledged Billie Holiday's "decisive influence on his singing." This synergism goes back to the roots of jazz, when New Orleans Italians were among the first "white" musicians to adopt and adapt that music in their performance. "Goombah blackness," a term coined by Ron Radano, recognizes "an affective alliance between Italian and African Americans based on mutual desires and pleasures, and grounded particularly in a tradition of boisterous male assertiveness...." That love-hate dynamic infuses Spike Lee's *Do the Right Thing* and *Jungle Fever* and Robert De Niro's *A Bronx Tale.* In the end, however, Italian Americans, fearing the lost of their hard earned "white" status, have pulled back from that embrace with "blackness."[34]

Like all Americans, Italian immigrants and their offspring have had to grapple with the nightmare of racial division, conflict, and violence. Having unwittingly become part of this American dilemma, they became both victims and victimizers. Learning by hard lessons the disadvantages of "blackness" and the privileges of "whiteness," it is not surprising that they opted for the latter. Paradoxically, having realized the prize of "white" status (although the stigma of criminality remains a question mark) many have found the rewards not to be commensurate with the price. "Whiteness" in essence was a synonym for assimilation. Much of their cultural heritage had to be jettisoned in the process ("don't be loud, expressive, or wave your hands when you speak"). Many Italian Americans are rejecting such reductionism which would relegate them to a deculturized "white" category. An increasing number are making unprecedented efforts to recover the memories, the history, and the language which constitute their authentic heritage as Italian Americans. By rejecting the binary racial classification, neither white nor black, they can be free to be themselves.[35]

---

[1] Winthrop, D. Jordan, *White over Black: American Attitudes Toward the Negro, 1550-1812* (Chapel Hill: University of North Carolina Press, 1968); Gary B. Nash,

Red, White, and Black: the Peoples of Early North America (Upper Saddle River, NJ: Prentice Hall, 2000).

[2] Matthew Frye Jacobson, *Whiteness of a Different Color: European Immigrants and the Alchemy of Race* (Cambridge, Mass.: Harvard UP, 1998); *U.s. Immigration and Naturalization Laws and Issues: a Documentary History*, Michael LeMay and Elliott R. Barkan, eds. (Westport, CT: Greenwood Press, 1999), 11; David R. Roediger, *Towards the Abolition of Whiteness* (London: Verso, 1994).

[3] "Whiteness and the Historians' Imagination," *International Labor and Working-Class History*, 60 (Fall 2001). This issue is devoted entirely to a critical assessment of "whiteness scholarship."

[4] Thomas F. Gossett, "The Idea of Anglo-saxon Superiority in American Thought, 1865-1915," Ph.D. dissertation, University of Minnesota,1953; *Idem, Race: The History of an Idea in America* (New York: Schocken Books, 1965); David R. Roediger, *The Wages of Whiteness: Race and the Making of the American Working Class* (London; New York: Verso, 1999); Dale T. Knobel, *Paddy and the Republic: Ethnicity and Nationality in Antebellum America* (Middletown, Conn.: Wesleyan UP, 1968); Noel Ignatiev, *How the Irish Became White* (New York: Routledge, 1995).

[5] John Higham, *Strangers in the Land: Patterns of American Nativism, 1860-1925* (New Brunswick, N.J.: Rutgers UP, 1988); Jacobson, *Whiteness of a Different Color.*

[6] Robert F. Harney, "Italophobia: an English-speaking Malady," *Studi Emigrazione*. 22 (March 1985), 6-43; Salvatore J, LaGumina, ed., *WOP: A Documentary History of Anti-Italian Discrimination in the United States* (San Francisco: Straight Arrow Books;1973); Joseph Albini, *The American Mafia Genesis of a Legend* (New York: Appleton-Century-Crofts, l971); Dwight Smith, *The Mafia Mystique* (New York: Basic Books, 1975); Richard Gambino, *Vendetta: The True Story of the Largest Lynching in U.S. History* (Montreal: Guernica, 1998).

[7] Peter D'Agostino, "Craniums, Criminals, and the 'Cursed Race': Italian Anthropology in American Racial Thought, 1861-1924," *Comparative Studies in Society and History*, 44:2 (April 2002), 319-43. For a comprehensive discussion of racism in Italy see Alberto Burgio, ed., *Nel nome della razza: il razzismo nella storia d'Italia 1870-1945* (Bologna: Società Editrice dil Mulino, 1999).

[8] William Z. Ripley, *The Races of Europe: A Sociological Study* (New York: D. Appleton, 1899).

[9] Edward A. Ross, *The Old World in the New: The Significance of Past and Present Immigration to the American People* (New York: Century, 1914), 97-119, 293-95.

[10] LaGumina, *WOP;* John B. Trevor, *An Analysis of the American Immigration Act of 1924, International Conciliation* (September 1924), no. 202; Rudolph J. Vecoli, "Chicago's Italians prior to World War I: a Study of their Social and Economic Adjustment," (Ph.D. dissertation, University of Wisconsin, 1963), 403-06; United States. Immigration Commission, *Dictionary of Races or Peoples* (Washington, Govt. print. off. 1911).This official publication not only distinguished between North and South Italians, but had a separate entry for Sicilians as well. The work relied heavily on the

work of the Italian anthropologist, Alfredo Niceforo, *L'Italia barbara contemporanea* (Milan: n.p., 1898); *idem*, *Italiani del nord e Italiani del sud* (Turin: Fratelli Bocca, 1901).

[11] James R. Barrett and David Roediger, "In-between People: Race, Nationality, and the New Immigrant Working Class," *Journal of American Ethnic History*, 16 (Spring 1997), 4-44; Robert Orsi, "The Religious Boundaries of an In-between People: Street Feste and the Problem of the Dark-Skinned Other in Italian Harlem, 1920-1990," *American Quarterly*, 4 (September 1992), 313-47.

[12] A. A. Roback, *A Dictionary of International Slurs (Ethnophaulisms) with a Supplementary Essay on Aspects of Ethnic Prejudice* (Cambridge, Mass.: Sci-Art Publishers, 1944); John R. Bartlett, *Dictionary of Americanisms on Historical Principles* (2 vols., Chicago: University of Chicago Press, 1951): Irving L. Allen, *Unkind Words: Ethnic Labeling from Redskin to Wasp* (New York: Bergin & Garvey, 1990). "Wop" on the other hand comes from a Neapolitan term , "guappo" meaning "a daring, handsome man-a dude." Typical was the newspaper description of two men arrested in Racine: "they are swarthy complexioned and have the appearance of being Italian." *Milwaukee Sentinel*, April 18, 1918.

[13] "Lynching," and "Italian Americans," *Violence in America: an Encyclopedia*, Ronald Gottesman, ed. (New York: Charles Scribnes Sons, 1999); Brian Evans and Bernard Waites, *IQ and Mental Testing: an Unnatural Science and its Social History* (Atlantic Highlands, N.J.: Humanities Press, 1981); Leonard C ovello, *The Social Background of the Italo-American School Child* (Leiden, The Netherlands: E.J.Brill, 1967); William McDougall, *Is America Safe for Democracy?* (New York: Charles Scribner's Sons, 1921). McDougall reported that Italians scored 84 on the IQ test, while "Colored" scored 83 as compared with the score of 106 of "All Americans," 64.

[14] Emory S. Bogardus, *Immigration and Race Attitudes* (Boston: D. C. Heath, 1928). George Gallup, *An Analysis of American Public Opinion Concerning the* War (Princeton: American Institute of Public Opinion, 1942). The fact that Italy was at war with the United States does not appear to have been a factor; Germans ranked much higher on all of these measures. Emphasis mine.

[15] Irvin L. Child, *Italian or American? The Second Generation in Conflict* (New Haven: Yale UP, 1943); Covello, *Social Background of the Italo-American School Child*. Autobiographies, novels, and oral histories are excellent sources for understanding the experience of second generation Italian Americans. See Fred Gardaphè, "The Evolution of Italian American Autobiography," and Mary Jo Bono, "The Italian American Coming-of-Age Novel," both in Pellegrino D'Acierno, ed., *The Italian American Heritage* (New York, 1999). As recently as the 1970s, the manual for prosecutors in Dallas, Texas read: "Do not take Jews, Negroes, Dagos, Mexicans or a member of any minority group on a jury, no matter how rich or ill-educated." Bob Herbert, "Countdown to Execution No. 300," NY Times. com, Article, March 10, 2003, WWW.

[16] Jacobson, *Shades of Whiteness*; Thomas A. Guglielmo, *White on Arrival: Italians, Race, Color, and Power in Chicago, 1890-1945* (New York: Oxford UP, 2003). Even official records conflated the categories of race and color. In a ledger of taxable property in Tallulah, Louisiana, Italians were identified as being *both* "White" and

"Colored." Cynthia Salvaglio to Ben Lawton, March 17, 2003, H-NET List on Italian-American History and Culture (hereafter H-ITAM), WWW.

[17] James N. Hill to F.I. Whitney, Duluth, August 18, 1897, Great Northern Railway Line Archives, Minnesota Historical Society; Vecoli, "Chicago's Italians," 330-31.

[18] The context was the Ethiopian War of 1896 in which Italy suffered a humiliating defeat. "Mrs. Taitu [wife of the Ethiopian emperor], Menilik [the emperor] doesn't want Menilik any more, she married [Oreste] Barattieri [the general in charge of the Italian army in Ethiopia], now she has white and black children." See also my unpublished paper, "The African Connection: Italian Americans and Race," American Italian Historical Association, Cleveland, Ohio, November 14, 1997; and Angelo Del Bosco, *L'Africa nella coscienza degli italiani* (Milan: Mondadori Editore, 2002).

[19] Orsi, "Religious Boundaries," 313; "The Italians of Chicago," and "Minnesota's Italians," Mary Ellen Mancina Batinich Oral History Collections, Immigration History Research Center, University of Minnesota. The following is from an e-mail of Rose Anna Mueller: "I grew up in Mazara del Vallo (pr. Trapani)... At some point the "others" the Turks, or Saracens, became the enemy. I remember being told to behave like a cristiana, not like a turca. Any bad behavior was called acting like a Turk. If guests were expected, we were told to get the house ready for the Cristiani — the people. As far as I know, the world of Mazara is separated into Turks and Christians. When I first came to the U.S. I saw two things I had never seen before — snow and blacks. I was told that I would see people with different color skin but that they were people just the same." H-ITAM, February 15, 1997, WWW.

[20] Jean (Vincenza) Scarpaci, *Italian Immigrants in Louisiana's Sugar Parishes, 1880-1910* (New York: Arno Press, 1980); Catherine Tripalin Murray, *a taste of memories from the old "Bush,"* v. I-II, (Madison: Greenbush...Remembered, 1988, 1990). Cookbooks with anecdotes accompanying each recipe, they are rich sources for the relationships between Italians and blacks.

[21] Growing up in an Iowa coal mining camp, Bruna Pieracci did not remember any prejudice against "Negroes": "in our home we did not hear the names, nigger, wop, dago, or Polack." Salvatore Lagumina, ed., *The Immigrants Speak: Italian Americans Tell Their Story* (New York: Center for Migration Studies, 1979), 41. Bruna's experience was not uncommon. For a discussion regarding terms Italians used for African-Americans see the exchanges on H-ITAM between February 14-18, 1997. For "cuns," A. B. Chiarello writing to comrades from Schenectady, New York, commenting on the opposition of whites to the hiring of blacks by General Electric. *L'Avenuenire Anarchico* (Pisa), July 12, 1917.

[22] African Americans and Italians confronted each other on both sides of the picket line. In June 1901 in Merchantville, New Jersey, Italian striker breakers, were attacked and beaten by blacks. Consul General of Italy in New York to the Italian Ministry of Foreign Affairs, June 26, 1901, Historical Archive of the Ministry of Foreign Affairs. On Spring Valley see Caroline A. Waldron, "Lynch Law Must Go! Race, Citizenship, and the Other in an American Coal Mining Town," *Journal of American Ethnic History*, 20 (2000) 50-77; idem, "'*L'Odio di Razza*': Identifications of Black and Italian Others during the Spring Valley Race Riot, 1895," Scholl Center Seminar,

Newberry Library, October 5, 2002. For an Italian perspective see the coverage in *L'Italia* of Chicago, August 10-11, 24-25, October 5-6, 1895.

[23] Jane Addams, *The Second Twenty Years at Hull House* (New York: Macmillan Co., 1930); William M. Tuttle, *Race Riot; Chicago in the Red Summer of 1919* (New York: Atheneum, 1970); Chicago Commission on Race Relations, *The Negro in Chicago; A Study of Race Relations and a Race Riot in 1919* (New York: Arno Press, 1968).

[24] Batinich Oral Histories, IHRC; for portrayals of Italian Americans see: Carlos E. Cortez, "Italian-Americans in Film: From Immigrants to Icons," *MELUS*, 14 (1987); Lester D. Friedman, ed. *Unspeakable Images: Ethnicity and the American Cinema* (Urbana: University of Illinois Press, 1991); Randall Miller and Allen L. Woll, eds., *Ethnic and Racial Images in American Film and Television* (New York: Garland, 1987).

[25] Rudolph J. Vecoli, "The Search for an Italian American Identity: Continuity and Change," in *Italian Americans: New Perspectives in Italian Immigration and Ethnicity,* Lydio Tomasi, ed. (New York: Center for Migration Studies, 1985), 88-112; Simone Cinotto, *Una Famiglia che mangia insieme: cibo ed etnicità nella Communità italoamericana di New York, 1920-1940* (Turin: Otto Editore, 2000) Social workers in the thirties attributed the "lightening" of the skin of Italian children to improved diet. Might it have been due to the fact that unlike their parents they did not spent their days in the fields under the burning sun?

[26] Fiorello B. Ventresco, "Italian-Americans and the Ethiopian Crisis," *Italian Americana*, 6 (Fall/Winter 1980); Stefano Luconi, "The Influence of the Italo-Ethiopian Conflict and the Second World War on Italian-American voters: The Case of Philadelphia," *Immigrants & Minorities,* 16 (November 1997); Nadia Venturini, *Neri e italiani ad Harlem. Gli anni Trenta e la guerra d'Etiopia* (Rome: Edizioni Lavoro, 1990); Rudolph J. Vecoli, "The African Connection." An Italian American garment worker in Boston recalled that following the invasion of Ethiopia, African Americans became angry, "shouting and throwing things" at the Italians. "We were good friends usually with those people...but that was a bad day...." H-ITAM, September 12, 1998, WWW.

[27]On Fascist racism, colonialism and anti-Semitism see: Burgio, *Nel nome della razza*, 145-214, 309-58

[28] Vincenzo Frazzetta, "I Fix the Railroad Tracks," Italians in Bridgeport, Peoples of Connecticut, Ethnic Heritage WPA Writers Project 1930s, Box 23, Historical Manuscripts and Archives, University of Connecticut, Storrs.

[29] George E. Pozzetta, "My Children Are My Jewels: Italian American Generations during World War II," in *Home Front War: World War II and American Society*, Kenneth P. O'Brien and Lynn H. Parsons, eds.(Westport, CT: Greenwood Publishers, 1995); Philip Gleason, "Americans All," *Speaking of Diversity: Language and Ethnicity in Twentieth-century America* (Baltimore: Johns Hopkins UP, 1992; Gary Mormino, "The House We Live In: Italian Americans and World War II," *Ambassador*, 26 (Summer 1995); Nadia Venturini, "African American Riots During World War II: Re-

actions in the Italian American Communist Press," American Italian Historical Association, Cleveland, 1997.

[30] Jonathan Reider, *Canarsie: the Jews and Italians of Brooklyn against liberalism* (Cambridge, Mass.: Harvard UP, 1985); Ronald P. Formisano, *Boston Against Busing: Race, Class, and Ethnicity in the 1960s and 1970s* (Chapel Hill, NC: University of North Carolina Press, 1991); Jim Sleeper, *The Closest of Strangers: Liberalism and the Politics of Race in New York* (New York: Norton, 1990).

[31] Tom W. Smith, "A Political Profile of Italian Americans: 1972-1994," [Report prepared for the National Italian American Foundation], National Opinion Research Center, University of Chicago, April 1996; Graziano Battistella, ed. *Italian Americans in the 80s: a Sociodemographic Profile* (New York: Center for Migration Studies, 1989).

[32] David A. J. Richards, *Italian American: The Racializing of an Ethnic Identity* (New York and London: New York UP, 1999). But see my review: "Racializing Italian Americans: Sources and Resources," *Voices in Italian Americana*, 12:1 (2001), 1-8.

[33] For radical views on race and racism see Rudolph J. Vecoli, "'Free Country': the American Republic Viewed by the Italian Left, 1880-1920," in *In the Shadow of the Statue of Liberty: Immigrants, Workers and Citizens in the American Republic, 1880-1920*, Marianne Debouzy, ed. (Saint-Dennis: Presses Universitaires de Vincennes, 1988). See also articles on "Radicalism," "Church Leaders," and individuals such as Carlo Tresca and Geno Baroni in Salvatore J. Lagumina et al, eds., *The Italian American Experience: An Encyclopedia* (New York & London: Garland Publishing, 2000).

[34] Jerome Krase, "Bensonhurst, Brooklyn: Italian American Victimizers and Victims," *Voices in Italian Americana*, 5 (1994), 43-53; Donald Tricarico, "Guido: Fashioning an Italian-American Youth Style," *The Journal of Ethnic* Studies, 19 (Spring 1991), 541-66; Lou Caro, Jr., "Mixed Relations: The Italian American-African American *Dis*-Connection," *Interrace* (May, June 1992); John Gennari, "Passing for Italian: Crooners and gangsters in crossover culture," *Transition Issue 72,* 36-72. See also "Intergroup Relations: Italian Americans and African Americans," "Jazz," and "Film Directors, Producers, and Italian American Image in Cinema," in LaGumina, *Italian American Experience.*

[35] Rudolph J. Vecoli, "Are Italian Americans Just White Folks?" in *Beyond the Godfather: Italian American Writers on the Real Italian American Experience*, Kenneth Ciongoli and Jay Parini, eds. (Hanover and London: UP of New England, 1997), 307-318.

Return Voyages: Rossellini, Scorsese and the Identity of National Cinema

Pasquale Verdicchio
University of California San Diego

Martin Scorsese's six-hour documentary on postwar Italian cinema entitled *Il mio viaggio in Italia* was first presented in a shorter version at the 1999 Venice Film Festival. Definitely a must for those interested in learning about that influential period in cinema, the title *Il mio viaggio in Italia* is doubly important to those of us fascinated by the cultural implications of a cultural exchange between Italians and the Italian diaspora. The publicity packet for Martin Scorsese's *My Voyage to Italy* (2002) states that the film

> serves as a tribute to some of [neo-realism's] greatest films and filmmakers. [As he offers viewers] a passionate look at the movies that have affected him so deeply throughout the years, Scorsese examines his own formation as a filmmaker and as a person. [...] The groundbreaking Neo-realist pictures [of directors such as] Rossellini, De Sica and Visconti not only opened up a whole new world for Scorsese when he was a boy — they also gave him a glimpse of his own origins. (Miramax Film Press Release, 3)

Scorsese has mentioned the influence of Italian cinema on his own work on a number of occasions. In *Scorsese on Scorsese* (Faber and Faber, 1989) he specifically refers to Pasolini's *The Gospel According to Matthew* as an influence in his biblical *The Last Temptation of Christ*, and a number of times he makes explicit references to Rossellini's cinematographic methodology and vision in general. Casino's juxtaposition of sacred and profane elements is perhaps most obviously comparable to Pasolini's own contrasts in films like *Accattone* (1961). And, direct correspondences and influences become apparent in viewing Visconti's Rocco and his brothers and Scorsese's *Raging Bull*, for example. Both are works that delve into interactive family relationships and the struggle for survival, recognition and individuality. Rocco and Bull stand as investigative pieces into the workings of each nation's social structures. As they are in most all Neorealist films, the boundaries between public and private life are blurred and, as such, they impose a strain on the main characters' adaptive powers. Boxing comes to be held up as an allegory for the struggles of life itself. The reality that Neorealist film-makers supposedly represented cannot truly to be said to find direct correspondence beyond the film screen except in very general terms and in their directors' desire to offer an alternative culture to the Fascism that had recently expired. Similarly *Mean Streets* and *Goodfellas* might be explicitly Italian-American in their references but how Italian-American are they? And, are other films such as *Alice Doesn't Live Here Anymore*, *The Color of Money* and *The Age of Innocence* any less Italian-American for their lack of Italian subject matter? These questions indicate the necessity for a reappraisal of the meaning assigned Neo-realism, that of a direct depiction of reality, and of its potential influence on a director like Scorsese.

Scorsese formulates an interesting distinction in his discussion of these classics of Italian cinema. He uses the expression "Neo-realism of the past" in reference to Visconti's *Senso* as a way of contrasting it to Neorealist films situated in a more apparently present time frame. In contrast to "neorealism of the past" we might extrapolate another, more direct Neo-realism of the present. It could perhaps be argued that, being aware of the strong influence that these films have had on his own cinematography, Scorsese seems to use the expression to establish distance between his productions and the Neo-realist films using the latter as a point of contrast.

And yet, we need only turn to Italo Calvino, whose 1946 novel *The Path to the Nest of Spiders* is signaled as the first postwar neorealist novel, for testimony regarding Neorealism's meaning for his generation:

> [...] it had never been so clear that the stories were raw material: the explosive charge of freedom that animated the young writer was not so much his wish to document or to inform as it was his desire to *express*. [...] to us the whole problem was one of poetics; how to transform into a literary work that world which for us was *the* world. [...] 'Neorealism' was not a school. (We must try to state things precisely.) It was a collection of voices, largely marginal, a multiple discovery of the various Italies, even — or particularly — the Italies previously unknown to litera-

> ture. Without the variety of Italies unknown (or presumably unknown) to one another, without the variety of dialects and jargon that could be kneaded and molded into the literary language, there would have been no 'neorealism.' (Calvino 1985, vi-vii)

It is obvious that for Calvino, as well as for all those filmmakers challenged to express themselves in the postwar period, a neorealism of the present was the most pressing concern. This is what I believe is at work in Scorsese, in his attempt to construct an Italian American *American* cinema. He is merely at work handling "the stories [h]e ha[s] personally enacted or [...] witnessed mingled with those [he] ha[s] already heard as tales, with a voice, an accent, a mimed expression." (vi) This is what makes *Mean Streets*, *Goodfellas*, and all the rest. Mingle *Italianamerican* with *The Last Waltz,* and you get Scorsese. Mix the *Stones* with religious fervor and you have the miracle of *Mean Streets* and a struggle of the self and its own difference that is *The Gangs of New York*. That is the uniqueness of Italian American culture.

The Italian films in *Il mio viaggio* are presented as part of a common global cinematographic legacy, which rescues Scorsese (the cinematographer) from a more direct nostalgic effect. Rather than being considered a cultural element that provided the drive or inspiration for him toward a collective Italian cultural sense, the Italian films gave Scorsese a head-start toward a personal assessment of his own inter-national relationship. The films, Scorsese reminisces, provided him with a here-to-fore unimagined context. However imported films might be construed in a foreign context, they gave him and other Italian Americans a sense of the elements on which to base much of their acquired Italian culture.

Of course, I am neither doubting nor qualifying Scorsese's Italian culture, but I am suggesting that the sense of *italianità* that one might have acquired through those films was a filtered and generalized one.[1] It was, in a sense, a Neorealist culture and not what might be considered a documentation of facts. This is particularly important since it was seen through the eyes of a second-generation child of immigrants from Southern Italy. In addition, for most of those immigrants the notion of an Italian nation with a unified culture and language was nothing less than foreign. These distinctions are important, in my opinion, in that they form the basis for the construction of that very specific cultural manifestation that is Italian American. In short, what I mean is that while Italian Americans might "feel" their roots, the historiographical concreteness of it was lacking. I believe that this is what Scorsese struggles with in his relationship with Italian culture in general and in the context of the documentary.

Scorsese, himself only a few years Bertolucci's junior, comments on the film *Prima della rivoluzione* (1963) as inspiring, and goes on to relate his feeling that he could not have made such a film. The reason for this may in part be due to Scorsese and other Italian Americans' own removed station from the currents of Italian socio-political history, including the historical context that generated their own condition. Scorsese says of Bertolucci, "he was raised in political thought, which was not the case with me. There were no books in my father's and my mother's house." This statement carries with it a great testimony as to the historical place of Italian immigrants. Bertolucci's politicized youth and Scorsese's less politicized one are not comparable as personal phenomena, because they are the results of social and political movements of their time and age. Italians of the period in question were in general more politicized than their American, and especially their Italian American, counter-parts. Having left the Italian peninsula as de-historicized peoples, Italian immigrants to the USA were initially marginalized peoples concerned with the business of survival above all else. The historicization of Italian Americans comes rather late in our history and is still in its formative stages. Therefore, even if there had been books in the Scorsese household, they would not have included those that most directly concerned them. Those books have only recently been produced and mostly by Italian Americans themselves. As such, the importance of *My Voyage to Italy* to Italian Americans is as a meditation on that historical gap and its stance as a pedagogical instigation.

Roberto Rossellini's *Viaggio in Italia* (*Voyage to Italy*) (1953) belongs to those films situated in the director's post-neorealist season. A number of those films from the 50s became vehicles for Ingrid Bergman and include *Stromboli* (1949) and *Europe '51* (1952). They differ from the director's earlier works in that they are more engaged with an analysis of personal relationships, marriages, emotional alienation and despair. Neo-realism in general, concerned as it was with a reconstruction of Italy on the socio-cultural level, represents the coincidence of a collective sense of responsibility, as is evident in Rossellini's own *Rome Open City* (1945) and *Ger-*

many, Year 0 (1946). The later films could be considered to represent for Rossellini a personal struggle for expression beyond the confines of the neorealist stage of which he is often named as father. The director's own statements regarding neo-realism ("There is no pre-conceived thesis [...] it refuses recipes and formulas" [...] "There are those who still think of neo-realism as something external, as going out into the open air, as a contemplation of misery and suffering. For me, it is nothing other than the artistic form of truth." [...] "The subject of neo-realist film is the world; not story or narrative." [...] "Neo-realism was born unconsciously dialectical film, after which it acquired a heart-felt consciousness of the social, human problems during the war and the post-war period." From "Due parole sul neo-realismo" in *Retrospettive*, 4, April 1953.) give us further insights into the necessities dictated by that period's often conflicted history. These might go to explain some of the perceived contradictions that a film like *Rome, Open City* might illustrate, even vis-à-vis the narrative that precedes the film. Projected over silhouetted scenes of the Eternal City, Rossellini outlines what amounts to both a credo and a plan of action. Others will later integrate many of these characteristics into what will come to be known as Neo-realism:

> While the Nazis held Rome in their firm grip after the summer of 1943 a group of Italian film makers were planning underground a motion-picture record of the terrors inflicted on their compatriots in the declared open city. Working behind barred doors in cellars and attics in ravines and hills outside Rome they prepared their scenario. The day the Allied Armies marched in the producers and actors went ahead using equipment, much of which had been stolen from the Germans at the cost of Italian lives. Without studio lights, with electricity often unobtainable, and restricted to old scraps of film they completed *Open City*, the 1st post-war Italian picture. Except for a handful of principals the cast consists of ordinary Roman citizens picked off the streets and the scenes were filmed at the exact location of the particular incidents.
> (Opening credits, *Rome, Open City*)

The rhetoric of this passage is easily decipherable. Rossellini lays out a cinematographic plan that is only covertly "partisan." Presenting his film as an act of resistance, acted out by "ordinary Roman citizen," "filmed at the exact location of the particular incidents" and, in doing so at the risk of their own lives, the film maker and his crew make sure that the "real" story is told. Rossellini liberates filmmaking as the peninsula has been liberated. And, while the conditions in which film has to be born and thrive are difficult, much like for everything else in the country, it is the plain labour of common and courageous people that makes its survival possible. This attitude touches all of Neo-realism and has been considered to represent the "nationalist" aspect of this period's filmmaking. Even though Rossellini received the support of individuals such as Rod Geiger (Gallagher, 159), a private first class in the US Forces in Italy, the cinema Rossellini helped initiate was the result of a particularly situated Italian experience.

Having established his vision regarding the need to film without the disruptive make-believe trappings of studios, Rossellini's post-neorealist films continue to maintain contact with many of the established precepts, such as filming on location, the use of non-actor, etcetera. Nevertheless, the films of the late 40s and early 50s can be read as a statement of the director's evolving interests and of his cosmopolitanism. He remarked as much in a 1954 interview with the journal *Cahiers du Cinéma*: "life has changed, the war is over, the cities have been reconstructed. What we needed was a cinema of the Reconstruction." In this regard *Voyage to Italy* stands as one of Rossellini's most important films. But there is more than that at work in these films. The reconstruction is representative of a more personal reconstitution of Rossellini's own attitude toward the function of cinema.

The Neorealist season served the needs of the immediate postwar period, as a way to re-elaborate a particular set of socio-political parameters that had been overwhelmed by twenty years of Fascism and World War II. However, after having passed over that ground, after having successfully addressed issues pertinent to an immediate post-fascist/post-war moment of national reflection, the need to re-elaborate the personal made itself apparent. That is when Rossellini and others aimed their cameras on the landscape of interpersonal relationships, seeking answers to the personal meditations that had ensued during the euphoric period of liberation and reconstitution.

Rossellini's *Voyage to Italy* is about an English couple's (Alexander and Katherine Joyce, played by George Sanders and Ingrid Bergman) visit to Naples. The couple is on the verge of divorce and they are visibly irritable and uncomfortable in each other's company. They are in Naples to dispose of some inherited real estate. Immediately, their English sensibilities are confronted with the inexplicable influence of the Neapolitan environment and social space in which they must function during this trying period. Naples stands in as a place of more basic emotional and sensual existence.

The film became a reference point for Rossellini in personal as well as artistic terms. His relationship with Ingrid Bergman had created a stir in the English language press, and his use of an English couple as a vehicle through which to oppose Mediterranean sensibilities to British or American Puritanism could be seen as a response to this. He in fact turns the situation inside out. The English couple is rescued by the sea of human sensuality that surrounds them in Naples. They find and define themselves within the crowd that surrounds them in the end. They emerge renewed and ready for a new future together. The allegorical relationship is, of course, as it has been all along that between Italian and American cinema. The struggle that pits entertainment against the need for the establishment of a cultural ground after the effects of Fascism. This is the same struggle that De Sica depicts in *Ladri di biciclette*, in the job he gives the unemployed father as someone who pastes movie posters advertising American films along the walls of Rome. De Sica, Rossellini and others immersed themselves in an exercise of comparative critical culture, a process by which their audiences were asked to make choices regarding the function and future of Italian culture and society. How does all this square with Martin Scorsese's own recent documentary *My Voyage to Italy*?

The process of discovery of Italian Americans is brought to stand by association close to that of the Joyces in Rossellini's film. In his own "voyage in Italy" while nodding in deference to the lessons of Italian film, Martin Scorsese announces his autonomy from it and makes a pronouncement for Italian American film as being expressly American. Not, mind you, in direct or explicit terms, but merely through his presence. He immerses himself in Italian cinema for his public and, while recognizing the importance of it both at the emotive and practical levels, he re-emerges from it revitalized for having acknowledged his inheritance. Like Rossellini's couple in *Viaggio in Italia*, Scorsese finds in Italian cinema the ground upon which to consecrate himself. He becomes American through the acknowledgment and distancing of his Italian origins.

In 1974 Scorsese made *Italianamerican* with the understanding that it would not dwell on some of the usual stereotypical recapitulations of the Italian immigrant experience. In other words, it would avoid some of the historical markers that defined the immigrant's first approaches into America (Ellis Island, the ghettoes, etc). The director chose his parents as the protagonists of the interview/documentary, as representative of a particular experience. He interviews them in their home, and reminisces with them about their life in their neighborhood as an illustration of a fairly common and comfortable, but not necessarily easy, assimilation into a new society. *Italianamerican* situates Italian Americans as unquestionably American through their assimilation quest.

Scorsese's choice to distance *Italianamerican* from the immigrant experience may have been intended to avoid the stereotyping that has hounded Italian American identity. But that was merely a rhetorical manner in which to illustrate the fact that there are indeed a variety of approaches by which the Italian American experience might be told, for in fact the short is deeply engaged in those aspects of Italian life that are misconstrued as stereotypical: family, community, food, communion and dialogue. But while the interview/documentary/film retains some obvious "ethnic" flavours, including the title itself, I believe that Scorsese succeeds, within the obvious limits of the film, in installing his family as a middle of the road, hard-working, strong American family. *Italianamerican* seeks to normalize the Italian American figure in the eyes of an American viewing public, and to give its Italian American viewers a sense of achievement and belonging within a level of social and cultural normalcy and assimilation.

In the end it could almost be said that *Italianamerican* is not an Italian American film, but a film that aims to end Italian American difference by declaring the legitimacy of Italian immigration and the installation of Italians in America as part of the hard-working, struggling masses who find in the ideals of the American republic a source of inspiration. And so, again, I should ask: where does Scorsese's *My Voyage to Italy* stand? It is not the documentary that it might have been had it not be preceded by Scorsese's documentary on American Film. The juxtaposition of the two documentaries gives each one a different shadow than they might have had as singular productions, and makes *My Voyage* less nostalgic by association.

As such, I would like to conclude with a rather contorted argument that I hope in the end might emerge as an intelligible reflection. I would propose that Martin Scorsese's view of Italian cinema represents a flattening gaze from afar. The effect is similar to that of a telephoto lens to which the optics of emigration might be compared. The resulting gaze overlooks social, political and other such currents within Italian society and cinema by the fact of their non-participation. While proposing a national cinematography through a direct reflection of life in opposition to Fascism, Neo-realism simultaneously proposed (mostly through language and therefore in an almost imperceptible manner for most non-Italians) a multitude that unmasks the preposterous masquerade of Italian nationhood. Italian national cinema in this manner became (and continues to be in its best manifestations) a critique of nationalism. The mere appearance of different languages on the screen exposed its artificial homogeneity. This is not to say that Rossellini himself did not cast a telephoto gaze on Naples, its peoples and culture. What is exalted are the myriad preconceptions outsiders have of that culture. Nevertheless, I must conclude that it is in these traits of valued diversity that are Neo-realist cinema's primary subject matter, that Scorsese finds the effective elements of Neo-realism and Italian national cinema. These are the elements that, paradoxically, make his own cinema American. Is it not American society after-all, at least rhetorically, the one that poses multiplicity and diversity as its national character? And these, being the ideological gifts of Italian national cinema and the very structure of Italian society, turn out to be the most important traits of this Italian American director.

As a footnote to everything I have said I would like to say a few words regarding another director, Gianni Amelio. Amelio and his work constitute another aspect of the culture of migration. Though not exclusively, his films (*Così ridevano*, *Il ladro di bambini*, *Lamerica*) have dealt with those who stayed, or were left, behind. His filmography could almost be considered *la vedova bianca*, the white widow, of Italian emigrant history. The three films I have mentioned ask of Italians a most difficult task: that of coming to terms with emigration (and, by extension, the new immigrations) as a domestic problem. The attitude, I'm sorry to say, has been quite the opposite. "Out of sight, out of mind" has been the guiding policy vis-à-vis Italians abroad (except of course when some political interests could be served, such as with the granting of the vote). Amelio's internal migrations and itineraries, his depiction of the relationship with Albania are more than tightly bound to the North/South dichotomy and its related problems, of which emigration is but one. The Italian / Italian American relationship has been less than familial, and Amelio is a valuable interlocutor for both sides of the equation. I shall close with a quote of a quote, Jake La Motta's quotation of Brando's character from *On the Waterfront* in Scorsese's *Raging Bull*. A quote that in the context of these musings goes to the heart of that missed opportunity for what Antonio D'Alfonso has called a culture "in italics" beyond nationalisms, culturalisms and linguistic barriers:

> It wasn't him Charlie, it was you. You remember that night at the Garden, you came down to my dressing room and you said 'kid this ain't your night, we're goin' for the price on Wilson.' Remember that? This ain't your night? My night. I could'a taken Wilson apart that night. So what happens? He gets a title shot outdoors in the ballpark, and what do I get? A one-way ticket to palookaville. I was never no good after that night Charlie. It was like a peak you reach and then it's down hill. It was you Charlie. You was my brother. You should'a looked out for my a little bit. You should'a looked out for me just a little bit. You should'a taken care of me just a little bit. Instead of makin' me take them dives for the short end money. You don't understand. I could'a had class. I could'a been a contender. I could'a been somebody. Instead of a bum, which is what I am. Let's face it. It was you Charlie. It was you Charlie. (From *On the Waterfront*)

---

[1] The term *italianità* is indicative of the process of self-definition involved in the cultural construct that is called Italian American. While *italianità* implies an essentialized national character, Italy's own perception of, and relationship to, Italians abroad is less than inclusive of their distant cousins. History bears out the fact that those who saw emigration as their last alternative were also defined as not quite fulfilling the idealized characteristics of an Italian citizen. This is closely related to the age-old North/South predicament that has tinged Italian society since unification. The definition of southerners as a lesser population has had long-lasting effects on the overall character of the country. As such, *italianità* appears to refer to an idealized Italian character that is primarily of North-Central origins. I tend to believe that the claims of *italianità* on the part of many Italian Americans is an attempt to extend a hand toward that country that bore them and their ancestors, and to which they feel an affinity. However, this act is hardly recognized in Italy, unless it can be politicized and

instrumentalized into something tangible such as the granting of the vote to Italians residing abroad. The machinations behind this granting of rights simply translated to a manipulation of the nostalgia that many Italians abroad feel. It is the assumption of some political parties and personalities that Italians abroad are all of a certain political stripe and that the granting of the vote will result in a change in the political hierarchy in Italy. Such assumptions are indicative of the patronizing and condescending attitude toward emigrated Italians; and they cynically sell *italianità* to those who long for recognition. It is my sincere belief that Italian North American culture is a self-defined culture that has grown at the interface between Italian regional cultures and the cultures (other immigrant cultures) that they interact/ed with upon arrival and beyond. It is neither Italian nor whatever American might mean, and it is both Italian and American by its hybridity. As a concept, *italianità* is bankrupt because it is a transparent attempt to sell nationalism for political gain to those it excluded. I would contrast D'Alfonso's concept of "italic" culture to that of *italianità*. The former is inclusive of cultural and linguistic diversity where the latter is not. The latter is normative in essence while "italic" culture tends toward multiple manifestations.

Works Cited

Boorman, John and Walter Donohue, editors. *Projections 7: Filmmakers on Filmmaking in association with Cahiers du Cinema*. London: Faber and Faber, 1997.

Calvino, Italo. *Introduction to The Path to the Nest of Spiders*. Translated by William Weaver. Fifth Printing. New York: The Ecco Press, 1985.

Corti, Maria. "Neo-realismo" pp. 33-36 in *Il viaggio testuale*. Torino: Einaudi, 1978.

D'Alfonso, Antonio. *In Italics*. Toronto: Guernica Editions, 1996.

Forgacs, David. *Rome, Open City*. BFI Film Classics. London: BFI, 2001.

Gallagher, Tag. *The Adventures of Roberto Rossellini: His Life and Films*. New York: DaCapo Press, 1998.

Thompson, David and Ian Christie, editors. *Scorsese on Scorsese*. With an introduction by Michael Powell. London: Faber and Faber, 1989.

Flags and Shopping Bags: Composing an Italian American Spectacle

Robert Viscusi
Brooklyn College, CUNY

I am an Italian. And let me be candid: I am an Italian without papers. I was born in the United States to a mother born in Italy. My father was born in the United States, and his parents, both Italian immigrants, separated when my father was still a boy. He was raised by his mother. As a consequence of this mischance, I have no papers to establish descent through my father's father. This leaves me only my mother's papers to depend upon if I want to call myself legally an Italian. These documents might be expected to suffice. After all, my mother was born in Italy. But not all such births are equal. My mother was born in 1916, but she did not acquire the ability to transmit to her children her rights as a native Italian until 1948, when the new constitution endowed her with legal equality. Since I was born before 1948, my descent through my Italian mother, howsoever amply documented and in every way attested, is not enough to establish me as an Italian. The law is very clear on this point, they have told me down at the Consolato Generale d'Italia on Park Avenue. According to the Italians, I am not an Italian.

And yet I am an Italian. Like many millions of other Italians who reside in countries other than Italy, I have lived my entire life claiming an identity to which I have no political title. Unless the laws change, unless I suddenly discover the papers that I need, unless someone does me a great honor — unless one of these things should happen, I will probably not become a citizen of Italy.

This is not an altogether unhappy state of affairs. After all, I am a native of the United States, where my citizenship has entailed obligations of tax and military service. I would hesitate before assuming another set of such burdens. Nonetheless, in Long Island City, Queens, the working-class melting-pot where I grew up, it made sense to call myself Italian as well as American. There have always been parts of New York where it seemed vital to claim membership in the commonwealth of Italians. Socially, politically, and culturally, the Italian colony of New York has been basic to my survival and nurture throughout my life.

In sum, then, I am an Italian to myself but not to Italians and, truth to tell, not to a lot of other people either. I am irreducibly two. Such two-ness has been indelibly outlined by W.E.B. Du Bois in *The Souls of Black Folk*:

> It is a peculiar sensation, this double-consciousness, this sense of always looking at one's self through the eyes of others, of measuring one's soul by the tape of a world that looks on in amused contempt and pity. One ever feels his two-ness — an American, a Negro; two souls, two thoughts, two unrecognized strivings; two warring ideas in one dark body. whose dogged strength alone keeps it from being torn asunder. (DuBois 8-9)

In the case of African Americans, the roots of this two-ness lie in the tangled history of slavery and capital. In the case of Italian Americans, the roots lie in the tangled history of nationalism and commerce. In both cases, the two-ness is irreducible. The Italian American discovers that immigrant Italianness is a category of the excluded and condemned, and historically is associated with visible signs of the migrant's extranational status, especially the Italian flag and its unmistakable heraldry of green, white, and red. Overcoming this status has often meant engaging in an upwardly mobile consumerism that demonstrates to the world that the immigrant or post-immigrant can afford the signs of the very prestige that has excluded him or her. The shopping bag with the legend *Armani*, *Benetton*, *Versace* can serve as a metonymy for this whole process in which the immigrant self learns to live with, and to transform, what it learns to see of its features through the eyes of others.

Flags

The lyrics of national anthems accustom us to the idea that flags represent blood sacrifices and border problems. These sacrifices include more than death on the battlefield. People who fly their national flags in foreign places often find themselves in the crosshairs of xenophobes. In the United States, the Italian flag has long served to mark Italian Americans as belonging to a socially abject group.

There was no easy way for Italian emigrants to escape the national heraldry that marked them with a stigma. Italian nationalism frequently worked at cross-purposes with itself. Indeed, it produced the Italian diaspora inadvertently, and with a great deal of weeping and gnashing of teeth. Depopulation was scarcely what the leaders of United Italy had intended when they started out, and they were determined not to lose sight or control of all their new nation's people. After unification, Italy's governments tried seriously to transform the many principalities of the Italian peninsula into a single nation, employing a program of war and empire (Duggan 770).[1] Italy's imperialist program did not succeed in producing an empire. What this program accomplished instead was to provide an appropriate ideology for the actual empire that Italians established — the system of labor colonies and export entrepôts that formed Italy's world trade network from Boston to Buenos Aires and from Sydney to Glasgow. The new nation could no longer support many of the people who had subsisted under the old arrangements; these people left Italy and found their way to settlements all over the world that the Italians called *colonie*.

These colonies had at their disposal international bankers and transatlantic shipping lines, as well as a copious flow of cheap labor from the Italian provinces. Their population justified the name *colonie*. But they did not have any military power of their own. Italy could not offer that kind of support. What Italy could and did supply was a spectacle of flags and military music, along with consular officials and other trained ideologues to explain it, keeping fresh and vivid the vision of Italy's glorious past and the image of its equally glorious intentions for the future. This spectacle provided the emigrants with an ideological identity that came to serve them well in the intergroup competition that characterized civil and political strife in foreign cities — and in none more than those of the United States. The *tricolore*, whatever it might mean in Italy, when it was unfurled along Fifth Avenue each year on the twelfth of October, spoke clearly to the Irish- and Spanish- and African- and German- and Polish- and Greek- and Anglo-Americans of New York City, announcing the presence, compactness, economic intention, collective memory, and firm political will that joined American Italians to one another and to that government in Rome which professed itself permanently interested in their welfare and prosperity. Italy was an aggressive country in those early years. In 1890 Italy's navy was larger than that of the United States. To Italian Americans, Italy's flag meant a powerful affiliation.

This affiliation came at a price, however. Insofar as they were Italians, the immigrants were second-class persons in the United States. To the degree that immigrants embraced the standard of the nation they had left behind, they reinstituted its orders of prestige, reminding themselves and others as well of the abject social condition that had led so many of them to abandon their places of birth. Language, economy, sociology, anthropology — the whole structure of Italian bourgeois learning collaborated to send these migrants into the world firmly ensconced in the lower part of the national pyramid. It was received wisdom that these immigrants could neither read nor speak proper Italian; it was frequently lamented that they scarcely began to command the same high culture they were expected to revere and to regard as a sign of their own deep abasement; and it was generally concluded that these disabilities were signs of much deeper faults: Italian criminologists provided ample evidence that these wanderers exhibited the undersized crania and sloping foreheads that accompany inherited degeneracy of all kinds, from sexual dysfunction to homicidal mania. American bourgeois institutions understood what to do with people who arrived carrying such recommendations, and they received the Italians into neighborhoods and lines of work suitable for a labor force that would remain legally dubious and culturally out of the question for generations — a condition of social debility that even today is neatly summarized in the term *Italian American* and generally signified by the presence of a *tricolore* hung on the wall of the establishment or printed on the letterhead of the association or carried alongside the stars and stripes in the parade.

When the Italian colony of New York City dedicated its monument to Christopher Columbus on the 12th of October, 1892, Carlo Barsotti, the editor of *Il progresso italo-americano*, who had promoted and led the project to construct the monument, speaking at the dedication, asserted in his discourse, "É la prima volta, dopo la scoperta del nuovo mondo, che il santo ricordo di Colombo, e la sacra bandiera tricolore, — ricevono così grandi onori sul suol d'America." And concluded with a triple salute "figli d'Italia, concittadini dell'Uomo che dette un nuovo mondo al mondo, ad acclamare con me al venerato nome di Cristoforo Colombo! All'Italia! All'America! Viva Colombo! Viva l'Italia! Viva l'America!" (*Il progresso italo-americano*, Domenica 16 ottobre, 1992: 2) This triple identification represents considerable force of willfulness. Columbus, for example, was no *concittadino* of any living Italian. Nor were the Americans, for their part, happy with the attempt of the Italians to lay claim to Columbus, whom the United States ideologues had long since elevated into an aureole of their own willful thinking, where he reigned, howsoever improbably, as a precursor of the reformation, the enlightenment, and the American Revolution. After the Columbus Circle monument was dedicated, "the *New York Times* observed that the circle had become 'a sort of mecca' where 'troops' of the 'swarthy sons of the Sunny South' wander about the bit of marble, looking it over with the deepest interest." (Bushman 182) The Italian *tricolore* retained, for the gaze of the Other, its power as a social stigma, something the Italian immigrants were slow to see and slower to incorporate into their own thinking.

A similar confusion reigns in the heart of immigrant spectacle as Garibaldi La Polla portrays it in his classic novel of 1890s Italian Harlem, *The Grand Gennaro*. Gennaro, the exuberant archetype of the Italian American *prominente*, leads a triumphal parade to celebrate Admiral Dewey's triumph in Manila. Gennaro appears as, in effect, the *tricolore* walking in the sunshine — "accoutred in a uniform of an officer of bersaglieri, shining green with a red sash across the chest from shoulder to hip." And he is saluted by the bands striking up *The Stars and Stripes Forever*. "There were all of six bands, and they had planned to start the triumphal procession with a concert of Italian and American patriotic pieces, to be played by the entire ensemble." (Lapolla 192) In Gennaro's case, as in that of many another, the two flags stand for notions of citizenship and of national mission that cancel out one another's meaning. Being both Italian and American in this hyperbolic spectacle is tantamount to being neither. In the rest of this novel, Gennaro rages through his political and personal careers like a man whose only real allegiance is to himself and his own interests.

Shopping Bags

Italy has not always had a flag.[2] Long before it had awakened and strapped on the helmet of Scipio, Italy had been known throughout the world of trade as a culture of commerce. Italian cities are organized around highly rationalized and articulated public markets. This form of urban planning has had long persistence in Italy. The markets of Trajan in Rome and Ostia, two thousand years old, would be recognizable as scenes of shopping today (Satterthwaite 16-17). The medieval Italian townscape organized around an open market actually provides the model for a contemporary shopping mall called the Borgata in Scottsdale, Arizona (Satterthwaite 17). The Galleria Vittorio Emanuele II in Milano has been called the "prototype for American shopping malls" of the late 20th century (Kowinski 166). And what has long been evident in public architecture has also been deeply woven into private practice of self-construction and display. Relics and fetishes have always played an important role in Italian personal and familial life. Local rituals with their roots in the mists of ancient practice still annually celebrate the grapes or almonds harvested in specific places. These liturgies of locality have persisted through many changes of regime and have never belonged exclusively to Ghibelline or Guelf. Such practices have given shape and purpose to the circulatory systems that have grown into the Italian world trade network. To this day, Italian neighborhoods in Brooklyn celebrate the feast days of the patrons of small cities outside Naples. But Italian markets in the United States now more frequently attach themselves to rites practiced in the Italian store and in the kitchen.

> In the store in the States
> I finger the can of espresso:
> Lavazza of Naples, Maimone of Sicily
> Danesi from Torino, Ciao from Piacenza
> I buy the Lavazza di Napoli, Mamma Giulia's favorite,
>   and make a late afternoon cup
> I think of my sister Pina in the pre-Alps of Lombardy
>   brewing each tazza in an automatic machine
> I sip, I taste, I remember
> my sister Luisa having her sixth cup
>   after the typing and telephones in Molise
>   her machinetta always handy
> Elena and Luca and Babbo at the crack of dawn
>   before work with the tiniest pots
>   aromatic steam rising in cold mountain air. (Fama 11)

Such celebrations of buying power have become a central ritual in Italian American spectacle. These spectacles incorporate many elements. This poem, entitled "Caffè Espresso," suggests how such a spectacle can serve multiple purposes: not only does it display the writer's familiarity with the varied coffees of Italy, but it also claims acquaintance with many of the country's principal cities, and the very recitation of their names works a powerful narrative effect: the members of the poet's immigrant family belong to a narrative of Italy as place where one buys things and acquires credentials of connoisseurship. The poet's fingering the cans of espresso enacts an overcoming of immigrant poverty and a healing of immigrant stigmata. Italian American literature is replete with second and third generation writers returning to Italy and brandishing their educations and their money in long processions of consumption. Helen Barolini's *Umbertina* constructs for its central character a well-articulated place in the heart of bourgeois Italy, with an apartment on Piazza Barberini and a wide acquaintance among leading novelists, critics, and arbiters of literary prizes. Perhaps the purest example of this style of spectacular travel is Barbara Grizzuti Harrison's *Italian Days*, wherein the knowledgeable shopper works her way from Milan and Bergamo, Venice, Florence and San Gimignano, down to the Mezzogiorno, where it concludes in her family's native place, a town in Calabria called Canna. There, the narrator has a vision of exactly what she has overcome:

> Above Grandma Rosie's bed hangs a picture of the Sacred Heart of Jesus. His heart looks like a radish with green stems. When I look at it my tongue hurts. (Harrison 459)

It is worth underlining that Harrison sees the hues of the *tricolore* in her Grandmother's picture of the Sacred Heart of Jesus. There are a lot of things one could say about this phenomenon, but in the context of Harrison's epic of discriminating taste it makes most sense to see the transposition as belonging to the phenomenology of shopping.

Shopping is a dramatic spectacle with its processions, places, and plots. An obligatory focus of every shopping plot is the consumer fetish, which can be read in many ways. The most familiar are those of Marx and Freud. Marx gives us the commodity fetish as a superabundance obscuring the slave/master relations that set the commodity on the counter for the consumer's inspection, acquisition, and use. Freud's fetish replaces something that is missing. But there is a third way of reading a fetish: in a commercial diaspora, every fetish may be the sign of perpetual displacement; the commodity fetish poignantly plays this role, standing in for a place whose language one no longer speaks, whose shores one no longer visits. The commodity offers something that the flag cannot. Its attraction to the post-immigrant narrator is that it overcomes the stigma of the flag by placing it in a long string of fetish substitutes that can subsume it, acquiring a new earnest of social prestige by drinking and eating Italian products that come marked with the cachet of Italian places emphatically *not* wrapped in the Italian flag. These objects come not with signs of shame attached but bearing certificates of authenticity. This wine was made from grapes that were grown in a specific vineyard. Look, there is a picture of it on the label.

Italian exporters understand the prestige of authenticity with a niceness of precision that is worth remarking. Recently, a delegation of merchants from Piedmont came to discuss the matter with the Italian Trade Commission in New York. They complained that too many so-called Italian restaurants there are selling food that does not merit the name *Italian*. They got quick action from the commission.

> "When someone serves you 50 different toppings on your pizza," said Augusto Marchini, Italy's assistant trade commissioner, "enjoy it, but don't call it Italian. I wouldn't even call it pizza at that point. We're approaching the absurd."
>
> New York is not the only city to stray from tradition. Of all the Italian restaurants nationwide, Mr. Marchini said only 10 percent can probably be deemed genuine. Some restaurants, for instance, unknowingly buy pasta packaged in red and green but made in Turkey. This irks Italy, which exports $1.6 billion in food products to the United States every year and wants to export more. (Crow 5)

Italian merchants have long struggled to maintain control of the regional and varietal names that mark their production. Now they are taking that onomastic expertise to a new level.

> Next fall, officials from the Italian Ministry of Agricultural Policy will begin scrutinizing restaurants and bestowing on the chosen a certificate called the Trademark of Authenticity of Italian Restaurants Abroad.

So much for the *tricolore*. Many restaurateurs are trembling in their boots, worrying that they may get caught serving Turkish *rotelle* or calling something *manicotti* when they ought to say *cannelloni*. It is clear, however, that this worry afflicts those who aim at producing fetishes of displacement. Those who are content simply to feed people and to do so inside the inherited abjection of Italian Americana have nothing to worry about:

> Others, like Louise Mitchell, who manages Pronto Pizza on West 42nd Street, are unsure, despite the red and green neon that decorates the premises and the $2 cheese slices popular among lunchers.
>
> "I bet we'll be O.K. with or without a certificate," Ms. Mitchell said. "I mean, our logo is an Italian flag, and we use only good cheeses."

I envy Ms. Mitchell. As for me, I admit that I belong to that class of Italian American that can neither overlook its own disqualifications nor keep itself from aspiring to the very codes of prestige that have consigned it to this vulnerable position. Part of any member of this class feels poisoned with exclusion and failure, and the other part takes as an antidote another taste of imported cheeses and wines *d.o.c.* and submits to another lesson in how to produce *lingua toscana in bocca romana*.

Portrayals of this doubleness are frequent in Italian American fiction, from the brilliant self-appraisals of John Fante's narrators in the 1930s down to the extraordinary self-portrait of the Italian American writer as someone on both sides of the working class in Richard Russo's story "Poison." The narrator, a successful writer from a working-class mill town, is Italian on his mother's side, and trades on that origin to help him secure a lucrative screenwriting project that allows him and his wife to buy a splendid beach house on an island off the New England coast. His double is another writer from the same town, who has an Italian name. Gene Ruggiero grew up with the narrator. Their fathers worked at the same plant. The narrator's father died of work-related poison, but Gene's father became a foreman and escaped the most deadly effects of factory work. Gene feels that he inherits the guilt of a class traitor. He makes an issue of emphasizing his relative failure as a writer, wearing sweaters with holes in them and in general accusing his friend of selling out. This intricate relationship is played out not as a minuet but as a dance of relative menu choices. The narrator's wife Grace, who understands all the dynamics in question, buys a lobster for their dinner. But she is carefully not to expose her husband to Gene's criticism by having a lobster dinner. Rather, she will simply make lobster sauce. Her lobster sauce is presented as famous. It is clear that she has used it this way more than once.

> The lobster sauce, when I think about it, is an inspired choice, given that it so deftly negotiates the shoals of Gene's personality. Whereas lobster for each of us would have been a conspicuous display, ill suited to the reunion of the sons of mill workers, the lobster sauce, served over pasta, signifies a sophistication that is nonetheless mindful of who we are. Until you get to know Gene, it's easy to offend him unintentionally. Which is why I laid in good but affordable Italian wines for his visit. He considers French wines an affectation, and imported beers are always sure to provoke a sarcastic comment. No, Clare's lobster sauce is just the right thing, its ethnic accent overpowering upward mobility. (Russo 156-57)

No one has explored this landscape of relative shame more fully than Rita Ceresi, for whom the *Italian* in *Italian American* is an inexhaustible source of bad feeling. In one of her most stunning stories, two sisters are trading memories. One of them confesses to stealing money from her husband to get an abortion. The recollection torments her:

> "Now when I fall asleep — God, I have so much trouble going to sleep — I dream about tidal waves. I read about them in the *Reader's Digest* at the clinic. They're called nightmare waves. They rush out of nowhere onto the shores of South Sea islands. They're supposed to be sent by a hostile god. Whole families, entire villages, get swept away."
>
> I felt the sharp corners of my fortune cookie melting in my mouth.
>
> "Do you ever have weird dreams?" Lina asked.
>
> "Sometimes I dream in Italian," I told her. "I'm talking, but I don't have the least idea what I mean to say." (Ciresi 182-83)

Dreaming in Italian: helpless and meaningless. For Ciresi's characters, the Italian Other often remains impossible to negotiate — dangerous, secret, and liable at any moment to tumble into view. At the opening of the same story, the sisters are meeting in a Chinese restaurant. The narrator suspects that her sister has chosen the place to be facetious. The décor is incredibly cheap and vulgar. She sees her sister waiting near a "tiny bentwood table for two that was toped by a red and black umbrella. The fabric on the umbrella looked spray-painted, and I suspected that if we stripped it we would find the tricolors used to decorate pizza patios, and maybe even a bold advertisement for CINZANO" (Ciresi 173).

Who's Better than Me?

Italian American double consciousness is very neatly dramatized in DeLillo's *Underworld*, where the hero takes the name of his Irish mother to leave behind the world of his Italian gangster father. DeLillo shows how the Irish half looks at the Italian. This is the Irish mother thinking about her husband's people:

> The Italians. They sat on the stoop with paper fans and orangeades. They made their world. They said, Who's better than me? She could never say that. They knew how to sit there and say that and be happy. Thinking back through the decades. She saw a woman fanning herself with a magazine and it seemed like an encyclopedia of breezes, the book of all the breezes that ever blew. The city drugged with heat. Horses perishing in the streets. Who's better than me? (DeLillo 207)

The question is a leitmotif that recurs whenever this long novel's winding narrative finds itself in the streets of the hero's Bronx boyhood, where the issue is most vividly joined.

One might construe DeLillo's sarcasm as an answer of sorts to the question implied by Giuseppe Prezzolini's notorious essay "*Perchè gli italo -americani sono permalosi*" ("Why Italian Americans are touchy") (449).[3] The Italian Americans are touchy because they are conscious of occupying a position that requires them to support a system of entitlements whose specialness rests upon, among other things, its unwillingness to include *them* within its magic circle of prestige. They are Italian when it is time to pay extra for real Italian ingredients. But they are not Italian when it comes time to talk about the splendors of Italian culture or to recount the great stories of Italian history or to recover a political *patrimonio* lost to them before they were born.

"Who's better than me?" Leaving the Consolato Generale with nothing except my United States passport in my hand, I might have looked up at the huge *tricolore* flapping in the wind and asked the same question. But you know I didn't do it. It occurred to me, as it always does, that the Consolato Generale may not yet know it, but this diaspora where I live is also Italian — if, that is, *Italian* is the name of a large historical narrative, full of surprises and always exceeding the boundaries it has itself erected and fed with blood.

---

[1] This seems like an extravagant policy to us, who know how disastrously it turned out, but the royal ministers looked with considerable despair upon their so-called nation. How could they make its people be the new self-conscious and dutiful citizens that a modern nation needed in order to take its place in the world alongside such successful examples of the type as France and England? The Italians, as Massimo d'Azeglio railed on a famous occasion, were recalcitrant: "gl'Italiani hanno voluto far un'Italia nuova, e loro rimanere gl'Italiani vecchi di prima, colle dappocaggini e le miserie morali che furono ab antico la loro rovina" (*Ricordi* 5).

[2] The conflict between national icons and other signs of social coherence in Italy has been a long one. The flag was a primary instrument of those who wished to resolve this conflict in favor of a single national unity. The struggle has never been settled for very long, for the very good reason that the term *Italia* refers to a geohistorical complex of institutions, practices, memories, forms, and trajectories impossible to confine within the framework of a single political idea, impossible to define within the terms and shapes of a single chronotope, howsoever rich and supple. Certainly, the ruling parties of United Italy have elaborated theories of action that appear to accommodate astonishing amounts of self-contradiction. Italy, during the past century and a half has often displayed a degree of adaptability that critics have assailed as a remorseless calculus of expedience and have called by the reductive name of *trasformismo*; others, however, have advertised this same adaptability as the political equivalence of a baroque geometry, all ellipses and convergent parallels.

For the first fifty years after the Risorgimento, the Italian nation suffered under a Papal interdict. According to the Popes of that period, Italy had no legal existence. In the former Kingdom of Naples, movements of resistance flourished frequently. The mass migration of most rural poor from all parts of Italy was a powerful vote of No Confidence in the Italian State. In the century following the Risorgimento, fully half the nation's population left to settle permanently elsewhere. All these entropic forces could thrive despite the powerful imperative to unity because all of them depended upon economic arrangements deeply rooted in the practices of the peoples of Italy — sometimes very ancient practices. The Catholic Church, with its independent system of global taxation, had the wherewithal to survive in a hostile environment and was sufficiently rich a source of income that the Italian government had no inducement to put it out of business. Rural movements of resistance depended upon the relative independence of barons and landowners outside the great cities. And the mass migration found its strength in Italy's long established networks of global trade.

[3] Ragusa 147 discusses this essay in detail.

Works Cited

Barolini, Helen. *Umbertina*. New York: Seaview, 1979.

Bushman, Naomi. *America Discovers Columbus: How an Italian Explorer Became an American Hero*. Hanover, NH: UP of New England, 1992.

Ciresi, Rita. *Sometimes I Dream in Italian*. New York: Delta, 2000.

Crow, Kelly. "Making Sure Food Is as Italian as Caruso," *The New York Times*, January 5, 2003, City Section: 5.

D'Azeglio, Massimo. *I miei ricordi*. Torino: Giulio Einaudi Editore, 1971.

DeLillo, Don. *Underworld*. New York: Scribner, 1997.

DuBois, W.E.B. *The Souls of Black Folk*. Introd. John Edgar Wideman. New York: Library of America, 1990.

Duggan, Christopher. *Francesco Crispi*. New York: Oxford UP, 2002.

Fama, Maria. *Identification*. San Francisco: Malafemmina press, 1991.

Harrison, Barbara Grizzuti. *Italian Days*. New York: Ticknor & Fields, 1989.

Il progresso italo-americano.

Kowinski, William Severin. *The Malling of America: An Inside Look at the Great Consumer Paradise*. New York: Morrow, 1985.

Lapolla, Garibaldi M. *The Grand Gennaro*. New York: Vanguard, 1935.

Prezzolini, Giuseppe. *I trapiantati*. Milano: Longanesi, 1963.

Puzo, Mario. *The Fortunate Pilgrim*. New York: Putnam's, 1964.

Ragusa. Olga. "Prezzolini's 'Transplanted' Italians" in Andrea Ciccarelli and Paolo Giordano, eds., *L'esilio come certezza: la ricerca d'itentità culturale in Italia dalla rivoluzione francese ai nostri giorni*. Italiana VII. West Lafayette, IN: Bordighera, 1998: 127-148.

Russo, Richard. *The Whore's Child and Other Stories*. New York: Knopf, 2002.

Satterthwaite, Anne. *Going Shopping: Consumer Choices and Community Consequences*. New Haven: Yale UP, 2001.

SECTION III

✦

THE LINGUISTIC AND LITERARY PERSPECTIVE

THE LANGUAGE OF EXILE

Fulvio Caccia

Paul Valéry described the Italian spirit with these words:

> Simple life — interior nakedness — needs reduced to the bare essentials. Dark soul and thoughtlessness; but always watchful. Insouciance and depth. Secretive. Pessimism confuted by action. *Depretiatio*. Tendency to go to extremes. Immediate passage *ad infinitum*. Ipseity. Aseity. The pros and cons of a marginal position. Readiness of familiarity. Be familiar systematically. *Becoming familiar with*, turns into a strong principle, extending to anything intellectual and metaphysical. Sense of method." (Valéry 1090)

Rather than defining some national characteristics, Valéry has captured a concatenation of attitudes, a way of relating oneself with the world that distinguishes a population. The Italian spirit would be for the Italian culture what the French spirit is for the French culture: its spirit. But if the spirit reflects an elevation of common sensitivity, it cannot be dissociated from its mediator, from its initial vector: the language. Can a writer of Italian origin disregard his mother tongue (or the dialect linked to it) or, rather, its memory? How can one deny this multiple and problematic identity which has led the Swiss writer Adrien Pasquali to call himself provocatively a "French-speaking Italian writer?"

Furthermore, is this definition able to describe the condition of the writers of Italian origin in North America and in Canada in particular? Posing the question involves facing the problem of multilingualism intrinsic to every language and the process of enhancement which leads it to become emancipated and establish itself as the predominant language. Dante was the first European to treat the issue. He acknowledged that the *volgare illustre* [standard Italian] could have two destinies: one within the borders of the country (national language), the other outside (the language of exile).

The first destiny was to materialize with the foundation of the nation five centuries later. Thus, the Court, legitimated by the Prince's will, would give the people living in a certain territory a common language which also becomes national. But in the same process, the other Italian destiny, in a proper and a figurative sense, followed another direction owing to the mass emigration of over 25 million Italians in just one century. This destiny was certainly linked to the development of capitalism in its most fruitful phase, leading to the transformation of the culture which we, within our group in Montréal, used to describe then as "the transcultural condition." This condition is still relevant, as shown by the current debate on cultural difference and its inclusion as part of "world heritage" by UNESCO. It is to be found earlier in the process of "national" crystallization and at the end of its development; moreover, it opens up to this "autonomy" imagined by Dante, of which Pierre Bourdieu, who has recently passed away, explains the intellectual condition, that is, the effectiveness of its political action.

In order to understand what is at stake, a historical reference is inevitable, because the conditions which allow a mother tongue to emerge are not always perceptible. A book often performs the linguistic function of both manifesto and "contract:" Dante's *De vulgari eloquentia* for the Italian language, just like Joachim du Bellay's *Défense et illustration de la langue française* for French a few centuries later.

Umberto Eco reminds us that the first documents written in Italian vernacular go as far back as the seventh century. They were *Auraceipt na n-Eces* (*Precepts of the Poets*), on the codification of the grammar rules of Gaelic written by some Irish monks. Its narrative structure follows the Tower of Babel story. According to the monks, the birth date of the Irish language would result from "cutting and pasting" the other languages which the seventy-two apprentices of the building corporations had learnt after the diaspora. "It was in Ireland," the Italian semiologist maintains "that this language was given its rules in such a way that the best and most beautiful features in each language were modeled on Irish." (Eco 31)

About seven centuries later, Dante himself was to use the same "cut and paste" technique and the same myth (the Tower of Babel) to describe his idea of the perfect language. On doing so he employed one of the resources of traditional Latin rhetoric: the *squaring of reality* (*quadratura del reale*), which was going to be used by all the founders of national literatures later.[2] His *De vulgari eloquentia* is written in Latin, because he, above all, wanted to convince his peers. He had to demonstrate that Italian could be as eloquent as Latin, provided that the same rhetorical methods were employed. "I have found that nobody else has dealt with the science of vulgar eloquence before me" (Dante 5), Dante makes as if insignificant, continues an anthropological and historical process which had pervaded the formation of languages in ancient times. Indeed, this process indicates two registers with one single movement:

We can call vulgar language what we learn by imitating our wet-nurse without any rules. There is also another language, which we learn later, called grammar by the Romans. The Greeks own this second language too, but not every one. Only a few are able to use it because it is only after long and constant years of study that we learn its rules and art. (Ibid. 7)

The language established by grammar is the written one, which is a privilege that only Latin, Greek and Hebrew still have. But Dante declares that the oral language, or vulgar, is on a higher level:

Between the two of them the noblest is the vulgar language, because it was the first ever used by human beings; also, because everybody uses it, even if pronunciation and words differ. Finally, it is natural to us, while the other has an artificial origin. (Ibid. 7)

In this framework, the transcription of vernaculars in Europe represents a relatively late phase per se in the evolution of the human language. Consequently, on the other hand, it allows us to hazard a guess at the complexity of its genesis, which refers to the creation of every literature.

In actual fact, Dante places himself in his works as the heir of this Latin antiquity, from which he can pass bits and pieces to the new Christian European paradigm in progress where standard Italian is the translator. This political-linguistic paradigm is based on the necessity to sever all links with ancient rhetoric in order to apply it to the emerging vernaculars. Such new humanism will develop on the fringes of scholasticism to be linked with Latin and Greek thought and, through them, to the heritage of sophism, neo-Platonism and Thomistic theology.

This is a double movement which has the effect of introducing critical thought, and promoting the modernity of the vulgar languages. In this way, the West began its process of secularization which would be achieved through the invention of printing in the fifteenth century, and end somewhat painfully in the twentieth century.

As soon as the oral language established itself in its written form it tried to take over the second one, especially when the latter was separated from its roots like Latin. But how does this elevation take place? Dante compares and chooses employing all the resources of classical rhetoric. He then analyses the triple idiom: *langue d'oc, d'oil*, and the different Italian vernaculars. Finally, he chooses what will become standard Italian and will deserve to be *grammatized* in order to keep its "identity in time and space." Therefore, he maintains:

"I can define illustrious, fundamental, aulic and courteous that vulgar of Italy which pertains to every Italian city but does not belong to any of them; and it is with this that all the other local Italian vernaculars are to be compared." (Ibid. 61)

Dante believes that any vernacular which wishes to rise to the level of a cultural and poetical language must become the language of the City, or the lingua franca. This is the sense that he immediately gives to the adjective "illustrious":

I must make clear why I call the vulgar language illustrious. When one uses the word illustrious one means something that enlightens or that, if enlightened, shines; therefore, we call illustrious those men who, either because they are enlightened by power enlighten others with justice and charity or, because they have a high teaching position, educate in a masterly fashion, like Seneca or Numa Pompilius. Now, the illustrious vulgar which I am talking about is elevated by teaching and power, and in its turn extols those who use it in honor and glory. (Ibid. 63)

It is here that Dante begins his introductory remarks of a "symbolic capitalization"[2] which would be resumed and developed later by all those who drew the guidelines of the great national literatures, including Du Bellay who would decline it in its nominal form.[3]

Magnificence and power are in effect different sides of the same reality. The power Dante refers to is the secular power of the Prince, who establishes and imposes language standards everywhere, but without claiming any idea of nation. Dante would explain this concept better by examining the "aulic" character given to this language:

> If there were a Court in Italy that is where our vulgar language should be spoken. Consequently all the courtiers speak a form of illustrious vulgar; and thus, moreover, our illustrious vulgar is like a pilgrim and a

stranger that finds hospitality in humble houses, precisely because we have not got a Court." (Dante 65-66)

Dante immediately foresaw the child's maladies of the Italian language, but also the necessary conditions for the development of the "illustrious language" whose importance was fully understood by Du Bellay. We can then state that French would be the first among the illustrious vulgars to materialize according to the optimal preconditions foretold by Dante. Its realization implies a territorialization[4] on which the whole idea of nation and literature would be built.

Nevertheless, the state of the *illustrious vulgar* was no less fruitful and would bring about the success of Italian literature for at least two centuries; It is the problematic state of the *language in exile*, resulting from a factual de-territorialization, which Dante was to outline.

Its vulnerability places it beyond politics, and turns the Italian spirit claimed by Dante, and beyond every national identity, not only into the result of a "national" awareness but also into an act entirely based on the *language experience*. By choosing the illustrious vulgar, Dante gives up the search for a perfect language model which cannot be found and opts for the *forma locutionis* "which allows the poet to adapt words to what they have to express and which would otherwise be inexpressible." (Eco 64) This *forma locutionis* is in effect the speaking act through which a language develops, depending on how its speakers change. On reconsidering this action *per se* within the individuation of the linguistic process, Dante reintroduces the figure of the poet, and an awareness of the elation of language, in the heart of that City from which the inventor of this philosophy had.

This line of thought, which Du Bellay would continue, is literary vocation "par excellence." It materializes through its rejoining with desire. This is why Dante reverses the order of priority of traditional poetic art by subduing the rhetoric methods to the choice of the linguistic material. All things considered, picking one's examples from among the "amour courtois" poets is somewhat reckless. Love for a woman and love for one's mother tongue coincide, and he enhances both in this transfer. The passage of a language to the written register helps to introduce that imperceptible gap that separates this very presence. This writing then includes the whole language field and becomes, according to Jacques Derida's formula, "the phantom of one word which dreams of replacing its double." This double phantom torments writing, and, all the more so, this vulgar written production which must by now be reconciled with the language. This is why in the second book, which was never finished, he established the necessary poetic techniques to succeed. They are mainly based on the art of singing, his melodic division (the stanza), the arrangement of its parts between them and the number of lines and syllables. We are in the field of classical rhetorics, revisited according to the most appropriate forms able to give richness back to the vulgar, that is song and stanzas.

The return of the desire of language in the actual writing, an important feature "shared by everybody but belonging to nobody in particular," is the basis of western modernity. It introduces relativity into the exiled language, which indirectly becomes a popular language, suitable to be learnt by a speaking community, unequally distributed in a territory.

> "Note these two conditions," writes Paul Valéry, "if we want cultural material to be a wealth of knowledge, it too demands the existence of men who need it and can use it, and on the other hand, know how to acquire or use the habits, intellectual discipline, conventions and experience that are needed to utilize the mass of documents and instruments piled up throughout the centuries." (Valéry 29)

In this respect, Dante seems to have been some sort of exemplary model ahead of his time. In the age of globalization and world literature, does a writer of immigrant origin who remembers his/her language, just like the Québec writers recalled their French origin, foreshadow the other destiny of the Italian spirit contained in its written language, that is to become the very condition of a universal literature?

Translated by Nick Ceramella, Università degli Studi di Roma, La Sapienza

[1] The squaring of reality deals with world order and would support it. World order can be achieved in three ways, which would make up as many as three categories of topics: by delegating the knowledge concerning the order, by getting it to make sense, or by defining it. If we leave the matter to chance, squaring can be reactivated by basing it on a priori division, on the sharing of values, or it will be an invention, recombination, in brief, a "resquaring." Breton, Philippe. *L'argumentation dans la communication*. (Paris: La découverte, 1966).

[2] I am referring to the notion of symbolic capital as it has been theorized by Pierre Bourdieu in *Régles de l'art*. (Paris: Pont Le Seuil, 1992).

[3] It is later, in the nineteenth century, that perhaps the most distinguished of French poets, Arthur Rimbaud, who by entitling his collection Illuminations thus concludes the European process of modernity started by Dante, but introduced into French literature by Du Bellay.

[4] I recall the notion of territorialization because it is a space chosen to legitimate a system of identity and belonging as Deuleuze and Guattari have developed it in Kafka ou de la littérature mineure. Paris: Editions de Minuit, 1982.

Works cited

Eco, Umberto. *La recherche de la langue parfaite*. Poli. 1989, 187-189; Paris: Le Seuil, 1994.

Alighieri Dante, *De vulgari eloquentia*, a c. di Claudio Marazzini e Concetto Del Popolo. Milano, A. Mondadori Editore, 1990, Libro 1°. (The translations from this book were done by Nick Ceramella).

Valéry, Paul. "La liberté de l'esprit," in *Regards sur le monde actuel*, Œuvres, Paris: Gallimard, 1960, Bibliot hèque de la Pléiade, vol. II, p. 1090, cited by Pascal Casanova in *La république mondiale des lettres*, Paris Le Seuil, 1999.

NOT ONLY MCARONE. NINETEENTH CENTURY ADDITIONS TO THE ITALIAN AMERICAN LITERARY CANON

Francesco Durante
Università di Salerno

Some time ago I edited, for the paper to which I regularly contribute, the serial publication of a novel by James Fenimore Cooper which has never been published in Italy and has nearly been forgotten even in America. *The Wing and Wing* or *Le Feu-Follet,* tells of the Italian mishaps of a French pirate.[1] The story begins on the Island of Elba and ends in the Bay of Naples where about two-thirds of the story is set; it is the year 1799, when the Neapolitan Republic came to a tragic end. I would willingly tell you this long story, with naval battles and repeated coups de theatre, with real characters like Horatio Nelson and Admiral Francesco Caracciolo and fictional ones like the two main characters, the brave, romantic pirate Raoul Yvard and his beautiful friend Ghita Caracciolo (*Caraccioli* in the original text), and above all an extraordinary second lead, the American adventurer, Ithuel Bolt — *a true homo novus* — in this theatre of complex European subtleties. However, even a simple outline of the plot would take too much space and it would take us off the track of this essay. I shall confine myself therefore to pointing out only one characteristic of the long novel, a certain fresco-like quality that illuminates the initial phase of the mutual discovery of two distant lands, Europe (Italy in particular) and America, two worlds between which Cooper moves with the critical subtleness and consciousness of a real connoisseur, charmed by so many differences and ready to register them with a spirit that is certainly more open than that of other contemporary American travelers who are most often horrified by the backwardness of the infernal Roman Babylon.

When Ithuel Bolt, a prickly and enigmatic sailor from the *Granite State* appears in the fourth chapter of the novel, we witness a scene that is extraordinary for its original yet puzzling disclosure. Bolt reveals his nationality to the authorities of Elba and everyone is astonished at the news that he is American, almost as though he were the inhabitant of another planet:

> "Uno stato di granito!" repeated the vice-governor, looking at the podestà with some doubt in the expression of his countenance — "it must be a painful existence which these poor people endure, to toil for their food in such a region......"

The astonishment of the inhabitants of Elba is such that Cooper feels the need to add a personal note:

> As recently as 1828, the author of this book was at Leghorn. *The Delaware 80*, had just left there; and speaking of her appearance to a native of the place, who supposed the writer to be an Englishman, the latter observed — "Of course, her people were all blacks." "I thought so, too, signore, until I went on board the ship," was the answer; "but they are as white as you and I are."

When we consider the events of the subsequent transoceanic emigration of the nineteenth century, and the discourse that it engendered, we are tempted to note that the author of the *Last of the Mohicans* could certainly not have imagined how the roles were going to be almost reversed in about fifty years, and it would be the Americans — or at least some of them — who were going to question the idea that Italy's inhabitants were really white.

In some ways, the struggle against racial prejudice has been the motor of the Italian American literary expression. But what is there between those two temporal poles, between those Americans seen as Africans and those Italians seen as Europeans of a different kind? In between there is the *Risorgimento*. For better or worse, that long-lasting historical event is destined to carve out a national image which will be referred to even later, when the misfortunes of the post-unification emigration will change it, but, unfortunately, in a negative sense for the average American. The *Risorgimento* is such a pervasive event that it shapes a considerably longer historical period, in fact it stretched over the entire period of the early emigration. What is peculiar is that there are very few Italian American studies on it. Indeed, on the whole, and merely on a chronological basis, the *Risorgimento* is usually placed in the limbo of the preceding events, as if it were possible to understand the birth of the first Little Italies without giving due reflection to events that had occurred before 1860.

In my book, *Italoamericana*, profiting from some valuable suggestions made by Giovanni Ermenegildo Schiavo, an important yet unjustly overlooked scholar, I have tried to bring some order into extensive subject, even though I realize that much remains to be done. I believe, however, that I have shown a certain continuity between first and second immigration, even though I am perfectly aware of the many gaps that still have not been filled in. Perhaps we continue to underestimate the vast network of texts linking the *Risorgimento* experience to the first mass emigration to America. I believe that greater attention should be paid to the very large body of literary work that deals with the *non* migratory relationship between America and Italy, in the Italian American studies. At the same time, we should focus particular attention on the literature produced in America during the first migratory waves from Italy, or immediately preceding them.

The Risorgimento Revisited

On writing this essay, I thought of using as a focusing point a small book by the poet George Arnold.[3] Under the pen-name McArone, the poet gathers fake correspondence from the various Italian war fronts during the *Risorgimento* in the New York weekly "Vanity Fair" (1806-61). Almost as a mirror confirmation of Cooper's "black" paradigm, George Arnold had never been to Italy, but, he was obviously familiar with the travel literature produced about our country and its bandits from the writings of authors such as Washington Irving. With the extraordinary freshness of his humor and his happily desecrating irony, Arnold managed to ingeniously overcome the fact that he had never been to Italy. McArone is a flamboyant, astonishing leader, who at the head of armies of *millions* of soldiers, fights side-by-side with Garibaldi. It is worth pointing out that until the start of the Civil War, when he was "detoured" onto the domestic front, McArone continued to write about Italian matters, an indication of how popular the *Risorgimento* movement was in America, with both its positive protagonists (Vittorio Emmanuele, Cavour, and Garibaldi), and its negative ones (Pius IX, King Francesco II Borbone). But Arnold's writings prove something else too. Above all, the idea of an Italy that, *mutatis mutandis*, is quite similar to "Freedonia" in *La Guerra lampo dei fratelli Marx (Duck Soup*, 1933): an old, bizarre, formal and bloody country — melodramatic in the most literal sense.

To talk about this country it was now necessary to substitute a more familiar and ironic register for the compelling, formal and solemn tones of heroism and civil passions that had been used only a few years earlier by poets like Tuckerman, Lowell or Longfellow. In effect, this is the classic voice of the great American humorists, especially Mark Twain of *The Innocents Abroad*, whose tone can also be found in the works of William Dean Howells or Bayard Taylor. This same tone is expressed in a bizarre, colorful happiness in *The Dodge Club, Italy in 1859,* written by the Canadian James De Mille in 1869; a picaresque book, and in some respects a very McAronean travel t ale practically told straight from the hottest season of the *Risorgimento.*[4]

While Arnold and all the other authors were writing, the Italians in the United States were building up quite a remarkable community. Their leaders came from the *Risorgimento* and had taken part in the struggle for national unity. By way of example, Cesare Moreno, a mercenary in Sumatra with Nino Bixio, appeared in New York ten years later. An adventurer very much like McArone, he even became Prime Minister in Hawaii. His biography was as incredible, fascinating and intriguing as those of many other Italians like Giuseppe Avezzana, Leonetto Cipriani and Luigi Palma di Cesnola, who fled to the United States because of the *Risorgimento* insurrections. In their bold destiny, there is inscribed what we could almost define a "Conradian" quality of the Italian character as found in the author's *Nostromo*.

All this occurs together with the growing Italian emigration, a phenomenon whose breadth at some point seems to sweep away the charm of the Italian personality, as if moving to America could erase one's legendary traits and replace them with a totally new identity. We see this so clearly in the "Italian American" pages of Henry James's *La Scena Americana,* where the Italians, though fitting in so harmoniously into their original landscape, in America appear to be so hopelessly out of place as to seem true aliens in the New World. This tragic loss of cultural image also features in other less popular novels like Arlo Bates's *The Pagans*.

The idea of the *Risorgimento*, formerly very vivid in the culture and in the consciousness of the Little Italies, is crumbling away inexorably in the American culture and consciousness For this reason new links that can lead us back to the glory of the *Risorgimento* need to be forged. I would argue therefore, that an ideal Italian American literary canon should also include the lesser-known, not to say unknown, works of those who can shed light on the subject. Two extraordinary but forgotten cultural mediators who can serve as witnesses of this complex and fruitful experience were American poets in their own right and the wives of the early *Risorgimento* Italian

American figures, Lorenzo Luigi Da Ponte, the son of the famous librettist, and of Vincenzo Botta.

Caroline A. Merighi

Caroline Augusta Frost, daughter of John, a professor of humanities and author of various scholarly works, married Count Merighi in 1854. They were both natives of Philadelphia, although the count's family, whose origins most likely could be traced to Le Marche, had had a role in the *Risorgimento*.

Caroline is known for her intense activity as a translator from French to English for Munro, the New York publisher of dime novels. Between 1882 and 1884 she translated novels written by Fortune Hippolyte Auguste du Boisgobey and one by Emile Erckmann. But Caroline Merighi is also an author in her own right; in fact, I found two of her poems set in Italy in the pages of "Harper's Monthly." These poems are, 'One Night in Venice,' (June 1872) and 'Roses of Florence,' (September 1874). Even more importantly, two short stories, 'My Little Newsboy,' (January 1871), and 'Breadcrumb Artist,' (April 1872), are among the first whose protagonists are Italian immigrants to America.

What stands out in Merighi's works is the obvious element of worldly elegance (something similar will be found at the end of the century, in the fleeting poetic career of Cora Randall Fabbri, the Florentine-American daughter of the rich New York merchant, Ernesto, and, niece of the banker Egisto Paolo Fabbri), that places into perspective the contrast between the upper class immigrants who live a life of privilege, and the new masses of immigrants whose existence is represented in a style situated somewhere between an eyewitness account and a *feuilleton*. These members of the elite are people who love Italy not only by reason of their national origins, but also owing to the knowledge that they have gained of Italy's history and culture acquired *as tourists*.

These are the very people who act as a link between Italy's privileged elite and its immigrants. The main character in Merighi's story, 'The Breadcrumb Artist,' is Luigi Vanessa, who at the age of ten had copied Michelangelo's *Pietà* using just breadcrumbs. Vanessa represents the personification of this continuity: the 'spontaneous' artist in whom the peculiar creative spirit of the Italian genius is naturally present. In this protagonist, who will be "adopted" and "sponsored" by an upper class woman, artistic genius is joined to an adamantine honesty and loyalty to his American benefactors. The marriage of these qualities is meant to suggest the wisdom of trusting in the Italians' ability to become model American citizens. In this sense, Merighi's story reproduces the same moral paradigm at the beginning of Italian American fiction as represented by *Il piccolo genovese*, published anonymously in 1869 in the New York paper *L'Eco d'Italia*[6] which was run by Giovanni Francesco Secchi de Casali. However, it should be pointed out that in the latter example the protagonist achieved success not in the world of art but in the more prosaic one of finance. Thus while the story that appeared in "L'Eco" is a direct expression of the world of immigration and of its social expectations, Merighi's story evokes a more rarified and idealistic setting.

Elizabeth Cavazza

Elizabeth Jones, daughter of an important businessman from Portland (Maine), who married the Modenese Nino Cavazza in 1885, is known as an outstanding mediator between the two worlds. Elizabeth was initiated into the world of journalism by Stanley Pullen, editor of the *Portland Press* who later became her second husband in 1894, several years after Nino Cavazza's death. She wrote a variety of articles for the *Portland Press* and, thanks to a particularly successful series of literary parodies, won the interest of some influential members of the New York Century Club, including Bayard Taylor and E.C. Stedman, who believing she was a man, went as far as proposing her name for admission to the Club. Later, Elizabeth Cavazza worked as the editor of the Italian Department of "Transatlantic" and for Boston's "Literary World," while contributing to various other magazines. In 1891, she wrote the introduction to the first American edition of George Meredith's *Modern Love*, published in Portland by Thomas Bird Mosher. Elizabeth's stories, set in an upper middle-class ambience, were written in the same period or a little earlier, and were published in the "Atlantic Monthly," "Scribner's Magazine" or in "The Century." Elizabeth Cavazza died in 1926.

Apparently Jones had been speaking Italian since childhood.[7] Her correspondence with the Dante Society of America is kept at Harvard, a likely indication of her serious knowledge of classic Italian literature. In addition to this, there is also clear evidence that she was well versed in the literature of her own time as well. Her article "Some Recent Studies of the

Sicilian People," where she reviewed the "Bibliographia delle tradizioni populari dell'Italia" by Pitrè, "Don Candeloro" by Verga and "Le Paesane" by Capuana as well as "Italian Popular Tales" by T.F. Crane, was published in the "Atlantic Monthly"in July 1894. In the previous month's issue, Cavazza had already published an article on the Sicilian "pupari" (*At the Opera di li Pupi)*

While we have no definite knowledge of why she preferred to study and write about southern Italian culture and its traditions, we can speculate that this choice may have been sparked by a wider interest in issues relating to immigration, which as we know, involved m ainly southern Italians. Moreover, southern themes are dealt with in Cavazza's two major works of fiction: a collection of Calabrian sketches, already partially published in various magazines under the title *Don Finimondone*, printed by Webster in New York in 1892; a Sicilian novel, *The Man from Aidone,* published in serial form in the "Atlantic Monthly" between October and December 1893, and never collected in one single volume. Some other works should be added to these, for example, the Sicilian tale, "A Doll on Mount Etna" (St. Nicholas Magazine, July 1888) and the Calabrian story, "Rocco and Sidora" ("Atlantic Monthly," October 1892). Finally, we can add various poems whose titles suggest that they too take Italy as their setting. Among these we find: "The Pupil of Cimabue," "Dante and the Young Florentine," and "Caterina and Her Fate," all published by "St. Nicholas Magazine" in June 1887, September 1887 and June 1888, respectively.

Don Finimondone is of particular interest for its realism and the image offered of the Calabrian peasants' *zeitgeist.* A reviewer of the time writes (in the "Overland Monthly," October 1892), that the short book:

> ...depict[s] with a simplicity that is almost baldness the colorless Italian peasant life. All of the tales are intensely realistic. They hug so closely the littleness of life that one lays down the book with a feeling of pessimistic discouragement. They seem more like animals than men, these peasants; and even the grim sense of humor that runs like an undertone through the stories fails to materially overcome the sense of depression. Any one who has been in Italy will recognize the striking fidelity to the fact of the descriptive work, and that the author has caught admirably the Italian point of view.

It is debatable whether this opinion should be considered either more harsh or more flattering. However, the overall impression is that Cavazza makes an honest attempt to keep up with the recent tradition of the Italian *verismo*, a sort of Verga in *sextodecimo*, on the other side of the Atlantic. Perhaps her intention was to depict the setting from which the thousands of poor peasants who were reaching America at that time, were fleeing. A good example in this regard is the "peasant" character who gives the book its title: *Don Finimondone* takes his name from the fact that wherever he turned his gaze, he saw omens of bad luck:

> Everything, according to him, was going to the bad. Did it rain, there would be another flood for the sins of the world, and that without the ark to put two beasts in. Did the sun shine, the grass was burning up, and the geese would die with their mouths open for thirst. If the olives were scarce, there would not be enough oil to fry the good things of heaven; and if it were a good year, he said it was a pity to see the branches loaded till they broke, and olive so cheap that it was indeed ruin. It was.

Return to Risorgimento

Thus literary women like Caroline Merighi and Elizabeth Cavazza effectively "explained" the existential journey of these poor Italians who arrived by the thousands at the gates of the New World; and their literary work is the result of a sound knowledge of the historical-cultural problems (besides the social one) that also struck the imagination of other authors like Horatio Alger in his documentary-novel, *Phil the Fiddler* (1872). However, other writers felt the need to clarify the connections existing between the desperation that was driving mass emigration and the heroic period of the *Risorgimento*. Indeed, this nostalgic backward glance at the *Risorgimento* is famously associated with Italian Americans whose "colonial passion for the past Italic glories and the generous enthusiasm of Little Italies in promoting the collection o f funds to erect monuments to key figures like Cristoforo Colombo, Leonardo da Vinci, Giuseppe Garibaldi or Giuseppe Verdi" is well known. This sentimental attachment to the glorious independence movement was meant to function symbolically as an antidote for the miseries of the present time. However, there are also numerous American novelists who have created characters taken from the Italian immigration to serve similar purposes.

Therefore, this forgotten literary work, published mostly in the magazines of the time, will have to be taken into some consideration. It is almost like a "heroic" contrapuntal melody from the politically correct ranks of the time to some pleading petitions of poetic brotherhood, originating from the most committed social fronts, as for example the Brooklyn Italian Settlement Society. In this context, and awaiting a more complete and systematic scrutiny, I wish to point out at least a couple of relevant narrative examples of the end of the century.

The first is the story "Domenico's New Year" by Thomas Francis Galwey, published in January 1886 in "Catholic World," a magazine whose affinity to Italians is obvious However, it would not be fair to consider Galwey's work mere clerical "tripe" overlaid by edifying overtones. Galwey (1846-1913), a journalist of Irish descent and a veteran of the Civil War, was also a professor at Manhattan College and an official of the New York City Council. To my knowledge he left only one book whose title clearly reveals the main interest of his life: *The Valiant Hours, Narrative of 'Captain Brevet,' an Irish-American in the Army of the Potomac.* Strangely enough, his Italian American story also deals with military life and the Civil War and makes "Domemico's New Year" delightfully unique. It is a story narrated with a wealth of historical, geographical and even linguistic references dealing with the valiant and loyal behavior of the fisherman Domenico Cafferata from Tropea (once again there is a Calabrian reference) during the Civil war. His loyalty will gain him significant gratitude, which is another recurring theme of the narrative.

The events take place in 1863, a meaningful year given the events narrated. Domenico will gain the esteem of a certain widow, Mrs Winslow (Mother Winslow, a "thorough Yankee," the ideal counterpart for a poor immigrant from Calabria), and the owner of a modest sailor's boarding house in Roosevelt Street, New York. Once Domenico is freed from detention in a Confederate prison camp, he wishes to return to his native Italy However, before he can achieve this objective Domenico feels the need to return to Mrs. Winslow to console her on her son's death. To his surprise, instead of the elderly lady (now deceased) that he expected to find, he is presented with a will rewarding him for the noble feelings and loyal behavior he had shown Mrs. Winslow's son during the War. The mother, who had been informed of Domenico's noble character by the son before his death, has named Domenico as the heir to the fortune that the son can no longer enjoy.

The war setting is most effective to exalt such virtues as honor, loyalty and courage. In that sort of Yankee version of the *Risorgimento,* an Italian character can in fact, recover the proud, manly dignity that prejudice denied the poor *dago* immigrants. Similarly, in the short story *The Romance of Miles O'Meara,* published in Boston's *The New England Magazine* in 1890, New York attorney and writer John Elliot Curran (1848-1890), fully restores dignity to two Roman siblings, Pietro and Maria Novara, humble greengrocers on Broadway, and to their friends and compatriots. Using the device of the long-lost narrative written by an old uncle (Miles of the title), we are introduced to the small universe of a handful of political exiles who cultivate a longing for the lost homeland, are very active in preparing its future freedom, and who though across the ocean, produce a newspaper, "The Exile." Their noble-mindedness is crystal clear, especially Maria's, a character who is strongly evocative of the proud girls depicted in the literature of the late nineteenth century Grand Tour. In the end, as a result of the patriot's victory in Italy and the release from prison of Maria's father and other companions, the young woman's life can change for the better and she can even envision the prospect of love.

What is more relevant in the story is the emphasis placed on the exquisite qualities of the Italian characters, an emphasis which, in a sense, is the story itself. While there is no "moral" to it, we can perhaps perceive it in that implicit equation, according to which poverty corresponds to tyranny, and only freedom can herald a radiant future, a future that for the young Italy is surely about to be achieved.

Translated by Grace Russo Bullaro, C.U.N.Y., Lehman College

[1] The first Italian edition of *Il pirata* was serialized *in Corriere del Mezzogiorno,* (July-September, 2002), Napoli-Bari, edited by Francesco Durante and translated by Paola Scippa. Another edition is that edited by Thomas Philbrick and prefaced by Dean King in 1998, for the series "Heart of Oak Sea Classics," New York: Holt.

[2] Durante, Francesco. *Italoamericana. Storia e letteratura degli italiani negli Stati* Uniti 1776-1880. Vol. I. Milano: Mondadori, 2001.

[3] Arnold, George. *Le avventure italiane di McArone.* Ed. F. Durante. Cava de' Tirreni: Avagliano, 2002.

[4] DeMille's book had been published in a serial form in *Harper's Monthly,* (March-October, 1867); the book form edition was published by the same publisher of the magazine.

[5] For this novel, published by Holt in 1884 in New York, cf. the excellent essay by John Paul Russo, "From Italophilia to Italophobia: Representations of Italian Americans in the Early Gilded Age," in *Differentia,* 6/7, Spring/Autumn, 1994, 45-75.

[6] You can read this short story in the above-mentioned *Italoamericana,* 442-446.

[7] I have extracted this scanty information from The *National Cyclopaedia of American Biography, 1893-1909.*

Voices From Canada

Alessandro Gebbia
University of Roma, "La Sapienza"

The title of this article is *Voices from Canada*. The choice of the word "voices" in the plural form is not at all casual because, in my view, Italian-Canadian poetry (or perhaps it would be more appropriate to call it Canadian poetry of Italian origin) consists almost entirely of words of voices, and ever-more articulate sounds, which have eventually substituted whispers with an expressive strength, capable of first drawing closer two opposite linguistic systems and then overlapping them. On making this statement my mind goes back to the image of Pier 21 in Halifax, Nova Scotia, the Ellis Island of Canada, where, before technological progress made them obsolete, hundreds of ships, filled with Italian emigrants, had been docking for decades. They were the least fortunate among our fellow citizens — Abruzzesi, Ciociari, Friulani, Lucani, Molisani — who in the flight for survival, had not succeeded in going forward to reach the most longed for destinations: the United States, Argentina, Venezuela or Australia. For these people, *'Merica* looked like a *terra incognita*, perhaps better than the mines of Belgium and France, but whose roads did not glitter with gold like those of New York, but only with snow and ice. Therefore, on these windblown docks, the notes of various dialects mingled, composing a terrified, sinister overture that never seemed to open itself up to hope. There was no wonder and astonishment in front of the New World, but *horror vacui*, the *Fryan* terror, to be swallowed up for good by that ultramarine Minotaur forever lurking: A tragic symphony rather than a joyful emancipation song:

> Pier 53 remembers
> ships and shadows
> coal-blue grey North Atlantic
> greets the eye and remembers
> the Conte Biancamano July 3 1952
> ...Who are we? Where are we?
>   return to Halifax for answers
> coal-blue grey North Atlantic remembers

Caboto, Verrazzano
an Italian who came later.[1]

And:

Trascinati d'antichi pesi
nel baratro dell'ingiustizia
stiamo sulle bocche
delle piste pronti allo scatto,
e sulle bocche dei "ramarri"
pronti all'agonia.

Figli di antica madre
che nelle doglie più sofferte
ha voluto partorire
migliori uomini, e ladri:
e noi con i primi esuli,
stanchi di un pane nero,
stanchi di correre, di cercare,
e nelle piatte città d'acciaio
ci lasciammo vincere, esiliare.[2]

These lines, by Joseph Pivato and Romano Perticarini respectively, aiming to retain the memory of that experience, reveal a sense of inevitable surrender to the will of fate. The majority of immigrants who are getting ready to undergo the violence of the immigration's red tape, see the incumbent Canadian experience as a moment of suspension, a sort of limbo in which they must earn, their emancipation to return to their native land.

When church bells ring
four thousand miles away
there in those hills that do not beat
the fruit of former years...[3]

Unlike other forms of immigration, due also and above all to the policy of the central government in Ottawa, in the case of Canada it appears in effect limited in space and time for a long period. Within the ghetto-neighborhoods in which Italians live, rigidly divided by their region of origin, as if in a *garrison*, on an island where they continue to speak Italian because English is useless, since any form of interaction with the surrounding society is excluded. In time, to save as much as necessary over the years, for the final trip back to their homeland.

For four years I dreamt of my father coming back.
It was a children dream.
He was aboard a little purple ship, returning
To our beautiful Calabria.
Phoenician's and Etruscan's land, bathed
by the sea of Ulysses.
For four years I waited for him on the stony beach.
From there I could see the almonds mingling with the olive trees,
in the hills, in the house where he was born.
He had gone to bring gifts to the world.
He would return, soon.[4]

The poetry of this island, just like that of Shakespeare's *The Tempest*, becomes the field where two opposed and parallel realities meet and diverge. The Italian Caliban with his rough and incomprehensible language, which is however magical and musical. The Canadian Prospero who wants to possess that music and spell, only to steal the secret of the perfect "spaghetti sauce." According to the theory of *survival*,[5] one is the "victim," the other one is the "victimizer" of that very survival which is the common denominator of every emigration story, on which Margaret Arwood has built her fortune.

Because life for him
has been labour and struggle,
Canadese, remember your father.
don't try to stifle your mother tongue,
in our cage, it is wrong;
do canaries smother their private song?

Be patient, don't rage,
Canadese, in time we'll belong;
we'll acquire our own sense of this land;
we'll record life and death of our million births;
we'll have families,
above and below the earth.

Canadese, you must never forget
what you are...never!
because when you do, they'll remind you.[6]

In order to survive, the Italian Canadian poet must disguise himself once again to take on Sheherazade's looks. He must continuously be able to recreate something that comes from overseas, images which are entwined, recollections of faded memories, far-away mountains, newly ploughed fields, small hill-towns: Something that the filter of absence has turned into ghosts of a past which is frozen in time, but cannot return.

Land of mountain pastures
        grazed by the sun
canopy of olive trees and vineyards
        you were coveted
        you were detested
Soldiers in exile haunt your paths
they will never forget your fragrances
        they talk about them
        in far away foggy ports
but the ones who do come back
        have different words for you
Calloused and bent with time
        they dress in black and say
"You aren't the same you've changed
        where are the wonders of younger days?"[7]

They are indeed the "wonders of the good old days," sensations already obsolete which we could identify with black bread, black like the dress of old ladies, "black madonnas" — hired mourners called on to cry the pain, the absence, the loss. Leaving is a little bit like dying, reads an old saying and, consequently, the theme of death and its celebration takes on a clear central role in the poetry.

In many of the remote villages in the Italian hills, it has been a custom to treat the departure of an immigrant in the same way as a death in the community. Funeral rites are performed for both the immigrant and the departed since both cease to be part of the village.[8]

These words of Alexandre L. Amprimoz and Sante A. Visel catch the meaning of this double centrality so well, which finds a further confirmation in the verses of Saro D'Agostino:

                                        I have been taught
death is the mother of beauty, but
my family takes death less seriously.

> The women will cry until the chant
> is broken and one of them collapses
> then some of the men will enter
> and try to help them, but the cries
> and chants soon begin again.[9]

It is evident here how the oral quality of the "chant" is identified with the written verse and, at the same time, how we shift from the real to the symbolic. The epitome of the immigrant then appears as that of a son lost to his community, which he abandons to become a ghost in the new community. Physical and psychological deaths become one, the contest in which they decide to compete with "the force of a double presence: that of their own generation and that of their ethnic group."[10] In fact, if at the beginning, death takes on a privileged role, because the memory of the departed dear one serves as a bridge between personal and collective memory, between Italy and Canada, as Pier Giorgio Di Cicco tells us:

> The man who lost his barbershop during the war,
> loves great white roses at the back of a house beside
> a highway. The roses dream with him,
> of being understood in clear English, or of a large
> Italian sun, or of walking forever on a
> Sunday afternoon.[11]

Later, it is used to combine the ghosts of the past ("little old men with the eyes of saints")[12] with those of our present condition, high and low history and, paradoxically, to give them back a transversal identity and a new visibility, notwithstanding the mimetic process which has taken place:

> Giovanni, ti hanno eretto
> un monumento, ma ti hanno cambiato nome:
> qui ti chiamano John.[13]

This *re-naming* process, so typical of contemporary Canadian literature, marks in fact a sort of implicit recognition which makes cultural death less bitter, in as much as it creates a linguistic duality which is the result of the "clash of the old language of life and the new language of death...The two languages must clash; Italian Canadian writers may work in English or French but many titles, images and expressions remain Italian."[14]

As Len Gasparini writes:

> The blood that moves through your language
> moves through mine.
> The heart that gives it utterance
> is ours alone.

And concludes:

> Let us string our mandolin and sing
> *O sole mio* every night!
>
> The joy is ours,
> strangled by a spaghetti stereotype,
> an Italian is supposed to lay bricks.
> You build poems with the stars.[15]

These final lines mark a sort of ritual of passing from a poetry of mourning and pain to one that justly claims its own right to work through this bereavement and this pain. That landscape, recalled with nostalgia and emotion many times, keeps on changing into an innerscape, an interior landscape:

> Out of my musical box
> spring the burnished grapes in wicker baskets
> of Italia, the Appennini breathe with lungs
> that are the bellows of my accordion.[16]

It becomes a mirror that reflects a new identity, old and new roots that intertwine and lead to that return journey of the mind which opens itself to new perspectives. Similarly painful, as Mary Di Michele shows us:

> My elder sister, Lucia, is not like me,
> she's not good, She's the first born,
> the stubborn one, who wears Italia
> like a cheap necklace around her throat,
> with a charm that makes her heart green
> with tarnish, Lucia, the poet
> who talks about us in obscure verses
> Nobody reads for sure.[17]

The only ones that are able to create a new poet, a citizen of the world, what Antonio d'Alfonso defines:

> Useless poet
> not white, not black, but in between
> black and white, more black by nature
> and love of black.
>
> Emigrants' son,
> an emigrants' son's son in quest
> of strong brave flesh for this blood of
> *contadino.*
>
> To emigrate.
> to make another soil one's own,
> to change not by choice but out of want,
> is to pretend,
>
> is feigning joy,
> is possessing the soul of sadness,
> is to smother the power of the heart,
> the pride of blood.[18]

Translated by Nick Ceramella, Università degli Studi di Roma La Sapienza

Notes and Works Cited

[1] Pivato, Joseph. "Return to Halifax."*Canadian Ethnic Studies* XIV, 1, (1982). Reprinted in *Italian Canadian Voices. An Anthology of Poetry and Prose (1946 - 1983)*. Ed. Caroline Morgan Di Giovanni. Oakville, Ontario: Mosaic Press, 1984. 185.

[2] Perticarini, Romano. "Emigrante." In Ibid., 177.

Dragged down by ancient weights
in the abyss of injustice
we are in the mouths
of the tracks ready to spring
and in the mouths of 'green lizards'
ready for agony.
Sons of an ancient mother
who in their hardest labour pains
wanted to give birth

to better men, like thieves:
and we with the first exiles
tired of black bread
tired of running, of searching,
and in the flat steel cities
we let them master us, banish us.
(Trans. N. Ceramella)

[3] De Iuliis, Celestino. "'Din Don', Love's Singing Song." Canadian Centre for Italian Culture and Education, Toronto, 1981.

[4] Mazza, Antonino. "Our House is in a Cosmic Ear." Op.cit. Ed. Caroline Morgan Di Giovanni, 54.

[5] Atwood, Margaret. *Survival. A Thematic Guide to Canadian Literature*. Toronoto: Anansi, 1972.

[6] Mazza, Antonino. "Canadese." Op.cit. Ed. Caroline Morgan Di Giovanni, 55.

[7] Caccia, Fulvio. "Irpinia." In *Aknos and Other Poems*. Trans. Daniel Sloate. - Montreal: Guernica, 1977. 53.

[8] Amprimoz, L. Alexander and Viselli, A. Sante. "Death Between Two Cultures : Italian-Canadian Poetry." *Comparative Essays on Italian-Canadian Writing*. Ed. Joseph Pivato. Montreal: Guernica, 1985. 103.

[9] D'Agostino, Saro. "Wake." *Roman Candles. Anthology of Poems by Seventeen Italo-Canadian Poets*. Ed. Pier Giorgo Di Cicco. Toronto: Hounslow Press, 1978. 65-66.

[10] Amprimoz, L. Alexander and Viselli, A. Sante. Op.cit. 104.

[11] Di Cicco, Pier Giorgio. "The Man Called Beppino." *The Tough Romance*. Toronto: McClelland and Stewart, 1979. 11.

[12] "Donna Italiana." Ibid. Ed. Caroline Morgan Di Giovanni. 68.

[13] Salvatore, Filippo. "A Giovanni Caboto." *Suns of Darkness*. Montreal: Guernica., 1980. 16.

Giovanni, they have erected you a monument,
but they've changed your name:
here they call you John.
(Trans. N. Ceramella)

[14] Amprimoz, L. Alexander and Viselli, A. Sante. Op.cit. 108.

[15] Gasparini, Len. "Il sangue." *Breaking and Entering: New and Selected Poems*. Oakville: Mosai Press/Valley Edition, 1980. 68.

[16] Di Michele, Mary. "Marta's Monologue." Op.cit. Ed. Caroline Morgan Di Giovanni.159.

[17] Ibid. 160.

[18] D'Alfonso, Antonio. "Life of Cross." *Black Cross*. Montreal: Guernica. 17.

America and Emigration in the Italian Fiction of the Past Twenty Years

Sebastiano Martelli
Università di Salerno

Italo Calvino went to the United States in November 1959 and stayed there until the spring of 1960; during this period he wrote many reports which were published in Italian magazines between 1960 and 1961. However, he never published *Un ottimista in America*, a book that, according to what he wrote in a letter to Armanda Guiducci on 6 April 1961, he himself destroyed:

> My American travel book [...] — after working on it for many months, when it was finally finished I destroyed it. — As time passes, I feel less sure about things.[1]

A Calvino scholar has recently written that the writer refused to publish *Un ottimista in America* "due to the clear gap between personal experience and fiction."[2] Perhaps this is the case but it does not take into account all the motivations underlying Calvino's self-censorship, referring to the wider chapter of the relationship between Italian writers and intellectuals and the United States, in particular in the two decades from the end of the 1950s to the end of the '70s.

Giuseppe Massara and Martino Marazzi[3] have retraced, through painstaking and original critical research, various phases of this relationship. Their findings confirm the fact that Italian writers, especially in the abovementioned period, were stubbornly silent both in their reports and fiction. In fact, they repressed almost completely the Italian American context and the phenomenon of emigration, taking place at about the same time as the last mass immigration in the fifteen years following the aftermath of World War One.

In the 180-page-long collection of Calvino's American reports, published in the Meridiani volume, there is only one reference to emigration, concerning the common stereotype of America, a country without a history, and of Americans devoid of any "sense of history." Calvino wrote that

America is "the country of men who have chosen geography and not history" and that in the 19th century "the poor Italians, like the Germans, Poles, Russians and the Irish, in the presence of hunger, not being able to conceive any mode of historical development for their own countries, chose a geographical solution: crossing the Atlantic."[4]

Notwithstanding this, Calvino maintained: "But I love New York, and love is blind [...] Shall I have written on my tombstone, beneath my name: 'Newyorker'?" He also expresses repression, uneasiness, and a certain difficulty in representing the reality of America and even more so the Italian American one, which was apparently considered a residual element of the past and not part of that modern America which, thanks to its social and cultural models, was conquering the world.

Calvino's experience must be read alongside Goffredo Parise's who, a year later, in 1961, went to America for the first time. He traveled far and wide, but was particularly attracted to New York, which, borrowing an image already present in Cecchi's *America amara,* he felt it had "the Babylonian aspect of a tomb," while, at the same time, he also considered "[the only] city in the world that has moved me." New York causes a "deep nausea" is a "city of fools" which:

> makes you feel sick as if you were intoxicated with alcohol and weariness. You walk snowed under by skyscrapers and lifting your head hurts. An incessant roar, the roar of all roars [...] The only real things are the skyscrapers and the factories covered with black coal-dust. All the rest is provincialism and madness. [...] Along the streets, wedged deep among these factories, which are in turn buried by clanging infernal bridges (hence by an iron oxide reddish light), all sort of waste coming from warehouses and factories was abandoned [...] and many thousands of other objects which seemed to me like those people imprisoned in warehouses and factories. It was a dreadful impression of torture, of incredible captivity, it drove you mad [...] All that was bathed in a light which I would rather call industrial, than natural, a light impregnated with pulmonary deposits, as if of an iron and copper mine, where a dim dirty brass sun sailed low amongst dense yellowish rivers of fumes beyond the crystal lattice, the swollen web of steel cables which supported the bridges.[5]

These are descriptions that reecho the imaginary vision of many European intellectuals who were in contact with the new American civilisation in the early 1900s, and which had a vigorous narrative rendering in Dos Passos's *Manhattan Transfer* (1925). This, in its turn, was a novel characterised by that "ambivalence" of attraction and repulsion,[6] which would be found yet again in Italian writers, like Soldati, Cecchi, Praz, Quarantotti Gambini, or Calvino and Parise.

The "sensory" style of Parise — which owes a lot to this American experience, a real "divide in expressive and intellectual life" — embraces that "smell" of America, the supposed essence of its true nature, the smell of distress an "inhuman, chemical, old distress, without being ancient [...] moral distress [...] slavery of slavery. The American is "artificial," a "second degree" man, a "murderer of tradition" who experiments the Darwinian "struggle for survival" in modern times.

Parise too — who traveled to America in 1975, by which time the "great" consumer "revolution" had already happened, in a civilization centered on the culture of objects and consumption that filled the historical and ideological void, resulting in some sort of "degeneration of western man, of his thought and tongue" — did not fail to see that double reading of American reality. While America appeared to him as a "demoniac image"[8] — with which 20th century Italian men and women of letters were also familiar — "a huge filthy place stricken by the wind [...] the degradation of a contaminated and unnatural hell, that is the new prehistory, in other words, the *American way of life* — at the same time he confessed he had "been tempted to go and live in America and lose himself in the new culture." A contradictory representation fed by the contemplation of the "aesthete heedful of decadence, dissolution, pervaded with a strong instinct to lose oneself."[9] It compared with Calvino's cold, geometric view, producing unexpected incursions stimulated by that "smell" which allows Parise to catch the different "smells" of a reality like New York's. This is what also happens during those brief insights into Little Italy which, although filtered by the sensory receptors of a "decadent," as he calls himself, materialize significant fragments of real life. Little Italy:

> is nothing else but a huge block of houses [...] looking all the same, grey, reddish, covered with soot, dust and dirt: I have never seen such a huge amount of filth in any other city in the world not even in the Arab neighborhoods: because you have to add to the dirt that moral misery, day after day in an absurd and unrecognizable slavery, which cannot be explained; a black, gloomy and hopeless melancholy.

A representation in which the figure of the unlucky little Sicilian trader enters as a functional piece of the mosaic, on whose face the writer reads the "disappointment" with the American dream, so marked that it "looks like death." Here is one of the victims of that America projected through films: "it is incredible how films have *built the image* of a slow-witted and inexistent America in the minds of so many Italians as if it spurred them to emigrate." A journalistic simplification of Italian emigration is partly redeemed by that "glance" at the Italian bookshop that is being remodernized in Little Italy:

> old records, old stuff [...] but the owners say this sentimentalism no longer exists, the new generations, which are already the fourth, the fifth, don't know what to do with Italian books and old things. On the contrary, they do not utter a word in Italian.

Parise did not have a different view of Little Italy, fifteen years later, at the time of his second stay there:

> Little Italy is an enclave and the poor old espresso coffee machines, operated by an Italian old lady who does not speak Italian any more, the wires with the white, red and green little flags put up between houses, nineteenth century Neapolitan haberdashers which sell statues of saints, fake coral horns, calendars and ribbons, delicatessen sellers with their hanging *mortadelle*, *provoloni* and *caciotte*, and which are, alas! The reconstruction, the set of an Italy which does not in any way exist any longer except in the hearts of those inhabitants.

They, like many other thousands of emigrants, fill their *vacuum* with signs, objects and illusions in a city and in a country which is "still a society of rootless immigrants," even if most Americans "want to forget of being or having been emigrants and, so to speak, they "censor" the reality of their origins according to the recurrent schemes of entrepreneurial morality which forgives any brutality and wipes out every memory in the name of the factory."

In this "ambiguous dynamic of attraction-repulsion" expressed by Parise and Calvino but also by Arbasino and Eco, as well as other cultured travellers of the sixties and seventies, the Italian American reality and emigration are absent or appear fleetingly without contributing to any narrative project. Moreover, in the Italian fiction of the sixties and seventies set in

America, the world of emigrants is absent: *Curriculum mortis* (1968) by Enrico Emanuelli, *Lungo equinozio* (1962) by Angela Bianchini, *Tempo lungo* (1961-94) by Gianluigi Melega, *Pene d'America* (1972) by Fabrizio Onofri, *Melampus* (1970) by Ennio Flaiano, *Il comunista* (1976) by Guido Morselli, *Romanzo Americano* (1979) by Guido Piovene, *La sposa americana* (1977) and *Addio diletta Amelia* (1979) by Mario Soldati, *Un don Chisciotte in America* (1979) by Alberto Lecco. Owing to a wide range of reasons, there was complete silence on such matters from the early sixties onwards. Italian society was projected towards modernization ruled by the belief that all present and past images of its own suffering be destroyed. The passage from the myth to the American model on which political and ideological nets were lowered; the new passwords of the intellectuals who, having abandoned the vital but contradictory season of neorealism, point out other paths that once again privilege — even if through new, avant-garde forms — a literature reproducing itself by parthenogenesis.

This silence seems to persist in the narrative of the eighties and nineties: from *Treno di panna* (1981) by Andrea De Carlo to *Una madre per l'estate* (1982) by Sandra Bonsanti to *America oh kei* (1984) by Giuseppe D'Agata. The list could include *A New York non si muore di vecchiaia* (1990) by Luigi Settembrini, *La mia America e la tua* (1995) by Aldo Rosselli, *L'attore americano* (1997) by Rossana Campo, *L'arcadia americana* (1999) by Gina Lagorio, *Dall'altra parte degli occhi* (1999) by Dario Buzzolan, *Come sono sbarcato in America* (2001) by Gianni Celati; *Saverio del Nord Ovest* (2001) by Giuseppe Ferrandino, up to recent novels such as *I veri nomi* (2002) by Andrea De Carlo, *Alborada* (2002) by Gianni Riotta, and Angela Bianchini's *Nevada* (2002).

America is the new center of the empire, whose socioeconomic system has spawned standardization, where the technological universe challenges imaginary science fiction in a continuous race, causing a real anthropologic mutation in the new generations throughout the empire. In these novels, America is above all elsewhere, the space-time of moving, the end of a journey during which you have to bring your cultural identity, and describe and understand the American universe or bury your existential geology in it.

Nevertheless, as is the case with all the Italian narrative production on American emigration,[10] starting in the 1880s, research reveals a significant output of fiction. Here the theme of Italian American emigration unfolds like history's genetic tissue, which, in some cases, is also adapted to unconventional narrative models.

Many social, historical, cultural and literary currents converge in this latest narrative revival of the emigration theme: new generations overcoming the repression of an important period of our national history when a biblical exodus had taken place, leaving its deep mark; the energy of the great Italian American cinema and the pervasiveness of American culture; not only the intellectual new mobility which has allowed ever more frequent plunges into the American world; and, at the same time, the massive return to rediscovery of one's roots. And, last but not least, the recent attention paid to the identity and the image of Italy abroad shown also by the institutions representing the Italian communities abroad, the other Italians without which an important part of our national history would vanish. Moreover, the reproposing of the theme of a weak Italian identity, which takes its strength from that very world of emigration, and the emerging that the emigratory experience itself can help build a pluralist identity of the new Italian and European citizen. The comparison between our old emigration and the new immigrations which have flooded into Italy in the past twenty years, as is so vividly evoked by the title of Gian Antonio Stella's best-seller, *L'orda. Quando gli albanesi eravamo noi* (2002). In the end, obviously, there are some more specific literary reasons, to say it with the Enlightenment thinkers of the *Caffé*, the return to a novel "of things and not words," meaning by "things" a grid of nuggets of reality, history, and condition, nourishing a non-minimalist writing, not bent over itself to auscultate its own feeble signs of life. Furthermore, they show, in the best cases, that linguistic creolization is not only a recovery of the Italian American condition but also an approach to the deconstructions and socio-linguistic contaminations which our multiethnic and multicultural contemporary society is imposing.

Through a synthesis of the Italian narrative map of the past twenty years, we can see how the above-mentioned themes have marked a turning point in contemporary historiography and, more in general, in the perception of Italian emigration.[11] Furthermore, they find confirmation in Italian fiction and in how literary representation, obviously with its specificity, conveys this changed perception.

I would like to start with Massimo Felisatti and Marco Leto, the authors of *O dolce terra addio* (1987), a novel with a traditional realistic structure, a rather common model in the narrative of the 19th and 20th centuries. It represents an attempt to write a whole novel on emigration, whose events are deliberately set in the last twenty years of the 19th century, and to reconstruct two emigration stories in an epic dimension, the destinies of two families, from the north and the south of Italy, cross the board a ship sailing from Genova to the New World. Two families marked by the stories of their lives whose differences are stressed by their original habitat: the Italy of the post unification period with the deep North-South divide, even if the destinies of the protagonists are united by their exodus. The novel ends with the landing in New York at the beginning of the new century, almost as if it were meant to underline the epic nature of the journey and the opening up towards the future: "poverty ends in America [...] 'America, America!'" A novel which, thanks to its structural and formal features, recalls an unproduced screenplay.

By contrast, Salvatore Mignano's novel, *Il tempo di Peter* (1981), which immediately shows the use of much more modern narrative solutions, not detached from a credible existential and ideological research, exemplifies the ideological and intellectual change with respect to the American dream come true between the end of the seventies and the beginning of the eighties. In this novel, the American dream is lived on this side of the Atlantic through the signs which it has left in the protagonist's childhood, the son of an immigrant who comes back with the American troops that landed in Italy. A father before never seen, except in faded photographs, whom the war provides the opportunity to meet in the flesh, almost a stereotype of the Italian American identity. But America would swallow the father up again, when the war was over, and the son realized he would never see that country because of father's refusal to allow him to emigrate. Thus, the American imaginary became the substitute of a reality which would be always far away and which, through the images recounted in his father's slang, becomes like a "fairy tale," materialized by the parcels full of goodies sent from America in the war's aftermath. But his father came back for good during the 1948 elections, and then rejection and rebellion crept in between them, while the son saw in his father's figure the embodiment of a "narrow-minded and racist America, mean and commercial, intolerant and warmonger." This rejection, taken to extremes with the symbolic murder of the father, becomes the rejection of the American dream. That is the time to depart, choose a life style, leave; it is distance itself that brings back the father figure who, with his presence-absence, had so deeply marked his life.

Then, in the conscience of that circularity, in the very days when his father was dying, Peter finds the complete identity, including the American part. Therefore, it becomes only natural to him to meet his father's desire to spread the American flag on his death-bed and wrap his body up in it before placing it in the coffin. That edge of the flag torn before burial is a symbolic-ritual gesture of the definitive recovery of the father-figure, of his acceptance as a whole, of the awareness that it is by then part of himself, and cannot be wiped out just like the furrows dug by his presence-absence in his life and personality.

Sicily is the background to the novel *Silvinia* (1997) by Giuseppe Bonaviri: a fairy-tale Sicily, richly imaginative, mythical and ancestral, a world in itself. Silvinia and the other little girls come in and out of a large Homeric cave at the foot of the volcano to collect and deliver the bread that their father Salvatore Casaccio has made with his assistants down there. Then one day, Cooper the wizard, who had come from the States with his extraordinary early cartoon shows, arrives in Idrisia, a village on the eastern coast of Sicily, which is where the story takes place, and Silvinia disappears, perhaps drowned, or kidnapped by Cooper. Along the frail thread of this metaphor of the Dysneian American fairy tale, which engulfs the real fairy tale of the Sicilian Silvinia, Bonaviri entrusts the girl's father — Salvatore was the writer's maternal grandfather in real life — with the task of collecting real stories of emigration and transform them into the tale of Silvinia, whose disappearance in 1922, was the source of endless sorrow to her parents and "a symbol creature, metaphor of the mystery of life and death."[12] Salvatore's transoceanic journey, entrusted with the visionariness and the fairy tale magic by an anti-realistic rejection, becomes a representation of oneiric worlds where storms, seaquakes, and sea currents push bodies towards a maelstrom which would swallow all of them up with a huge tide of decomposing human mortal remains that come from all over the world. It must be underlined that this happens as if Silvinia's death had triggered a process of purification and that current carried along all the evil on earth.

Once in New York, Salvatore stays with his children, absorbed by their American life style, while he spends his days alone at home:

> in the evening, he felt like looking at the trees and the moon. He drew the curtain of the only window with its blackened shutters, and looked towards the street. Along the sidewalks you could see some leafless

> limes with their withered branches, some niggers lying on torn blankets slept beneath their scrubby tops. And then he looked up to search for the moon, but he hardly saw the strip of sky turned reddish and smoky by the shining of the street bulbs.

In that American solitude, Salvatore, who had become already a burden to his children, continues to follow mentally the little Silvinia whom, every now and then, seems to send him a message, a request for help, from another world. Ten years after his wife died of a broken heart after Silvinia's death, Salvatore ends his days too at a hospice in New York in 1933. However, Salvatore's funeral is transformed into Silvinia's. Bonaviri entrusts the American dream with the task of giving peace to little Salvinia eventually; a fairy tale-show funeral attended by all the authorities one can think of, including the mayor Fiorello La Guardia, great cinema stars like Charlie Chaplin and James Stewart and cartoon characters such as *Arabella*, Donald Duck, Snow White and Peter Pan. While the funeral procession is passing by, bread, just like that carried by Silvinia, is thrown on the mourners. The ship is at the port ready to sail off for its last trip under captain Bussino's command: Salvatore wuld return to his Sicily because "after death everyone must return to his/her homeland!" In Fact, he does return to his native land, but it is as if Silvinia too went back with him. The "American" fairy tale allows her to have a softened death, which had been made impossible by her tragic passing away. The novel ends with this unanimous "American" participation that only the fairy tale, almost in retaliation, can achieve, especially in that port which had seen so much heart-rending grief and the acceptance of bereavement and memory had been impossible for many decades:

> All the ships towed into port at that moment had been decked with black flags. The Statue of Liberty, which the reflections of the sea got to fade into a blue halo, on the right, stretched towards America. It had a very dark satin flag with the forty-eight stars in deep purple.

In the past decade or so, other writers too have focused their attention on some of the most important real and symbolic places of the Italian American dream and emigration, as if they were temples to which the memory is entrusted, namely Ellis Island and Little Italy. In *Lettere a Manhattan* (1997) by Manlio Concogni, Phil and Titus, the two elderly friends so attached to the old Little Italy of New York, real and symbolic space of Italian emigration, try to stop the destiny of decadence and extinction, as it is invaded by the Chinese expansion and the new immigrants, besides the dispersion of the Italian nucleus. Titus, an old monologist actor, wants to save the memory of this Italian "colony," epicenter of the Italian American dream, and give it back its dignity. Titus's project unfolds between exaltation and irony while he wants the world of exodus, which had given up its cultural-linguistic identity, to remain in the American dream, to speak up again in the suburban abandoned theaters. His tour around the Italian communities, acting out Dante and Manzoni in improvised small theaters while looking for a theater of his own in Little Italy, becomes a metaphor for a project of cultural repossession and salvation of a world on the threshold of an extinction that is both real and part of memory. This is a course which inevitably exaggerates its obsessive and prophetic tones, to which the first person narrator does not miss the opportunity to add an evangelical "substratum" meant to mark not only Titus's story, but that of all the people involved in the Italian American exodus. The extinction of Little Italy and of its memory would imply the symbolic place of that mass migration. The story is well paced and agile, merging irony, melancholy, and the grotesque with narrative wisdom.

The availability of a capacious store of autobiographic memories between Italy and America allows Marcella Olschki in *Oh, America* (1996) and Giosi Lippolis in *Getta il tuo pane sulle acque* (2000), to present women's narration of a culturally aware emigration enriched by special family routes by focusing on the experience of their own American dream, which is at the same time open and available to other people's experiences.

By contrast, the writing of other texts, which recover fragments of life lost along the ways of the exodus, is turned into autobiography: Ferdinando Maurino (*Dal cavo delle mani*, 1968), Carmine Biagio Iannace (*La scoperta dell'America*, 1971), Antonio Margariti (*America! America!*, 1979), Pietro Riccobaldi (*Straniero indesiderabile*, 1988), Tommaso Bordonaro (*La spartenza*, 1991), Joseph Tusiani (*La parola difficile*, 1988; *La parola nuova*, 1991; *La parola antica*, 1992). In other autobiographical writings the emigration journey links up with more complex reasons: Carol Lunetta Cianca (*Un'anima in viaggio*, 1999), Pasquale Manduca (*New York, perdonami*, 2000), Eric Salerno (*Rosso a Manhatan*, 2000).

The recovery of the American dream through short flashes by Alessandro Baricco, in *Castelli di rabbia* (1991), and in more substantial forms in *Novecento* (1994), takes place on a completely different front. It is recovery with a metaphoric and symbolic slant realised through a writing style of refined literariness where the real, historical, anthropological outlines of the American dream dissolve like in Pavese's *La luna e i falò*. Again, in *Novecento* — from which Giuseppe Tornatore has drawn the film *La leggenda del pianista sull'oceano*, in which the American myth-dream impregnates the whole story of the pianist who refuses to leave the ship, where he spends all his life, while the vessel continues to sail the ocean from Italy to America loaded with emigrants and visitors. What is left at the end is a metaphor of another American dream, happiness and the impossibility to achieve it. However, what must be underlined is the fact that the American dream of the emigrant pianist is presented by a writer who, in terms of generation, formation and narrative typology, is the most distant we can think of from the emigrationist imagination.

Any narrative map of the past twenty years cannot ignore a writer who lived in America for about fifty years, although it is just in the past twenty years that he has been discovered in Italy thanks to the revival of some of his novels, including *Tiro al piccione* (1953). However, ever since the 1950s, he was considered one of the most original voices of the post-war new generation of writers,[14] and, in that very decade, he published *Peccato originale* (1954), *Biglietto di terza* (1958) and *Una posizione sociale* (1959), which are still widely considered among the most significant works in the Italian emigration literature.

Rimanelli in the 1960s and 70s had continued to follow his immigrants, in an America divided by racial riots and protests of youth, in *Tragica America* (1968), *Graffiti* (1977), *Il tempo nascosto tra le righe* (1987), *Detroit Blues* (1997). Here, the immigrants of the old generation, weighed down by the rootlessness that comes from disillusionment, and suspended by feelings of refusal, irony, and integration, find themselves living side by side with new emigrants and blacks. Here they are seen within new generations, in times marked by crisis with outbursts of racial, social and political violence, in years "when my father's beautiful America was becoming the blind America of the children."

In the past twenty years it was poetry, especially that written in dialect (*Moliseide*, 1990,1992,1998), which absorbed Rimanelli's writing. The emigration themes took shape through a plurilingualism structured on a studied musical rhythm, where the different worlds of the intellectual emigrant are put together in a poetic *Koinè* in which various languages flow (i.e. Italian, English, dialect), and nuggets of existential and cultural experiences, memories, voices of far away worlds are represented and continuously reinvented.

In the nineties, Rimanelli, besides his narrative in English, produced works in Italian, especially critical stories, a kind of writing which embraces various genres: autobiographical memory, essay reflections, and narrative reinvention.[15] In *Dirige me Domine* (1996) and *Familia* (2000) the set of family memories leads to a recomposition of some significant autobiographical fragments, voices, figures, landscapes, events, and heart-rendering grief caused by the long period of emigration; the shadow of illness and death enters, in a continuous dialogue with the writing, thus extending the life line. The many existential, cultural, linguistic, and memorial layers which emigration has nourished find a functional merging point in Rimanelli's polymorphic writing (short stories, diary, essays, poetry, theatre, and music) that once again block life and artistic creativity on the threshold with an inextricable knot.

The latest generations of writers, by ending the long season of repression and absence, have rediscovered the great transoceanic emigration from a varied set of motivations. That is to say, a ritualized recovery of memories from one's family and community background, the confrontation with the American dream and the pervasive American cultural hegemony conveyed above all by cinema and television, the formative voyage, nomadism and the search for unconventional destinies to which one should link one's identity. Moreover, the limitless mobility in the new globalized multicultural dimension, the multiethnic communal life that is gradually imposing itself in Italy too, and which emigration and the literature linked to it were the first to introduce and represent in the Italian sociohistorical and literary horizon.

The novel by Rodolfo Di Biasio, *I quattro camminanti* (1991), is apparently a very late attempt of a novel about emigration, which seems to be confirmed by the memory option of settled autobiographical nucleuses. It is an emigration story beginning from the brink of War World One, when the youngest child of a large Italian family from Central Italy emigrates to America to be followed in the next couple of decades by his three other brothers. The life fragments of the four brothers are not disjointed, but are kept together by the memory of their parents who remained in their hometown. This is a peculiar memory entrusted to their mother a "modern Niobe," who, "doomed from the moment her children left to wait on the threshold of time," pulls the strings of their stories and destinies on this side of that ocean which she will never see. Stories and destinies which to her were only "made of paper," letters and photographs, piling up through the years, but which thanks to her are woven into the same cloth of which she holds the threads. A mother figure who is not only a Mediterranean *mater* but is also a metaphor of the word itself, in its anthropological dimension, not an abstract sign but a concentrated universe of feeling and co/feeling, memory, "vital sap," the ability both to exist in the present and cross through it.[16] Here, then, is a peculiar linguistic blend: a crossbreeding of popular and dialect Italian, jargon, idiomatic phrases, Italian American slang, especially in the dialogues and letters, which alternate with a refined learned language, not in a mimetic-realistic sense but rather on a course of modern poetic conscience which entrusts the word with the task to create epiphanies, look at and reconstruct reality through flashes of inspiration and fragments that would blend on the same palette.

The destructuralization of the realistic novel, plurilingualism and the absorption and recreation of popular oral expression belong to the same story plan in which the poetic experience of the author has a crucial role because it allows the development of a highly concentrated writing style although it is genetically made up of fragments and flashes of inspiration. The intense polishing has exalted further the stylistic qualities of the story, thus making it acquire essentiality and evocativeness. The flow of Italian American slang terms indicates the changing of an inner and sociolinguistic condition which is nourished from its original source, left at home, where the modern Niobe puts together all the various threads turning them into a single life programme-project. As time passes, the "walkers" (*camminanti*), integrated into American society, lose their exclusiveness of being emigrants even if they keep the heart-rendering feeling of rootlessness and the values tying their destinies to the original world in a confrontation with the America of their first landing w hich was accepted and never avoided. America — written with a small letter as if they wanted to reduce symbolically the emigrationist totemic macro signs of the Other World — becomes then a metaphor of somewhere else towards which many "walkers" take their trip, the place of myth and memory to try to understand and interiorise.

America appears and disappears through fragments of stories and flashbacks in the novel by Silvana Grasso, *Ninna nanna del lupo* (1995), a novel about a female world is told through protagonist Mosca Centonze, who emigrated to America as a child in 1910, and was incarcerated for five years in Bloomfield sanatorium, the woman of a *Mafioso*, who eventually went back to Italy in 1936. Once she was plunged back into the archaic Sicilian world with its rituals and atavist laws, Mosca would take a heinous revenge on the *podestà* [i.e. mayor] of the village, a cruel, violent rapist. Not even the second long period spent in America, of about twenty-five years, would help to change the mental and existential universe of the protagonist. By then, she is in her nineties, living in solitude with her servant Clementina, thinking of the terrible revenge whose plan she had mulled over in the American sanatorium and of which she now sees the "uselessness." "She did not repent, it just seemed useless." A concentrated horizon, a perennial penitentiary climax which is not affected by the emigration experience, such is the gravitational force of the archaic world where they originally came from. All that is rendered through a baroque form of prose, virtuoso and flamboyant, to represent the exaltation of moods, pulsions, instincts, sensuality and anthropologic stratifications, typical of the Sicilian universe.

Givanna Giordano's *Trentaseimila giorni* (1996) is another novel about the female experience. Again, its protagonist comes from Sicily, and at sixteen in 1888, she was already a wife and mother when she immigrated to America. She was driven to emigrate, like many thousands of people in those years, by the pressing need to escape from misery and backwardness, but she has a higher level of awareness, a love for life, and a capacity to imagine and take risks. Her American life becomes a "Catherine-wheel" of meetings, stories, situations, experience, a passing of time which, once on American territory, has wiped out the static and cyclic time dimension of the home country. An imaginary reality which wipes out the traditional emigrationist vision to substitute it with pyrotechnic succession of many-sided representations; a picaresque and "magic realism" which literarily feeds itself from a variety of sources, going from *Don Quixote* to Calvino's *Barone rampante*, from films on the prohibition to Hitchcock and *Blade Runner.*[17] The protagonist lets herself be absorbed by this new dimension, experiences it thoroughly without sparing anything because "life changes and does not stop an hour, like the wind." She experiences success and failure with passion, wonder, and courage, and rises up again before having to come to terms with those broken threads that cannot hold together love, happiness, or fellow travellers. A woman of whom the American dream has exalted certain qualities by making her "extraordinary" and which the author proved to be able to write about with "a sulphurous, resounding, changing and soft language.[18]

Comparison should be made with respect to the narrative that in the past fifteen years has dealt with emigration to Latin America with its affinities but also the remarkable distances compared with the narrative set in North America. The Latin American continent of emigration is present in three novels between the late eighties and the early nineties: *Le donne divine* (1988) by Renzo Rosso, *La Fiera Navigante* (1990) by Livio Garzanti, and *Un altro mare* (1991) by Claudio Magris; these are Conradian journeys of young people bitten by existential anxiety, running away from their fathers or seeking for an unknown father. Three young bourgeois intellectuals at odds with society, family and institutions embark on a voyage marked by the search for adventure, freedom and borderless lands, a geography of some possible alternative existential models, a space-time where one can drown out the homeland. Echoes of emigration, different in form and consistency, flutter in and out of the three novels. To put it more straightforwardly, in *Le donne divine*, where the young protagonist on talking to his uncle, an old immigrant by then seriously ill in a hospital in Caracas, meets "the emigrant's lost and re-found time and the profound emotional and psychological reasons of that adventure-fracture, of that trip without a horizon and perhaps with no return,"[19] but also discovers the real identity of his unknown father, revealed by a mechanism of recognition typical of the popular emigration novel.

The world of emigration enters Livio Garzanti's novel much more marginally, both during the sea trip in the aftermath of war as well as the protagonist's few contacts with the Italians of Brazil and Argentina. This is because he is so absorbed in the shell of his existential bourgeois condition with the conflicts and the choices he needs to find a landing place; an initiation trip with a predictable return.

In Magris's novel, only the images of the ocean and the forlorn and wild South American landscape draw the existential adventure of the protagonist, the young Greek scholar and philosopher Enrico Mreule near to the emigration world. He leaves Gorizia and becomes a *gaucho* in Patagonia, where, in anonymity and solitude, he consumes his restlessness and impatience to live — fed by a Central European highly intellectual imprint, Carlo Michelstaedter's — which he coherently transforms into an escape "to vanish, retire [...] exist less."

Regarding the narrative emigration to Latin America, a new voice is Laura Pariani's, who published the novel *Quando Dio ballava il tango* (2002), but first drew attention to herself with two collections of tales: *Di corno o d'oro* (1993), *Il pettine* (1995). Distant memories of early emigration to South America take shape in *Di corno o d'oro*; for the young peasant, the protagonist of the story, South America is the place where he hopes to drown the remorse for loving his immigrant brother's wife and for not trying to save him from drowning in the Parana River. Reduced to the state of a "wandering Jew," he crosses deserts, "barren, grey and dusty lands," *pampas*, cardoon fields and villages, while getting drunk and playing his *arm-mandolin*, "a little music to death," while everything worth living for was over, and the images of his brother and sister-in-law, who come to forgive him and drown the remorse, belong only to a dream.

Later, Laura Perini drew on this recovery of a memory of emigration as lethean space-time in a more complex referential narrative with the tale *Lo spazio, il vento, la radio* (*Il pettine*, 1995). The fifteen-year-old girl's journey to Argentina does not just mean the recovery of a family memory to come to terms with, that is meeting Louis, the anarchist grandfather, who had emigrated from Italy in the 1920s, and who continued to live his life unconventionally also in South America by disappearing into the vastness of wild Patagonia. He is a figure who can be compared to the protagonist of Claudio Magris's *Un altro mare*, Michelstaedter's friend, who abandons Italy in 1909 to emigrate to Argentina and become a cowherd in Patagonia. The protagonist's trip, the first person narrator, of Pariani's story, as time goes on, becomes a comparison between two worlds, Europe and Argentina, two cultures, the white and the indigenous, into which the grandfather is immersed. The comparison is now transferred within the girl herself between the culture from which she comes — that of her mother, symbol of the European, authoritarian — white culture — and the South American, symbolically tied to the nature where the grandfather has found a state of equilibrium as an unconventional rebel. That transoceanic trip and meeting Luis, her old immigrant grandfather, would become for the young protagonist, the space-time of her self-discovery and first maturity. She opens her mind and the sensitivity to the pain of the world, injustice of history, deep social and economic differences, the need of an ideological conscience and of coherently taking sides for someone like her, a daughter of the white culture and of the affluent European society. On returning to Italy, the memory of her grandfather "would find its place" in the culture and wave of the 1968 protest in which the protagonist would plunge herself.

In her latest novel, *Quando Dio ballava il tango*, Pariani re-proposes the South American world of emigration through some feminine figures, like the protagonist Venturina, who happens to be the very memory of the exodus and heart-rendering grief that it caused. She too, like her mother, protagonist of *Quattro camminanti* by Di Biasio, is a modern *Niobe* who pulls the strings of the destinies of immigrant males: fathers and sons of immigrants marked by the instinct of escape and nostalgia, which along the ocean routes, pile up disappointment, treason, remorse, grief and mourning that the American dream encircles, preventing escape. But Venturina is not only a Mediterranean *Mater*; she holds in herself the reactions of a modern, conscious, contrasted femininity: "Only mountains do not make a move. Mountains and we, women, we are always here waiting, never asking, never expecting, never bothering." They fix, tidy up and save from the wreck of emigration the scattered shipwrecks by tying them together through the ability to narrate entrusted to the mother tongue, the "last shelter" of time which flows and wipes everything out. Only the feminine memory can create a vital circuit between historical fragments and destinies dispersed on both sides of the ocean. However, these are feminine figures who do not exhaust their role in waiting, like those who remain, or in the discrete shadow, like those who follow their men to the other side of the Atlantic, or rather in the soothing of their solitude for those who cannot "expect" anything from men who dream of returning to Italy, a return which is always in the background of their days as desire or remorse. Stories of the long lasting emigration which stretch as late as the time of the generals and the *desaparecidos* [i.e. missing], and even further until the latest serious economic crisis that afflicted Argentina.

At this point one wonders if these really are the last vital flares of the Italian narrative on emigration and the American dream, or if there is something that can nourish the collective and individual memory and pass from there to narrative writing. According to Marco Rossi Doria,[20] if the greatest sociohistoric phenomenon that has passed through Italy for over a century is to feed memory, especially that of the new generations, symbols and signs that provide "matter and spirit to the 'collective memory'" and may preserve it are needed. Failing the presence of places, symbols, signs in our country, in Naples or Genoa — from where a few million Italians sailed off towards the American dream — we can turn our eyes towards the real and symbolic places of the Italian American dream: Ellis Island, Little Italy. Going on some sort of a pilgrimage to Ellis Island to find out about "wanderings, dispersion, diaspora," in the words of George Perec in his diary *Ellis Island. Storie di erranza e di speranza.*[21] Writers too can only go to Ellis Island and nourish a new writing of emigration by wondering about the same things as Perec did in his diary:

> how can one describe?
> how can one narrate?
> [...]
> How can one recognise this place?
> give back what it was?
> how can one read these traces?
> [...]
> How can one grasp what is not shown,
> what has not been photographed,
> placed on files, restored, staged?
> How can one find again what was flat, banal, daily,
> What was normal, what used to happen every day?

And Ellis Island is the whole space of the opera with the same name, lyrics and music composed by Giovanni Sollima and Roberto Alajmo, which premiered at the *Massimo* Theatre in Palermo in October 2002. This is a work with an imprinting which is more evocative than narrative, crossing different languages and voices, just like they used to cross in that chaotic universe of Ellis Island, where only the shared condition of being emigrants gave them common ground, thus overcoming ethnic and cultural barriers.

Sergio Campailla, in the central chapter of *Romanzo americano* (1994), entitled *Album di famiglia*, bases the story on the traces of an emigratory event that can be found in the large computerized archive of the Ellis Island Museum. The protagonist goes there to look for the memory of his grandfather, Carmine, who landed in New York in the 1920s, leaving in Sicily his two daughters and his wife who was expecting a baby whom he would never see. The young man wanted to dispel the fog which had always surrounded the figure of his grandfather, whom he had met only through the words of his own mother, who, in turn, had been haunted by the "shortcoming" of never having seen her father, and who would cling till the end to the hope of seeing him on the threshold of her house all her life long. And now the young Carmine goes with the old immigrant Partanna to the "memorial" of emigration at Ellis Island to look for an answer to his own and his mother's questions; perhaps that is where "the ultimate secret of that story" is kept. But there is nothing. It is left to the old immigrant villager "to break the web" of silence and reveal what had happened to grandfather Carmine, whose destiny had been marked by his own "nature" and his being an emigrant. A story like that of many other thousands of Sicilians, Italians "a story of emigrants [...] sank into the past: a story of individuals forced to leave their land, naked, without any means, without even knowing the language. From the old to the new world. They died and were reborn. But they were reborn old, already old"; or as Partanna concludes, a story within the much greater History where "there are ... those who win and those who lose."

In the novel *Parenti lontani* (2000) — which we can define as the response of a Southern narrator to De Carlo's *Treno di panna* — Gaetano Cappelli, in the long American chapter after that on Lucania, despite the inclusion of figures, like the rich American uncle, and emigration circles, follows above all the hypertrophic self-narration of the Picaresque narrative I who is determined to get even with the mean days back in Lucania. It was there that Carlino had toyed with his American dream bombarded as he was by a thousand lights, images, sounds, words of an America which had reached even the worn out back streets of that land, just like generations of immigrant peasants who had been dazzled by the bills of the shipping lines. Like many of them Carlino too would live his catastrophe at the end of his American dream in the dispersion and waste of a civilization which would remain alien to him.

Through a writing style bent to the different rhythms of the three periods of the protagonist's life, narrated by three different narrative I(s), Giuseppe Lupo with his *L'americano di Celenne* (2000) has written a novel about an American, Danny Leone, from Lucania, who had left for New York after the Great War, but who suddenly decided to return home in the mid-thirties even though he had been successful. By developing some segments of the "Levian" pages, Lupo focuses his narrative on the memory of the American dream, which occurs like a film with alternate flash-backs: a pleasant narrative of Little Italy of the roaring twenties, made up of atmospheres created through lightness, melancholy, and irony, but also through a rigorous reconstruction. If the return to the homeland, which is constantly in the background, reveals the impossibility to heal the hidden heart-rendering grief caused by separation, and, therefore, the acknowledgement of "one's failure" as an emigrant, it does, however, not lend itself to any recrimination. By contrast, Danny would fascinate his fellow villagers in Celenne with his captivating American stories, thus transforming the myth into a journey of discovery for others, as used to happen with the narration in the days of the peasant civilization. Danny Leone managed to change the emigrant condition, a *bird of passage*, into an opportunity of great life experience and knowledge of the world, where the return does not necessarily imply a rejection or a defeat of the American dream, but space-time to arrange life's ins and outs. It seems that Lupo indicates with this novel one of the possible ways through which, once the stereotypes and repressions are overcome, but also the scowling claims of civilization and the ideological interpretations which have marked the imaginary and the representation of emigration for over a century, all that can still be narrated today.

The latest literary season has offered a narrative production which in some cases goes through the American imaginary pursued by the narrative of the 1980s, starting from the experience on the road, as in *Chemical Usa* (2003) by Daniele Brolli, a diary of an "absent traveller," terminal of real experiences and mental images, or a multi-medial universe, merged in a continuous swinging, without a possible distinction.

In *Tutto brucia* (2003) by Dario Buzzolan, the fantastic adventures of two trios unravel among a crowded mass of characters and stories, through a continuous merging of times, genres and narrative registers in the overflowing American space, from the South to the North, from Mexico to Alaska. American space and imaginary reality compared with those which seem to be familiar and taken for granted in a Turin out of the canons of a popular representation.

If it is partly true that America in Buzzolan's novel represents the conveying space-time through which "the ambiguous border between memory and oblivion, present and past, between repression exercises and surprising wonders"[22] can be recounted — thanks to a circular route which unites it inextricably to contemporary Italy, city and province, especially in the south — all that is more visible in two other novels, *In viaggio con Junior* (2002) by Angelo Morino and *Così ti ricordi di me* (2003) by Nicola Gardini. The former is a travel diary which takes place between New York and Matera touching most of the Italian peninsula, in the search for a father excluded from the life of the protagonist, always travelling between America and Australia, a figure recovered together with the lines and sense of family memory during the visit to the "fathers' land."

Whereas, the story of Oreste, an eight-year-old boy, fits into Molise and America, in the novel *Così ti ricordi di me* by Gardini, but America is only in the background. In fact, all the story is centred on a sunny summer in the seventies which Oreste spends at Ponte Nero in Molise, as decided by his mother, who had emigrated years earlier, owing to a dismal episode of paternal violence she had been the victim of at home. A return, after the little boy's father's death and the failure of the American marriage, meant to search for a conciliation with his own past, while the present ensures that he, left alone with his relatives in the village, learns the treacherous depths of that past. It is a present when the time of the peasant civilisation is torn apart, dissolved by the coming of television and the consumer age. There are only phantoms left, petrified faces and, especially, in the new generations a void filled by sounds, images, degraded imitation of the new life models as conveyed by television. In this crossing of past and present, conditions and languages — Gardini uses a plurilingualism (Italian, Molisan dialect, English) typical of the novel of emigration — Oreste is initiated to life and discovers his identity along a route which cannot possibly escape from being marked by that past from which his mother had fled.

The latest literary season has offered an important novelty, Melania Mazzucco's novel, *Vita* (2003), which is a *comprehensive* novel on emigration, with an imposing structure on which the epos of an emigratory story is developed. It begins in 1903, when Vita and Diamante, ten and twelve respectively, both from Tufo di Minturno, sail, with two thousand emigrants on board the White Star Line, from the port of Naples to New York. It is in this American city where thousands of immigrants land every day that the two children rejoin the rings of an emigratory chain, Vita's father and Diamante's uncle. They would live in one of the degraded houses in Prince Street, in a Little Italy embracing a mass of people who, in escaping from the misery and hunger of their country of origin, must go through a hellish reality made up of fighting for life and marked by violence, the very condition enabling them to enter into the paradise of the American dream later.

A hypertrophic reality which draws individuals closer, brings them together and leads them to clash with their ethnic and linguistic imprinting. Their destinies will take different directions sooner or later, and not all of them will find the American dream. Vita and Diamante would survive the hellish period of Prince Street supporting each other with a sympathetic nearness, which seems to be destined for a life lasting love and links.

No Italian writer had succeeded up to now in telling the story of Little Italy at the time of the great emigration. Many tried and as many gave up, hinting at a failure which was not just individual but referred to a more general shortcoming of our literature which is often weak, incapable of dealing with great sociohistoric themes and thorough environmental reconstruction, thereby bravely facing the impending risk of falling into the stereotypes represented in Italian American literature and cinema in particular. I think that the secret consists in entrusting the vast documentary research carried out on both sides of the Atlantic to a polyphonic vigorous writing style, supported by family memory — Diamante was the grandfather of the writer — which as time goes on expands, collecting new fragments, the bare bones remaining of the shipwrecked memory of emigration. The family memory of the experience of emigration was shipwrecked too, then the opportunity of a trip, meeting again in a street, Prince Street, where grandfather Diamante had experienced his American dream, unchains a reaction, the need to learn, know the weaving of destinies, repressed stories which demand to be brought back to life. It would be history that weaves the thread of those stories, links scattered fragments coming from archive documents, newspapers, letters and photographs, the memory of the survivors, and fills in the voids with its imaginary.

But there is not only Little Italy, there are the endless inland American spaces, where Diamante goes to work as a water boy in the railway worksites, an outpost of the mobile American frontier which thousands of emigrants contributed to push ever more forward.

The "spiral" writing, which unravels like an assembled puzzle, offers the reader a mobility which wipes out the stillness of the realistic novel and leads it along the roads of Diamante and Vita which destiny will separate. Vita driven by her vital energy would follow the American dream and would come through successfully; whereas Diamante is the weak link, after ten years he went back to Italy, taking with him his failure, the remorse for the end of the American dream and the love story between him and Vita. A charming story that becomes a metaphor of the experience and the failure of the American dream that goes beyond the story of the two protagonists of the novel. In the vast frame of the novel enter two stories, which fit well to weave the epos of an emigratory event, such as that of the arrival in Italy of Vita's son with the Fifth American Army during World War Two. Or, the first and only trip Vita, an aging widow, took to Italy to meet Diamante whom the American dream seemed to have destined her for her life-companion. But by then everything was over, the only thing left was the time of memory and words, the only things that can make her live again. The novel closes with the images of the trip on the ocean as it had began: to Vita and Diamante that had been their initiation into life; in that night on the ocean which they spent together in a lifeboat, perhaps there were already the signs of a different force which would drive or stop them on the way to the American dream:

> He takes her hand because otherwise he is not sure she is next to him. The vivid glimmer of the lights penetrates through the oilcloth. The painted letters on the side of the lifeboat repeat obsessively the syllables that they have never known how to read. Next to her, against her body, there is a boy wearing a stiff cap. He clasps her hand. Diamante says, why do you look at me like that, Vita? I told you I would come. She says why didn't you do that sooner? He said, I've done it now.

We can conclude that Italian literature eventually has produced the great modern novel on the transoceanic emigration, as has been the case with other literatures as with Ireland in Frank McCourt's novels, *Angela's Ashes* and *'Tis: A memoir.*

Melania Mazzucco has succeeded in rendering a dated and repressed subject matter into a wide-ranging narrative, spread over a complex architecture thanks to the successful assembly of the puzzle breaking linear time, just like the transoceanic trip breaks the cyclic time of the peasant civilization from which emigrants withdraw. A vigorous and copious writing, nourished by a narrative capacity which is rare in the weak panorama of Italian narrative, through which we have acquired the modern novel of the emigratory epic. A writing style that handles with great ability the contamination of literary genres and registers, as well as the contaminations of various linguistic registers, Italian, dialect, Italian American slang. Hence, an inevitable recovery of the different models which for over a century have dealt with the history of the great emigration but freed from the literary and sociohistoric stereotypes that have collaborated for a long time to the repression of this subject matter.

The twenty-year-period of the last flares of the narrative on the transoceanic emigration ends then with an important event, the novel that was missing from Italian literature. The novels and short stories that I have mentioned here have in a sense paved the way for this, together with the historiographic and literary studies of the same period. The success of Mazzucco's novel with readers and critics alike closes significantly the circle for a debt that Italian culture owed to an exodus that has had so many repercussions for the history and experience of our people.

Translated by Nick Ceramella, Università degli Studi di Roma La Sapienza

[1] I. Calvino, *I libri degli altri. Lettere 1947-1981*, a cura di G.Tesio, Torino, Einaudi, 1991, p. 365.

[2] D. Scarpa, *Dieci lemmi calviniani*, in *Italo Calvino newyorkese*, a cura di A. Botta e D. Scarpa, Cava de' Tirreni, Avagliano Editore, 2002, p.180.

[3] G. Massara, *Viaggiatori italiani in America (1860-1970)*, Roma, Edizioni di Storia e Letteratura, 1976, ID., *Americani. L'immagine letteraria degli Stati Uniti in Italia*, Palermo, Sellerio, 1984; M. Marazzi, *Little America. Gli Stati Uniti e gli scrittori italiani del Novecento*, Milano, Marcos y Marcos, 1997.

[4] I. Calvino, *Diario americano 1960*, in *Saggi 1945-1985*, a cura di M.Barenghi, tomo secondo, Milano, Mondadori, 1995, p. 2652.

[5] This and the following passages are taken from Parise's new edition of his "American", *New York*, a cura di S. Perrella, Milano, Rizzoli, 2001.

[6] P. Gelli, *Canto per New York*, in J. Dos Passos, *Manhattan Transfer*, Milano, Baldini & Castoldi, 2002, p. 13.

[7] S. Perrella, *Fino a Salgarèda. La scrittura nomade di Goffredo Parise*, Milano, Rizzoli, 2003, p.65.

[8] G. De Pascale, *Scrittori in viaggio. Narratori e poeti italiani del Novecento in giro per il mondo*, Torino, Bollati Boringhieri, 2001, pp. 51-55.

[9] I. Crotti, *Tre voci sospette. Buzzati, Piovene, Parise*, Milano, Mursia, 1994, p. 181.

[10] Cfr. S. Martelli, *Letteratura contaminata. Storie parole immagini tra Ottocento e Novecento*, Salerno, Laveglia, 1994; E. Franzina, *Dall'Arcadia in America. Attività letteraria ed emigrazione transoceanica in Italia (1850-1940)*, Torino, Edizioni della Fondazione Giovanni Agnelli, 1996; S. Martelli, *Letteratura ed emigrazione: congedo provvisorio*, in *Il sogno italo-americano*, Napoli, Cuen, 1998, pp. 405-443; ID., *Dal vecchio mondo al sogno americano. Realtà e immaginario dell'emigrazione italiana*, in *Storia dell'emigrazione italiana*, a cura di P. Bevilacqua, A. De Clementi, E. Franzina, Roma, Donzelli, 2001, pp. 433-487.

[11] Cfr. *Storia dell'emigrazione italiana*, a cura di P. Bevilacqua, A. De Clementi, E. Franzina, I, *Partenze*, II, *Arrivi*, Roma, Donzelli, 2001-2002.

[12] M. Collura, *Dall'Etna a Manhattan cercando la piccola Silvinia*, in "Corriere della Sera," 2 aprile 1997.

[13] Cfr. E. Paccagnini, *Utopia della parola*, in "Il Sole-24ore," 22 giugno 1997.

[14] Cfr. *Rimanelliana. Studies on Giose Rimanelli*, edited by S. Martelli, Stony Brook-New York, Forum Italicum Publishing, 2000.

[15] L. Fontanella, *Giose Rimanelli e il viaggio infinito*, in *La parola transfuga. Scrittori italiani in America*, Fiesole, Edizioni Cadmo, 2003, pp. 101-174.

[16] Cfr. L. Fontanella, *A proposito de «I quattro camminanti» di Rodolfo Di Biasio*, in "Misure critiche," luglio-dicembre 1991, 80-81, pp. 147-150.

[17] Cfr. P. Treccagnoli, *La vera felicità è cogliere l'attimo*, in "Il Mattino," 13 marzo 1996; A. Fasola, *In America con la capra*, in "l'Unità," 20 maggio 1996.

[18] C. De Michelis, *Nota critica*, Giordano 1996.

[19] D. Puccini, *E la nave va in America Latina*, in "Il Messaggero," 7 luglio 1990.

[20] M. Rossi-Doria, *Ellis Island. È possibile ridestare memoria nei bambini in questo nostro tempo dell'usa e getta?*, in "Parolechiave," 9, dicembre 1995, pp. 145-154

[21] G. Perec, *Ellis Island. Storie di erranza e di speranza*, a cura di M. Sebregondi, Milano, Archinto, 1996.

[22] G. Tesio, *Buzzolan: dov'è finito quel figlio un po' magico?*, in "La Stampa-Tuttolibri," 28 giugno 2003.

Bibliography

Arbasino, Alberto. *Grazie per le magnifiche rose*. Milano: Feltrinelli 1965.

_______. *Off-Off*. Milano: Feltrinelli, 1968.

_______. *Fratelli d'Italia*. Torino: Einaudi, 1976.

Baricco, Alessandro. *Castelli di rabbia*. Milano: Rizzoli, 1991.

_______. *Novecento*. Milano: Feltrinelli, 1994.

Bianchini, Angela. *Lungo equinozio*. Milano: Lerici, 1962.

_______. *Nevada*. Milano: Frassinelli, 2002.

Bonaviri, Giuseppe. *Silvinia*. Milano: Mondadori, 1997.

Bonsanti, Sandra. *Una madre per l'estate*. Milano: Rizzoli, 1982.

Bordonaro, Tommaso. *La spartenza*. Torino: Einaudi, 1991.

Brolli, Daniele. *Chemical USA*. Milano: Rizzoli, 2003.

Buzzolan, Dario. *Dall'altra parte degli occhi*. Milano: Mursia, 1999.

_______. *Tutto brucia*. Milano: Garzanti, 2003.

Calvino, Italo. *Corrispondenze dagli Stati Uniti (1960-1961)*, in *Saggi 1945-1985*, a cura di M. Barenghi, tomo II. Milano: Mondadori, 1995.

Campailla, Sergio. *Romanzo americano*. Milano: Rusconi, 1994.

Campo, Rossana. *L'attore americano*. Milano: Feltrinelli, 1997.

Cancogni, Manlio. *Lettere a Manhattan*. Roma: Fazi, 1997.

Cappelli, Gaetano. *Parenti lontani*. Milano: Mondadori, 2000.

Cecchi, Emilio. *America amara* [1939]. Padova: Muzzio, 1995.

Celati, Gianni. *Come sono sbarcato in America*, in *Cinema naturale*. Milano: Feltrinelli, 2001.

Cianca, Carol Lunetta. *Un'anima in viaggio*. Leonforte: Lancillotto e Ginevra Editori, 1999.
D'Agata, Giuseppe. *America oh kei*. Milano: Bompiani, 1984.
De Carlo, Andrea. *Treno di panna*. Torino: Einaudi, 1981.
_______. *I veri nomi*. Milano: Mondadori, 2002.
Di Biasio, Rodolfo. *I quattro camminanti*. Firenze: Sansoni, 1991.
Dos Passos, John. *Manhattan Transfer* [1925], trad. italiana di A. Scalero. Milano: Baldini & Castoldi, 2002.
Eco, Umberto. *Dalla periferia dell'Impero*. Milano: Bompiani, 1977.
Emanuelli, Enrico. *Curriculum mortis*. Milano: Feltrinelli, 1968.
Felisatti, Massimo-Leto Marco. *O dolce terra addio*. Milano: Rizzoli, 1987.
Ferrandino, Giuseppe. *Saverio del Nord Ovest*. Milano: Bompiani, 2001.
Flaiano, Ennio. *Melampus*, in *Il gioco e il massacro*. Milano: Rizzoli, 1970.
Gardini, Nicola. *Così ti ricordi di me*. Milano: Sironi, 2003.
Garzanti, Livio. *La Fiera Navigante*. Milano: Garzanti, 1990.
Giordano, Giovanna. *Trentaseimila giorni*. Venezia: Marsilio, 1996.
Grasso, Silvana. *Ninna nanna del lupo*. Torino: Einaudi, 1995.
Iannace, Carmine Biagio. *La scoperta dell'America* [1971]. West Lafayette: Bordighera, 2000.
Lagorio, Gina. *L'arcadia americana*. Milano: Rizzoli, 1999.
Lecco, Alberto. *Un don Chisciotte in America*. Milano: Mondadori, 1979.
Lippolis, Giosi. *Getta il tuo pane sulle acque*. Roma: Empirìa, 2000.
Lupo, Giuseppe. *L'americano di Celenne*. Venezia: Marsilio, 2000.
Magris, Claudio. *Un altro mare*. Milano: Garzanti, 1991.
Manduca, Pasquale. *New York, perdonami*. S. Eustachio di Mercato S. Severino, Il Grappolo, 2000.
Margariti, Antonio. *America! America!*. Casalvelino Scalo: Galzerano Editore, 1979.
Mazzucco, Melania. *Vita*. Milano: Rizzoli, 2003.
Maurino, Ferdinando. *Dal cavo delle mani*. Cosenza: Pellegrini, 1968.
Mc Court, Frank. *Le ceneri di Angela*, trad. italiana. Milano: Adelphi, 1997.
_______. *Che paese, l'America*, trad. italiana. Milano: Adelphi, 2000.
Melega, Gianluigi. *Tempo lungo*. III. *Eravamo come piante* [1961]. Milano: Baldini & Castoldi, 1994.
Mignano, Salvatore. *Il tempo di Peter*. Foggia: Bastogi, 1981.
Morino, Angelo. *In viaggio con Junior*. Palermo: Sellerio, 2002.
Morselli, Guido. *Il comunista*. Milano: Adelphi, 1976.
Olschki, Marcella. *Oh, America*. Palermo: Sellerio, 1996.
Onofri, Fabrizio. *Pene d'America*. Bari: Dedalo, 1972.
Pariani, Laura. *Di corno o d'oro*. Palermo: Sellerio, 1993.
_______. *Il pettine*. Palermo: Sellerio, 1995.
_______. *Quando Dio ballava il tango*. Milano: Rizzoli, 2002.

Parise, Goffredo. *New York* [1961-1976], a cura di S. Perrella. Milano: Rizzoli, 2001.
Pavese, Cesare. *La luna e i falò*. Torino: Einaudi, 1950.
Perec, George. *Ellis Island. Storie di erranza e di speranza*, a cura di M. Sebregondi. Milano: Archinto, 1995.
Piovene, Guido. *Romanzo americano.* Milano: Mondadori, 1979.
Praz, Mario. *Cronache letterarie anglo-sassoni*, voll. 4. Roma: Edizioni di Storia e Letteratura, 1950-1967.
———. *Il mondo che ho visto.* Milano: Adelphi, 1984.
Quarantotti, Gambini Pier Antonio. *Neve a Manhattan* [1939-1957], a cura di R. Manica. Roma: Fazi, 1998.
Riccobaldi, Pietro. *Straniero indesiderabile.* Milano: Archinto, 1988.
Rimanelli, Giose. *Tiro al piccione.* Milano: Mondadori, 1953; nuova edizione con Introduzione di S. Martelli. Torino: Einaudi, 1991
_______. *Peccato originale.* Milano: Mondadori, 1954.
_______. *Biglietto di terza.* Milano: Mondadori, 1958.
_______. *Una posizione sociale.* Firenze: Vallecchi, 1959; nuova ediz. con il titolo *La stanza grande.* a cura di S. Martelli, Cava de' Tirreni: Avagliano, 1996.
_______. *Tragica America.* Genova: Immordino, 1968.
_______. *Graffiti.* Isernia: Marinelli, 1977.
_______. *Il tempo nascosto tra le righe.* Isernia: Marinelli, 1987.
_______. *Dirige me Domine.* Campobasso: Edizioni Enne, 1996.
_______. *Detroit Blues.* Welland-Lewiston: Soleil, 1997.
_______. *Moliseide and Other Poems* [1990-1992]. New York-Ottawa-Toronto, 1998.
_______. *Familia.* Isernia: Cosmo Iannone Editore, 2000.
Riotta, Gianni. *Alborada.* Milano: Rizzoli, 2002.
Rosselli, Aldo. *La mia America e la tua.* Roma: Theoria, 1995.
Rosso, Renzo. *Le donne divine.* Milano: Garzanti, 1988.
Salerno, Eric. *Rosso a Manhattan.* Roma: Quiritta, 2000.
Settembrini, Luigi. *A New York non si muore di vecchiaia.* Milano: Rizzoli, 1990.
Soldati, Mario. *America primo amore* [1935], a cura di S.S. Nigro. Palermo: Sellerio, 2003.
_______. *La sposa americana.* Milano: Mondadori, 1977.
_______. *Addio diletta Amelia.* Milano: Rizzoli, 1979.
Stella, Gian Antonio. *L'orda. Quando gli albanesi eravamo noi.* Milano: Rizzoli, 2002.
Tusiani, Joseph. *La parola difficile.* Fasano: Schena, 1988.
_______. *La parola nuova.* Ivi, 1991.
_______. *La parola Antica.* Ivi, 1992.

KING OF HARLEM: GARIBALDI LAPOLLA AND GENNARO ACCUCI "IL GRANDE"

Martino Marazzi
University of Milan

-What's his name?
-Garibaldi.
- What kind of name is that?
Bernard Malamud, *The Assistant*

The intention of this paper is simply to pay well-deserved tribute to an Italian-American writer of the early years, Garibaldi Mario Lapolla (b. 1888 in Rapolla, province of Potenza, d. 1954 in New York City) , author of three novels published in rapid succession at the beginning of the 1930's. The last of these, *The Grand Gennaro*, should unquestionably be considered one of the cornerstones of Italian emigration literature and one of the most convincing and absorbing narratives devoted to that epochal mass exodus. A work that is wide-ranging in scope, the culmination of unmistakable artistic maturity, *The Grand Gennaro* (published in 1935 by New York's Vanguard Press, publisher of Lapolla's two previous books) presents a powerful portrayal not only of the title's proletarian hero figure, but more generally of the entire local, domestic world of Southern Italy in its complex, troubled encounter with American modernity. The novel, which chronologically stands out as one of the earliest noteworthy endeavors in English originating within the Italian diaspora, may undoubtedly give the impression of looking backward in terms of narrative structure and writing style, relying on a realism that at times could actually be said to be of the late 19th century *Veristic* period; certainly not unusual in American literature, much less in those works that at the beginning of the century had to all intents and purposes launched an "ethnic" literature (one is reminded of an Abraham Cahan).

Although it did not pass unnoticed in the months immediately following its publication, *The Grand Gennaro* soon fell into oblivion. As mentioned in one of the rare pieces written about Lapolla, the novel of the Thirties had left behind that style of depicting the emigrant experience through broad "ghetto" frescos: after the pomp and splendor of the turn of the century, the so-called *immigrant ghetto fiction*, with its consequent linearity, its mixture of minute description of surroundings and lurid characterization, in short its Balzac-like approach, had been marginalized by a literary milieu that had, on the one hand, veered toward extreme experimentation and, on the other, justified its attention to social issues through increasingly distinct political positions.

The fully drawn character of Calabrian Gennaro "il Grande," a tragic protagonist, a typical "manly" figure like no other at the center of an epic tale of ascent and sudden downfall, could to a certain extent be considered anacronistic. Yet he would have risked being responsible for such a heavy, unanimous silence at all costs. It is necessary to call attention to him, though, since in fact in the aftermath of his greatest book, one that was more successful and more satisfying, Lapolla disappeared from the literary scene, though continuing his not insignificant publishing activities in the two specialized areas of textbooks and cookbooks. The scope of Lapolla's reception is still more amazing when observed from the viewpoint of Italian and Italian-American scholars: in Italy, unless I have missed something, the East Harlem novelist was mentioned only three times throughout the entire twentieth century. Nothing more, until the appearance in 2002 of the translation of an unpublished story, *La Ribellione di Millie* (Millie's Rebellion), as part of a small, precious volume of miscellaneous works edited by Francesco Durante.

The ways in which this hidden presence nevertheless manifested itself are instructive. In 1934, in Turin's newspaper "Gazzetta del Popolo," Giuseppe Prezzolini traces with absolute timeliness a very early panorama of Italian-American prose, emphasizing among other things its composite nature and strong autobiographic and commemorative foundation, well represented by the names of schoolteacher Angelo Patri and Ellis Island commissioner Edward Corsi. For narrative prose the names cited are those of Louis Forgione, one of the most notable Italian-American novelists writing in English in the Twenties, Bernardino Ciambelli, journalist and author of endless appendices, and, of greater prominence, Lapolla, at this stage still the author of only two books: *The Fire in the Flesh* (1931) and *Miss Rollins in Love* (1932). Even within the limits of such recognition, the choice of these names is sufficient to attest to Prezzolini's critical intelligence, were there a need to do so. That such clarity could later be distorted by a broader vision, in part prejudicial and in part dispositional, of an Italian culture outside its "natural" borders, is a discussion that for now would lead us far afield from *The Grand Gennaro* — up to a certain point, however, since Lapolla's name re-emerges in the *Trapiantati* (the Emigrants), the book that is the sum of Prezzolini's Italian-American diligence, this time linked to his masterpiece and earning only a dismissive mention.

Also associated with Prezzolini's name is the ground-breaking project brought to completion by his student Olga Peragallo (and following her death, by her mother Anita), who in the Forties compiled the first alphabetical index of Italian-American writers worthy of the name (in the overwhelming majority of cases, they were authors writing in the English language). Among the fifty-nine entries listed in this study, commendably positivistic for its exclusive attention to the facts, appears that of Garibaldi Lapolla, along with those of Mayor LaGuardia and Jerre Mangione (rediscovered in the Eighties by Sciascia, no less), names that at first glance might seem more prominent. And in the wake of Peragallo, with the rebirth of serious Italian-American scholarship beginning in the Seventies, others also at least indicated the existence of this work that had been rendered more visible meanwhile by the reprinting of *Fire in the Flesh* and *The Grand Gennaro* in 1975. Nevertheless, the few critical references made by *outsiders*, no matter how prestigious their names, do not seem to have encouraged a more long-lasting, contextualized interest. There are two notable exceptions: the pages devoted to Robert Orsi's best novel in 1985, within a broad ethnography of Italian Harlem, and several interpretive attempts by Robert Viscusi, who with remarkable critical intelligence emphasizes the mythical vividness of the Gennaro character. Among Italians, however, Alberto Traldi was essentially the only one to have shown any real interest, in 1976. But Traldi tends to observe emigration literature through the "lens" of contemporary journalistic criticism: the result is to diminish Lapolla's art, though he acknowledges the substance of the narrative and attentively traces its coordinates. In short, Lapolla remained unheard of, or nearly so, up until the above-mentioned, recent translation in Italian. And this while Italy, at least, experienced the rediscovery of John

Fante from the end of the Eighties and a rebirth of interest with respect to the history and culture of emigration.

But here we are back to where we started from, or almost. So let's adopt as our own the confident, though short-lived, judgment of the early Prezzolini, who spoke of the "power and ... keenness of the writer," and for a moment enter into Lapolla's fascinating creative workroom, conserved thanks to his wife's bequest to the Balch Institute, a center for ethnic studies in Philadelphia. Not a location chosen by chance, if we consider the fact that the rather numerous documents of an Italian-American colleague of Lapolla, Leonard Covello — an educator and sociologist, and a central figure of Italian Harlem — are also found there. Along with Covello, LaGuardia, Corsi and others, Lapolla was among the first descendants of Italian immigrants to emerge from the ghetto in every sense, and earn a higher education (in his case, a university degree) by attending courses at nearby Columbia University. Moreover the theme of education, of acculturation in an American sense and conquest of the citadel of New York knowledge, returns punctually in his three novels, and constitutes one of the pivotal points of the second, *Miss Rollins in Love*. Similarly, the main incidents of all three novels develop *roughly* in the forty year period ranging from the large migratory wave from Southern Italy in the 1890's to the crisis at the end of the Twenties and the closing of American borders to lower class peasants of Eastern and Mediterranean Europe, focusing on themes in the areas of family, work and education. Just so, their author, having landed in New York as an infant in 1890, almost the same year as the sons of Gennaro Accuci, earns his university degrees very early, in 1910-1912, and becomes part of the city's life by making a career in the academic world.

My intention is not, however, to trace a mechanical parallelism between the author's life and his works. At best what really matters is that the profile of a true writer emerges from his unpublished papers. Lapolla pursued the art of verse with perseverance and style, and left a considerable number of poetic endeavors that varied widely in meter and subject, often of such an expressive confidence as to make the output not at all casual. Such seriousness of creative intent is confirmed by the existence of seven short stories set for the most part in Little Italy, though they are far from having a purely descriptive appeal. Rather, in their concision, they are rich in dramatic moments and in views at odds with the current mentality (to summarize briefly: a brilliant clerical career suddenly ended by an inexplicable fatal attraction between a head clerk and an immature, disturbing young woman; the failure of a proxy wedding between two immigrants that actually results in infanticide caused by lack of attention and indifference; and so on).

The existence of another unpublished novel (or perhaps two) is particularly striking: namely *Jerry*, a book that unfolds through the interaction of fifty or so characters duly listed in an introductory outline. At the center of attention, as elsewhere in this narrative, are the youths from the East River ghetto: and among the most successful pages are those whose setting is not far off from that of *Call It Sleep* (the same river, a few miles further south; the same young men, having come there from the Jewish ghetto downtown; the same time frame, even with regard to composition and publication). In a couple of pages attached to typewritten manuscripts Lapolla proposes at least three different endings for a story that would bring his readers back to already familiar places and situations: a school for orphans and maladjusted youths (the Juvenile Protective Asylum) and a relationship that can be perceived as almost incestuous between a young man and his benefactress.

The world that we encounter in Lapolla's books and unpublished works is in large part one that is only apparently limited in its horizons, and that finds its justification, its etiology, in having abandoned the narrow, rural Italy of the South: an Italy dedicated to sheep-farming, its perspectives leveled by a subsistence economy, and suffocated by an atavistic respect for the customs and hierarchies that condition the relations between the sexes as well as social relations in general. That which results is the foundation, the κτίσις of the overseas colony, portrayed not only with skill and vividness, but, what's more important, with a very lucid, rigorous, layman's sense of its achievements and losses, its thousands of variations, contradictions and subtleties, its setbacks, its reversals (both geographic, as all the statistics on Italian emigration confirm, as well as emotional and irrational), and its unexpected turns, all portrayed on a canvas broad enough to take individual destinies into account. Lapolla leaves a powerful depiction of his own exodus, if you will, because he has the courage and feeling to go into personal details without hesitation: from the personal and the specific, he allows social issues to emerge.

From an outsider's standpoint, this is quite evident in his first two works, which at the time earned him the applause of a difficult Italian literary critic like Prezzolini, with definite, anti-rhetorical tastes: no small honor indeed. Looking back, thanks to a perspective made possible by the success of *The Grand Gennaro* and the consciousness of a not undistinguished production attested to by his unpublished writings, the first two works can only be considered as stages in his progressive literary development. Within the course taken by Lapolla, they perform the function of extensive sketches placed one on top of the other, in which the author lays out the figures and backgrounds to which he will give much greater prominence later on. Not that *The Fire in the Flesh* and *Miss Rollins in Love* are valuable solely as attempts or indefinite approximations: if anything, one notices a certain rigidity in them stemming from a desire to portray their respective themes with irrefutable clarity. Novels of ideas, starting with their titles that define and summarize, which for that matter is a characteristic they have in common with the linchpin of this narrative triad.

A triad, rather than a cycle: one of the more obvious constants in Lapolla's narrative is the almost identical repetition of novelistic measure, both in general results (the three novels essentially have the same number of pages), as well as in the articulation of an internal rhythm, dictated by brief numbered paragraphs. Here too, however, *The Grand Gennaro* appears more ambitious in its sturdy, three-part division (*Gennaro*; *Rosaria*; *Carmela*) that suggests the existence of a more solid vaulting over the tumult of events; by contrast, *The Fire in the Flesh* and *Miss Rollins in Love* had been split up into approximately twenty brief chapters, to the detriment of an overall epic effect.

But the point is that reading through the first two novels, it is not at all difficult to discover in them compositional elements of the third, with respect to situations, ideologies (both the author's and those of the depicted surroundings) and character profiles. In the first novel, *The Fire in the Flesh*, such parallelism is so strikingly obvious that one might easily get the impression of dealing with an exercise of variations on a theme. Certainly, from the lurid *incipit* it is clear that southern folklore and anthropology play a more direct role here than in *The Grand Gennaro*: the protagonist Agnese makes her appearance in the church of Villetto, and in front of the congregation, interrupts a Sunday Mass by accusing the priest, Father Gelsomino, of having abused her and of being the father of the child she holds in her arms. The original sin, or more mildly if you will, the misstep underlying the reparative flight to America, is portrayed in no uncertain terms. Everything turns not so much on the inevitability of that passion, but on the sensual charge of the young woman, to whom all the principal male figures (including, at a reasonable distance in years, her son) must yield. Once settled in Harlem, with a convenient husband, her father Gesualdo, a fiery brother always ready to defend her honor, and an introspective artist son, Agnese will know perfectly well how to control the "fire in the flesh" as required, and will look after herself and her men quite nicely. A gallery of main characters is launched, characterized by a striking, ardent sensuality and clear ideas, who find in America the only terrain suitable to make their personalities flourish. Without simplistic theologizing, but reckoning instead on human and material losses often endured by others (such as what happens to the splendid Carmela, Gennaro's second wife: raped as a young girl, as an adult she will give birth to a dead child and witness the violent end of her two husbands), as well as internally, when the internal coherence of the work requires it (this is the case with Amy Rollins, the psychologically tormented heroine of the second novel). Agnese and Carmela, both first generation Americans, atone for their own precocious carnality through a prolonged renunciation of true affections, rendered more problematic by the encounter with a new culture. Yet the period of deprivation is also a time of social maturing: they learn a trade and are proud of their own enterprise, while the maternal role, though always present, is experienced in bursts and frustrations, in a way that is very different from that of the mothers of the previous generation.

Everything in these novels proceeds from and continues to revolve continually around well defined nuclei: these strong, hot-blooded women attract both their male counterparts (that is, those who, though in difficulty, untiringly pursue their mission consistent with "making it in America," accumulating money and property or even merely maintaining their own distinct social status) as well as a heterogeneous group of those who are different. Among the latter are those who, on the one hand, delude themselves that they are able to preserve a shaky, petit-bourgeois identity in the

New World, often though not necessarily arriving at a painful undoing (they are figures of landlords and military men, priests and artists), and on the other, those who, experiencing for themselves the transition between first and second generations, seek new paths to success in America, counting above all on education and their own creativity. This makes for interesting openings toward worlds that are parallel to those of manual labor and domestic intimacy: primarily a university and scholastic environment (a choice also motivated by Lapolla's biography), both one of secular orientation, as well as that related to Protestant missionary efforts among a Catholic population prey to insecurities and troubled by vague desires for change. And alongside institutionalized instruction, the world of artistic apprenticeship: sculpture, painting, puppet theatre and female fashion. All of this, as may be easily understood, the result of Lapolla's intent to pay scrupulous attention to the facts of the surrounding reality: the role played by Methodist educators is very well documented in the colonies of Little Italy, along with that of the extremely active representatives of an artistic "middle class" that found not a few clients in the United States at that time.

Alongside or beneath the large group of main characters then lies a bustling understory with specific features that essentially guarantees both continuity and a relatively peaceful day to day life, as well as a more respectable induction into "affluent" American society. Here we have an entire series of mediation figures: from the more traditional figures of priests, landlords or "boarders," and numerous "aunts" busy feeding everyone and straightening up the rooms; to the more "modern" figures of teachers, instructors of some specific art, exceedingly American do-gooders or even directors of prison institutions.

The events narrated by Lapolla in a sweeping, expansive way are "small," meticulously individual incidents that rise to the level of typical case histories, representative in turn of a larger History, the dramatic culmination of a long period of social marginality and deprivation. For this reason, the two main agents of mediation between the individual and society can only be the home and family. Both are shown to be central to the development of the plots. Though they signify continuity of affections and preservation of customs, transplanted to such a different space-and-time, they also constitute a shell tendentially open to renewal. To reconstitute the family and make a new home across the ocean in itself meant having the ability to accumulate capital. And therefore, in perspective, the ability to invest: to invest in the building of new houses (the centrality of the construction trade in Italian-American society), to open the home to other individuals or families, and to expand therefore one's own contacts within the domestic walls themselves. All of this modified the internal arrangement of the traditional family even before young people became the bearers of new values; and herein lies the silent, poignant crisis of the wives-mothers who arrived from the Old World, often recalled after years of forced separation. Catarina in *The Fire in the Flesh*, Donna Angela in *Miss Rollins in Love*, Gennaro's wife Rosaria and many others: they are women who suffer from *maladjustment*, between angry outbursts and hypochondriacal mute spells, or who fade away in sorrow. Sometimes, as in Rosaria's case, by turning their back on America and choosing a return that is literally equivalent to death (the daughter Elena will repeat the mother's fate by becoming a nun in a Calabrian convent).

A destroyed Verghian lair, half a century away and a continent apart. But it is the dizzying energy of change that occupies the forefront, more than bitterness (though it too is present): from beginning to end the objective remains focused on the home or family ties, in order to recount the changes that, in the span of a generation, will give birth to a new type of humanity. As for what will follow, Lapolla will not want to, or will not think he is able to recount it with as much meaningfulness. This is not the southern Italy of *The Leopard* but one in which, in the end, nothing remains as it was, beyond "cues" of a sentimental, folkloristic nature, and in which everything changes for real. But is it really and simply America that causes everything to change?

One of the things about Lapolla that scandalized people, perhaps one of the reasons why he was so little understood and read, is the very fact that he did not take refuge in a comfortable anti-modernist, anti-American abhorrence in the name of popular, Catholic accord or of individualistic vitalism, as was not infrequent in authors close to him. Passages in which characters dialectically discuss the advantages and disadvantages, the miseries and splendors, respectively, of their home towns and a *'Merica* discovered through sacrifice are not rare; but the dialectic has no resolution, even if it is understood that to turn one's back on America, and go back to the Apennines, undermines the very reason for the story at its foundations, and jeopardizes not only the characters' destiny, but this literature itself. Lapolla is too human and too intelligent to suggest a historical-civil Manicheism. What makes the world go around, what brings about changes and transports families from one side of an ocean to another, is first and foremost the desire to put an end to poverty experienced as an unfathomable fate, and the equally insuppressible driving force of the senses. The first a masculine principle, the second feminine, though they are shared at times with different intensity by characters of both sexes: it is clear that these are the characters who really matter, the ones at the center of our attention and that of their author. Money and sex, to simplify further. These are the realities that, from one generation to another, from Calabria or Basilicata to Manhattan, challenge social conventions: especially that of marriages arranged by the family, forever bound to failure. On American soil, on the other hand, it was possible to start over again from zero, that is, very pragmatically without moral or material debts, as well as to marry by first of all heeding one's own intimate feelings.

The world of the past, that is the Old World, reacts by expressing an atavistic violence, counteracting the initiative for success with the blackmail and abuses of an old Mafia-type gangsterism (as in *The Fire in the Flesh*, where Agnese refuses to pay the protection money and sees the yards devastated by fire) and vindicating the role of honor and the use of force, knives included, against "free" unions based on passion. While pertaining to that world, Gennaro, though illiterate, is able to detach himself from it with full awareness: his novel originates as the result of a decision, formed in nearly total secrecy, to leave that world, explicitly rejecting the appeal of banditry. These and other ancestral traditions also function as the *deus ex machina* of a novelistic device that is ideologically courageous but not always immune to a certain predictability.

In any case, American modernity is not the deity solely responsible for this civil metamorphosis — a metamorphosis, among other things, that although tragic, appears inevitable to Lapolla and yet "progressive." America brings to fulfillment aspirations already present at the time of departure: this can be seen in those characters of a more solid mettle at least, while the fate of those transplanted against their will (wives and children) turns out to be much more unforeseeable.

The second novel, *Miss Rollins in Love*, is the exception that proves the rule. It is the most "topical" of Lapolla's books (roughly covering the period 1919-1932), in which the attempt to portray the popular epic of emigration is less all-encompassing. Italian Harlem plays a role through the figure of the young student Donato Contini, with whom a very American Amy Rollins, his teacher, falls in love. While it is true that Donato, the members of his troubled family and the world they incorporate constitute one of the two poles between which events shift, looking closely, it is the one that is least necessary and least felt.

In *Miss Rollins in Love* Lapolla shows that he is interested in capturing the psychology of the two main characters, but above all in tracing a vibrant, richly nuanced profile of an "average" heroine, a painstaking yet emotionally fragile teacher who is slow and undecided about opening herself up and giving herself to others. Amy's self-analysis pervades the novel from beginning to end, with a surprisingly explicit, at times nearly lewd, frankness that brings into focus a tangle of unresolved sexuality, fraught with renunciations, sacrifices and guilt feelings. Like the illegitimate son whose appearance in the final pages seems somewhat forced, her salvation stems from the handsome young Italian: Amy's internal torment, not to mention her difficulties in relationships (with colleagues and aspiring lovers), is resolved with full sensual satisfaction, at the same time succeeding in uniting the Old and New Worlds, art (Donato sets off to become a successful sculptor) and a bracing freedom of spirit (Amy, after a nervous breakdown and a teaching trip to Italy, will decide to move to New Mexico with her child, at that time already a refuge for artists and "non-conformists"). And yet, even this squaring of the circle confirms the nature, in its own way experimental, of the work in question, in which Lapolla, rigorously adopting a female and American (or let's say wasp, to simplify somewhat) point of view, recounts in an oblique way *the* story that constitutes the foundation of his narrative. Moreover, there are at least three other central themes dear to him that emerge, which Lapolla treats with sensitivity and the makings of a true novelist and creative prose writer: the insuppressible urgency of a loving, unreserved union that satisfies the sexual instinct above all; the modern problematics of teaching, caught between a true pedagogical vocation and the stagnant millstream of a grey, wretched non-career; and the eccentric dimension of a popular tradition that is glorious but perennially less important than that of the Sicilian puppet theatre. Even in *Miss Rollins in Love*, then, as had already happened in *The Fire in the Flesh*, Lapolla clearly "shows his hand." In the first novel he had stressed colors and *tableaux* of a late nineteenth century cast: a main theme à la *Cavalleria Rusticana*, the story of the ocean crossing, and the intense impact of the unprecedented sounds and spaces of Harlem. In the second effort, less restricted, more oscillating and bipolar, Lapolla's English advances toward the terrain of the irrational and psychological incoherence, attempting a *stream of consciousness* and several night "visions." In both cases, the narrator's attention, though in different ways and with different results, is consistently focused on the destiny of the female protagonists.

All the more mature and comprehensible is a novel like *The Grand Gennaro*, majestic in its way, when considered as the destination point of such a journey. To begin with, the "male" choice made here, at a distance of a few years, is equally determined: if it sacrifices (though only in part) the supporting female characters, it does so intentionally, precisely to be able to delve more deeply into the protagonist's situation in a more uninhibited way. From its *incipit*, *The Grand Gennaro* exhibits a narrative style that is fully confident in its methods: this is evident in the rigorous unilaterality of the adopted viewpoint, in the splendid straightforwardness of the author's voice, in the virtuoso orchestration of events and individual characters, and in the consistent choice of an "ethnic" inflection of the language (that of the narrator, with its circumlocutions and syntactically heavy English, as well as that of those of his characters who express themselves in *broken English*). The energy deriving from the protagonist, who oversees everything and towards whom everything converges, quickly penetrates the bloodstream of the story and sustains the narration. *The Grand Gennaro* is one of those novels that immediately wins over the reader, like a world apart that opens up, complete in itself and historically and geographically rooted (all the more so in its twofold nature, Italian and American); nearly organic, I would say, in its intense sensory charge that goes hand in hand with a psychological virtuosity applied to the "lower," uncultured strata of the population. Cohesion and consistency are among the first words that come to mind, not only to try to explain the coarse fascination of this work, but also to do justice to what was not a slapdash, accidental outcome, but the result of protracted, masterly effort.

In *The Grand Gennaro*, then, Lapolla includes with a precise sense of rhythm the characters, situations and broad themes that we have already talked about: all revolving around the *larger than life* figure of the *cafone* Gennaro Accuci, a Calabrian peasant from Capomonte, who emigrated from Reggio at age 32 in the early 1880's, and whose experiences we follow step by step through the two economic recessions of the early 1890's and 1907, the arrival of his wife and three children at Ellis Island around 1890, and the Spanish-American war of 1898 (that claimed the life of his oldest son in Cuba). Gennaro *makes it in America* and reaps success without letting himself be held back by scruples. He does so with pride, intelligence and an awareness of his limits, knowing how to hammer and push fortune: he deals in rags and discarded metal scraps that he collects, crushes and re-sells to Jewish wholesalers downtown; over the course of the years he perfects his trade, mechanizes the warehouse and makes it more efficient, and becomes a modest boss who has to answer to the union and meet the requirements of his employees. He starts out from zero in a rented room shared with other people, then with a violent ploy he steals control of operations from a fellow countryman, Rocco. But the injustice is only the initial spurt that allows him to complete the leap toward true entrepreneurship. Soon Gennaro invests in the real estate market, acquiring a small house that will become the center of romantic and family intrigues. Meanwhile he never stops adapting to technological progress: in the early days, he carries his merchandise, covering on foot the long miles that separate him from downtown; later on he uses horse-drawn wagons (the notorious, deafening elevated train of New York is reserved instead for individual transportation); by the end of the story, he supplies the company with motorized vans and electrical machinery, and allows himself the luxury of riding in a car. He is always looking ahead, works constantly, and never allows himself a break; what's more, even in his private life (though this is a distinction superimposed by us out of a need to analyze) he sweeps over everything, and tries to *do* and *undo* with his all-absorbing "masculine" energy. Success is not assured here however, on the contrary. The four women who share his journey in different ways prove this to be so with splendid humanity: Nuora, the northern Italian landlady, will follow her husband Bartolomeo in his return to the homeland. Dora Levin, the beautiful daughter of the Jewish merchant, boldly confesses her relations with younger men to Gennaro. His wife Rosaria, by coming to join him, only makes plain the unbridgeable distance between them, and after ten years of painful estrangement, shattered by her failure and by her firstborn's death, finds the strength to turn her back on Gennaro and America, and goes to live out her life in her native Calabria. And finally Carmela, who although she loves Gennaro dearly, is unable to give him a son, and indeed cannot resist a passion — though borne in silence, without betraying him — for his second born Emilio (a young, typical *second generation figure*). At different times, in different ways and for different reasons, all these women go away and leave Gennaro: nothing is stable, everything is mutable. But while this can be an incentive to progress in one's work and in society, it signifies loss, abandonment and solitude in the sphere of affections. Not surprisingly, at a certain point Gennaro will explore the path of prostitution with blind determination.

And the issue is not just one of erotic ties and domestic affections; interpersonal relations catalyzed by the two *avatars* of home and family reveal themselves to be equally problematic. Gennaro in fact forms a connection with the destinies of two other southern Italian families, the Dauri and the Monterano families: father, mother and numerous offspring engage Lapolla in additional efforts at characterization and plot (successful but undoubtedly laborious), and immobilize the protagonist in a generous but impossible inspection job. Beneficence succeeds if one's objectives are "traditional" and inanimate as it were: and here we have Gennaro allocating time and money in the construction of a church dedicated to the patron saint of his home town, Saint Elena. But inside the walls of the little house in Harlem, within which surge the lives of three families and dozens of individuals, an odd accumulation of affections and interests, time-honored and modern, it can only create imbalance, change and not a few tragedies (the Monterano couple will die, and the Dauri will decide to leave the city). So that one of the possible keys for reading the novel is one which underscores the generational and intrafamily contrasts between fathers and sons (Gennaro and Domenico, Gennaro and Emilio), or between mothers and daughters (Sofia and Carmela), with foreseeable supersensory interpretations of a psychological and social nature.

In any case, Gennaro is "grand" and a "man" even in his mistakes and defeats, such as the illusion of being able to maintain traditions in a totally changed context, or of being able to direct his passions toward assured, programmable goals. And naturally he is "grand" even in his death, which is both brutal and mechanical, bloody and silent, "deserved" but unexpected: after twenty years, his old co-worker Rocco takes his revenge for the abuse he suffered at the start of their career by harpooning him in the neck with one of the new hooks in operation at the modernized warehouse. Gennaro, like a head of cattle, dies on the spot, spilling his blood on the bales of rags on which his wealth was founded.

Such a tragic end with all of its suggestiveness marks the end of a sweeping life span that, to be convincing, had to attract other destinies and other stories during its course, committing to and being open to new prospects. This simplicity within complexity is one of the keys of the novel, and the element that, even at a first reading, makes it "grand" like its protagonist, all the more so after those that preceded it.

What's more, Lapolla builds up the coherence of the overall vision little by little, resorting to a series of effective stylistic constants. It is not only Gennaro's presence and the fascination radiating from his story that is convincing, but also the expressive maturity that has been attained. The *fresco* is painted with much greater assurance and fluidity with respect to the first two novels because the narrator has learned how to stand aside when required, letting the words of his characters "act on their own" and making objects "speak." In this way the social portrayal gains immediacy and displays the elegance of a "guided" improvisation, one that is planned rather than extemporaneous. At the same time, thanks to a convincing use of language, it is as persuasive as something "fully formed," like an instantaneous event we see happening before our eyes.

Of great effect, for example, is the precision with which Lapolla "disconnects" one scene from another, especially when dealing with irreversible, epochal changes in his characters' lives. These can certainly be foreseen and imagined by the reader, but they are not presented and prepared for in the narration, which tends to reveal them suddenly, in all their harshness. Gennaro knows that his wife Rosaria and their three children are finally arriving after a wait of nearly ten years; he arranges their journey, and talks about it with his friends. Meanwhile nothing is said to us about what is happening in Calabria. Then, all of a sudden: "Rosaria had landed. Gennaro first saw her through a grilled fence in the new immigrant station at Ellis Island" (94). A remark that is all the more powerful in that Lapolla deliberately "buries" it in the middle of a long paragraph, without giving it any importance. The arrival of Don Tomaso Dauri and his family later on is treated similarly: this time the personal and economic reasons governing their departure are being discussed when, all at once, in the New World, comes the impact of reality and the unexpected end of illusions: "In New York he discovered very soon that the several thousand *scuti* he had realized on the sale of his possessions were not going to last any length of time" (123). More generally speaking, it is the appearance and vicissitudes of the Monterano and Dauri families within Gennaro's "peripeteia" that have a disconcertingly fulminating effect: as though the nature of that "narrow" micro-community of three nuclei in the neighborhood was marked by a violent, unintentional destiny.

This is a world in which the materiality of existence leaps into the very forefront. Often, relationships between individuals are rendered explicit through the mediation of objects, and it may even be said that Lapolla's narrative style, late-Balzachian as it is, is all the more so to the extent that it relies on objective correlatives. The entire memorable scene of the end of Gennaro's relationship with the young woman Dora Levin revolves around mumbled words and a few "things" — a hat, a hair pin, a defective gas lamp — that slow down the verbal exchange and add a note of tension (67-68). Even more significant are the two gold earrings handed down from father to son and finally to Gennaro, that from beginning to end contain intensely within themselves the attachment to roots, the character's pride and — after a violent, unforeseen act forces him to part with them — his awareness of the distance he has come and of the metamorphosis and Americanization that has taken place. The earrings will re-emerge in explicit form as the talisman-charm that Carmela gives to the last of the Accuci, Emilio.

Things but also, even more so, words. In *The Grand Gennaro* much occurs in the degree to which something is said, articulated, during the frequent dialogues between the characters. Verbal exchanges that, given the social standing of the characters, are for the most part quick and essential, almost stichometrical. Dialogues abound, but real, full-fledged conversations are scarce. The tensions between the characters are all "told," expressed; but for the most part the task of reconstructing the psychological dynamics underlying them is left to the reader. Notable also is the presence (of no minor importance) of a middle zone between external, third person narration and copious recourse to direct discourse. We might call it the "Verghian zone" of *The Grand Gennaro*, in which the discourse slips naturally from the narrator's consciousness to the thoughts and feelings of the characters, leading to fragments of interior monologue and unrestrained indirect discourse. So it is in the following passage, where the focus is on Rosaria's state of mind as she proposes to take her firstborn Domenico's side against her husband and Carmela's mother (Domenico is Carmela's rapist and as such forced to "make amends" by marriage): "His mother had gone shopping deliberately. She had for the first time summoned enough courage to offer some kind of opposition to the dictates of her husband. She had spoken against the enforced marriage. Let women keep their daughters home. It was, after all, the mother's fault. Oh, Domenico had really done no harm. Certainly, it might have been a vicious attack. He had intended all the harm there could be, of course, of course. They were both young, however, babies both. To pummel the lad, beat him into a whimpering pitiful animal crying out for mercy — what for?" (149).

Thanks to stratagems of this type, even characters on the brink of literacy, or unquestionably below the threshold, receive full dignity precisely because their intentions have a way of being expressed without always having to resort to the intermediation of the omniscient narrator. Moreover, they are figures who are themselves fully conscious of what they are doing, as well as being aware of their historical condition. The events of time shape their journey and change its features: the failure of the Bank of Naples, the memories of Garibaldi (the hero of the Two Worlds, not our author) wounded at Aspromonte, the echoes of the defeat of Adua, the invasion of Cuba.

The Grand Gennaro, perhaps like no other work emerging from the culture of the Great Migration, rests solidly on two feet, from the Mediterranean to the Atlantic. That was not the case with the serial novels produced in Italian in previous years; nor would it occur later on, not even with the finer names (Fante, di Donato, Mangione, Pagano, D'Agostino) whose Italian origins were taken for granted, a feature of their own diversity within a culture that was now different, in which one had in fact been included. For Lapolla, and for the "grand" Gennaro, on the other hand, Italy (Calabria, the "paese") is *close by*. First of all because it represents the goal of returning for many of his characters; not only that, but all of those who broke away from it *know precisely what it is*. They know it with passion: they suffer their origin; all of their actions are a direct, explicit consequence of it. Theirs is a nation that was newly created at the end of the nineteenth century, that has behind it a culture and deeply rooted customs: pizza, yes, arranged marriages, and devotion to patron saints; but also Dante, Leopardi, Manzoni, Giusti, remembered and read deliberately, not as mere ennobling labels. Italy here is not a nostalgic background, an empty cause for pride (and if it is, it is challenged and ridiculed as such): rather it is an ever present foundation, even at a distance. From it, certainly, come contradictions and suffering: but also the potential for tragedy and heroism, resulting from a fractured identity that we observe in its making and unmaking, in its continual, day to day renegotiation. Profound reasons — artistic, historical, and cultural — that seem to compel a serious reading of this masterpiece and the discovery of its author.

Translation by Anne Milano Appel

[1] Mario Garibaldino Lapolla, as recorded in the municipal birth records, was born on April 5, the son of Biagio Oreste, "age 31, occupation café owner" and Maria Nicola Buonvicino. He emigrated to the United States with his family at only two years of age, in 1890. The Lapollas settled almost immediately in the Italian section of East Harlem that is the setting for all of the author's novels. The variant "Marto," adopted as a middle name, is to be considered an editorial *lapsus calami*. The few biographical facts come in part from the documents of the Lapolla archives preserved at the Balch Institute in Philadelphia, and in part from the home town municipality thanks to the courtesy of Donato Rapone; among printed sources, Peragallo and Durante (see Bibliography under *La Ribellione di Millie* — Millie's Rebellion) provide the main outlines. My thanks to Salvatore Salerno and Beagan Wilcox for their assistance in retrieving materials.

[2] It quickly received favorable mention, for example, in the columns of the "New York Times" (by Fred T. Marsh, "'*The Grand Gennaro' and Some Other Recent Works of Fiction*," The New York Times, September 1, 1935), and of the "New Republic" (by a friend such as Jerre Mangione, "'*The Grand Gennaro,' by Garibaldi M. Lapolla*," The New Republic, October 23, 1935).

[3] Thus in part argues Richard A. Meckel, "*A Reconsideration: The Not So Fundamental Sociology of Garibaldi Marto Lapolla*," MELUS 14, Nos. 3-4, Fall-Winter 1987, 127-28 and 138. With regard to political commitment, it is well to recall that in

New York Lapolla, at the height of his most prolific season as a novelist, was a front line militant of the Socialist Party (Elisabetta Vezzosi, *Il socialismo indifferente. Immigrati italiani e Socialist Party negli Stati Uniti del primo Novecento* [Indifferent Socialism. Italian Immigrants and the Socialist Party in the United States in the Early Twentieth Century], Rome: Edizioni Lavoro, 1991, 182).

[4] Between 1929 and 1943 Lapolla authored a series of anthologies and English grammar texts for use in the schools (he was a teacher and principal his entire life, in Manhattan and Brooklyn), and the year before his disappearance from the literary scene, he wrote two cookbooks that were not without interest precisely because of their "ethnic" nature (imagine a title as suggestive as *Italian Cooking for the American Kitchen*). It would not be totally pointless to mention here that, after the studies by Franco La Cecla and Donna Gabaccia, *The Fire in the Flesh*, of 1931, contains, for example, what is perhaps one of the earliest descriptions of pizza (in italics in the text as well) in the United States: "a dough-cake flattened out and spread with anchovies, slices of tomato, and cheese, all seasoned spicily and baked on hot ashes" (67). More generally speaking, it is now possible to profitably place Lapolla's activity within the framework of a social history of Italian-American food: Simone Cinotto, *Una famiglia che mangia insieme. Cibo ed etnicità nella comunità italoamericana di New York, 1920-1940* (A Family That Eats Together. Food and Ethnicity in the Italian-American Community of New York, 1920-1940), Turin: Otto, 2001.

[5] Mere mentions, more frequent from the 1990's on, in the more important historiographic studies on Italian-American issues, both in Italy and in the United States.

[6] We possess three typewritten versions of *Jerry*, drafted between 1941 and 1954 (the one which appears most complete consists of 115 pages), and a manuscript contained in eighteen notebooks: the first eleven bearing the title *The Light That Never Was*, the last seven a different title: *The Journey Homeward.*

[7] And that's not all. The archival documents contain, among other things, the typescripts of three theatrical works, part of the correspondence, and the most interesting testimonies regarding the profession of educator.

[8] Thus, in those years, he replied to his sociologist friend Covello with the full awareness of experience: "You ask me to send you my manuscript of the novel I have been fortunate enough to find a publisher for and lo and behold you want it merely for a sociological document. Well, it ain't such a beast. It is just a yarn that happens to have the Italians living in Harlem doing a lot of things which they should not do and some they cannot help doing, and I am afraid of no more sociological interest than the numerous flies and bugs that infest Little Italy" (letter dated October 22, 1930, Balch Institute, Philadelphia). Lapolla is referring to his first novel, *The Fire in the Flesh.*

[9] Lapolla puts in the mouth of this minor, but very well delineated, male character the most explicit condemnation of a society, like that of the United States, in which everything "seems upside down and crazy," in contrast to another in which "everyone knows his place and things are orderly and decent" (37): for this reason too, the choice

of name makes one think of homage paid to one of two martyrs of working-class Italy, the Piedmontese Bartolomeo Vanzetti.

[10] "But he, he, the grand Gennaro, he had become a somebody [...] And now that he had as his own such an accumulation that would put to shame the holdings of the baron of his Calabrian countryside, he, Gennaro Accuci, by his own right, was not Gennaro Accuci who had the farm at the foot of the hillslope but just plainly Gennaro Accuci, a man" (98): where it is hardly worthwhile to point out the absolutely predominant position of the name and pronoun that form a whole with the iteration of his successes. Further on, the positive nature of the impression will begin to crumble: but not the identity of the person.

Works Cited

The Fire in the Flesh. New York: Arno Press, 1975 (anastatic reprint of the edition: New York: Vanguard Press, 1931).

Miss Rollins in Love. New York: Vanguard Press, 1932.

The Grand Gennaro. New York: Arno Press, 1975 (anastatic reprint of the edition: New York: Vanguard Press, 1935).

La Ribellione di Millie (Millie's Rebellion), in *Figli di Due Mondi* (Children of Two Worlds). *Fante, Di Donato & C. Narratori italoamericani degli annia '30 e a '40* (Italian-American Novelists of the '30's and '40's), ed. by Francesco Durante. Cava de' Tirreni: Avagliano, 2002.

Archival Material

Garibaldi Mario Lapolla Papers 1930-1976, Mss. Group 64, The Balch Institute for Ethnic Studies, Philadelphia.

Critical Works

Oliver, J. Lawrence, "'*Great Equalizer*' or '*Cruel Stepmother*'? *Image of the School in Italian-American Literature*," The Journal of Ethnic Studies 15, No. 2, Summer 1987.

_____. "*Beyond Ethnicity: Portraits of the Italian-American Artist in Garibaldi Lapolla's Novels*," American Studies 28, No. 2, Fall 1987.

Orsi, Robert Anthony. *The Madonna of 115th Street. Faith and Community in Italian Harlem, 1880-1950.* New Haven and London: Yale University Press, 1985.

Peragallo, Olga. *Italian-American Authors and Their Contribution to American Literature*, ed. By Anita Peragallo. New York: S.F. Vanni, 1949.

Prezzolini, Giuseppe. "*Stati Uniti: autobiografia e romanzo*" (United States: Autobiography and the Novel), Gazzetta del Popolo, December 19, 1934.

_______. *I trapiantati* (The Emigrants). Milan: Longanesi, 1963.

Rouge, Jean Robert. *Les Métamorphoses de l'espace ou l'espace récuperé dans The Grand Gennaro*, in Jean Beranger - Jean Cazemajou - Jean-Michel Lacroix - Pierre Spriet, *Multilinguisme et multiculturalisme en Amérique du Nord: Espace seuils limites*. Talence: Presse Universitaire de Bordeaux, 1990.

_____. "*Una Tragedie à l'italienne ou la resistance du moi dans The Fire in the Flesh de G. Lapolla*," Annales du Centre de Recherches sur l'Amérique Anglophone 17, 1992.

Traldi, Alberto, "*La tematica dell'emigrazione nella narrativa italo-americana*" (The Theme of Emigration in Italian-American Fiction), Comunità 30, August 1976.

Viscusi, Robert, "*The Text in the Dust: Writing Italy across America*," Studi Emigrazione 19, No. 65, March 1982.

_____. "*Il Caso della Casa: Stories of Houses in Italian America*" (The Case of the House...), in Richard N. Juliani, ed. *The Family and Community Life of Italian Americans*. Staten Island, NY: American Italian Historical Association, 1983.

"*Gli dei: l'allegoria dell'America italiana*" (The Gods: The Allegory of Italian America), in Ignazio Baldelli and Bianca Maria Da Rif (eds.), *Lingua e letteratura italiana nel mondo oggi* (Italian Language and Literature in the World Today). Florence: Olschki, 1991.

FROM "ITALIANO 2000" TO THE PERMANENT LINGUISTIC OBSERVATORY FOR ITALIAN DIFFUSED AMONG FOREIGNERS AND IMMIGRANTS

Massimo Vedovelli and Monica Barni
Università per Stranieri di Siena

---

1. Objectives

The main objective of our contribution is to present some important aspects of the current situation of the Italian language diffused among foreigners by referring to some recent initiatives such as the research project *Italiano 2000* and the work done by the center for advanced studies known as the *Osservatorio Linguistico Permanente dell'Italiano diffuso fra Stranieri e delle Lingue Immigrate in Italia* housed at the University for Foreigners in Siena. Data found in these sources enable us to get a general picture of the status of the Italian language worldwide, including the specific condition of Italian in North America. These initiatives, promoted by several Italian governmental agencies, are designed to analyze the contemporary dynamics of the diffusion of our language among foreigners. In the case of CILS (Certification of Italian as Foreign Language), given its pedagogical and linguistic mission, has been able to gather data and information that puts it in a privileged position in the process of identifying trends affecting the current status of the Italian language in the world.

Italiano 2000, a research project sponsored by the Ministry of Foreign Affairs (*Ufficio I, Direzione Generale per la Promozione e la Cooperazione Culturale*) was assigned to the Department of Linguistics and Literary Studies at the University of Rome "La Sapienza." The project director, Tullio De Mauro, was assisted by a team of researchers and faculty from the University for Foreigners in Siena: Massimo Vedovelli, Monica Barni, Lorenzo Miraglia. The research took place between July 2000 and July 2001 and its findings are contained in Tullio De Mauro, et al, *Italiano 2000: Indagine sulle motivazioni e sui pubblici dell'italiano nel mondo* (Roma: Bulzoni, 2003).

The *Osservatorio Linguistico Permanente dell'Italiano Diffuso fra Stranieri e delle Lingue Immigrate in Italia* is a center for advanced studies established in 2000 by the University for Foreigners in Siena and funded by the *Ministero dell'Università*. Out of twenty-three centers for advanced studies applying for funds to pursue research using innovative technologies as applied to human science the Sienese proposal was selected for funding alongside another proposal by the University of Perugia to create a computerized catalog of artifacts damaged by earthquake. These are the only two projects funded in the humanities. The Ministry's decision to fund two centers for advanced studies in the so-called 'soft science' area was criticized by some representatives of the hard sciences. (This reflects an ongoing debate about what constitutes scientific research, a topic discussed by Carlo Bernardini and Tullio Mauro in *Contare e raccontare. Dialogo sulle due culture*, Roma, Laterza, 2003.)

The various sources used in our study enable us to examine the subject of our investigation through a methodology of 'triangularization' that makes it possible to explain the complex phenomena of changes in linguistic identity by drawing parallels with concurrent changes in Italian society over the last ten years. A true linguistic revolution that affects the status and public image of the Italian language has taken place both within Italy itself as well as beyond its national borders. (We do not intend to describe the situation of the Italian language in North America since most of the conference speakers will be dealing with this theme. No one knows this situation better than they do.) The goal of our investigation is to try to put this in a global context in order to adopt a systemic method of identifying specific characteristics determined by an interplay of complex factors. By using different points of view, we can elaborate a theoretical model suitable for examining empirical data. The point of departure of our presentation is to define as clearly as possible a theoretical model that will enable us to clarify the current worldwide status of the Italian language (henceforth referred to as *L2*).

2. *A theoretical model*

2.1 *The conceptual frame of reference*

The main intent of *Italiano 2000* is to place complex aspects and problems of a language with international diffusion — such as Italian — within a single interpretive framework. To reach this objective, we did not limit ourselves to simply acknowledge the status of Italian language spoken by foreigners (*L2*) through quantitative analyses (e.g., statistics) and qualitative analyses (e.g., linguistic/glottodidactic) of social and cultural processes. We had to refer to an adequate theoretical model that resulted from a combination of other examples in different areas of research. The intrinsic bond between language and culture makes it difficult to determine which area our research should address. Since the two are intertwined, our investigation had to be oriented toward cultural phenomena that become concrete through a process of linguistic codification. In other words, we entered the realm of semiotics, dealing with issues such as the production of meaning and the creation of modes of identity. To answer the question of what the future of L2 will be, we utilized the instruments, methodology and interpretative models of semiotics. Among the language sciences, socio-linguistics has been our point of reference both at the conceptual and methodological levels. We have placed the investigation of *Italiano 2000* within the field of socio-linguistic sciences, looking for models and methods suitable to our objectives. This choice is motivated by the fact that the relationship between language and its political dimension has become the subject of an area of socio-linguistic research known as linguistic politics. The socio-linguistic perspective enabled us to reconcile quantitative and qualitative analyses in a manner suitable to this initiative, even though most socio-linguistic research in Italy has focused on problems of teaching and learning Italian as this was of interest to the governmental agencies that sponsored the research.

Theoretical models, far from being reduced to formalized structures, often make use of metaphor in order to define themselves. In the model used for *Italiano 2000*, we applied three guiding concepts: the sistema Italia, social usefulness, and the language market. The choice of these three elements has been dictated by an awareness that, in order to define the conditions of L2, it is not enough to consider merely the linguistic aspect. Using concepts drawn from other sectors allowed us to construct a framework which, thanks to the interaction among its own elements, enabled us to develop hypotheses necessary for the pursuit of research on L2.

2.2 *Sistema Italia*

In recent years *sistema Italia*, a popular and somewhat chauvinistic concept, presents a positive non-critical image of today's Italy. In our opinion, this reinforces the need to develop a systemic view of how the interrelationship among economic, political, social and cultural factors can affect a language's capacity to appeal to foreigners. By examining the link between language and culture, we can assume that any change in these sectors will affect the status of the Italian language around the world.

2.3 *The social usefulness of languages*

An incentive to study a foreign language is its usefulness, either as a means of everyday social communication or as means of personal cultural enrichment. In the first case, there several important factors: the presence of speakers of a foreign language in the community with whom there is a high probability of engaging in some form of conversation; the ability of native speakers to communicate in an alternate language; the desire to establish relationships with business partners whose native language is used in commercial transactions; the marketing or trade of merchandise associated with a specific language or cultural group.

With regard to the number of native speakers, Italian language ranks nineteenth in the world with about 70 million speakers, according to an estimate made by Philip Baker and John Eversley, Multilingual Capital, London, Battlebridge Publication, 2000. This situation is the result of increased mobility of Italians through emigration as well as tourism. In view of Italy's productivity and the fact that it is one of the most industrialized countries in the world, more interaction with native speakers of Italian is inevitable, even though the international language of business is English. In fact, in certain sectors, such as food and wine, Italian is used as a means of communication with many Italian words and phrases becoming part of an international lexicon. The social usefulness of a language refers to social interactions and intercultural exchanges which motivates foreigners to choose which language to study.

2.4 *The language market*

The third and most controversial element of the model is the term 'language market' as if the word market used metaphorically pollutes the purity of ideas and therefore does not belong in intellectual humanistic circles. However, the expression 'language market' is used more frequently especially in relation to languages with an international diffusion. For instance, the term used by Louis-Jean Calvet is le marche aux langues (in Marche aux langues, Paris, Plon,200) which has a pejorative connotation. By *mercato delle lingue* we mean the process through which the study of a language by foreigners spreads internationally. This is the result not only of the intrinsic semiotic identity of the language itself, but also from the convergence of the social dynamics of its native speakers, the role played by governmental agencies in language promotion, and the ability of a society to project its own cultural image as being successful and prestigious to the international community. The language market, therefore, reveals the non-neutrality of the process of the international diffusion of language and how much it depends on non-linguistic considerations. Indeed, any social-cultural-language system that becomes popular does so only when it succeeds in representing something deserving respect and admiration.

The *mercato delle lingue*, thus, becomes a metaphor for the capacity of a society's value system to appeal to foreigners. The attractiveness of a language depends on the socio-economic and cultural system of which it is the vehicle. As we have indicated above, though in terms of the number of native speakers, Italian ranks 19th in the world, it is the fourth or fifth language studied by foreigners: from the USA to the UK, from Japan to the Mediterranean and Eastern Europe. The popularity of Italian obliges us to reassess its position in the world market of languages.

With the term *mercato delle lingue* we are not referring exclusively to the cultural industry which is concerned with the dissemination of languages in the form of publishing and multimedia for pedagogical use. This component plays a considerable role in the diffusion of a language, since it enhances its appeal by contributing to its image. In research done in connection with *Italiano 2000*, however, we have not used the metaphor of the language market in this sense; we only cite it in order to explain phenomena that characterize Italian whenever comparing it with other internationally diffused languages. Using the term, the language market, in a metaphorical sense, allows us to develop a sort of systemic vision that encompasses the dynamic dialectic among various languages as well as linking language with socio-economic factors and values within a language community. This process, however, requires clarification. The notion of language market can appear simplistic when one tries to explain linguistic discourse by means of the logic and criteria of market economy. Cultural dimensions are intrinsic to language because language enables us to communicate in a creative mode. Individuals and communities find identity, that is, their cultural essence, above all, in the structure and use of their own language. Were we to reflect on all the intellectual activities organized by means of language, it would become difficult to apply an economic perspective. We should be careful about using the market metaphor, particularly at this point in time when economics seems to be the sole criteria by which everything, including cultural and intellectual processes are measured. Concepts of diversification and variation of cultural values associated with a language seem less important than the concept of mass homogeneity which aims at justifying the worldwide diffusion of a handful of languages for purely pragmatic reasons. The tendency — favored by many — of abandoning minority language in favor of adapting a global language system can be justified by the fact that the popularity of a language increases in proportion to the economic and political stature of the social values of its speakers. Such an approach primarily values the communicative function of the language (what one needs to communicate) rather than the language as an means of self-expression and cultural identity.

The condition of Italian L2 has some things in common with open-air markets and country fairs. This is a place where buyers and converge. The vendors boast about the quality of their beautifully displayed merchandise arranged in such a way on carts to catch the attention of buyers. Price is not important. What counts are the products' appeal to the public and the rapport between buyer and seller; impulse, personal preference or advertising can stimulate as much motivation as genuine need. All these factors combine to guide buyers in choosing which products the would like to purchase. In the spirit of competition, each seller presents his products in the most attractive way possible way in order to make the most profit and tries to persuade buyers that his beautifully displayed merchandise is the best, which requires establishing rapport with the buyer. A similar situation exists in today's language market. Each language strives to gain popularity with the public by stressing its utility and importance. In the competition among languages of international diffusion, the selling point is that knowledge of one or two languages benefits both individual and society and that a certain language has become indispensable for recreational and business travelers. Sellers — that is, the combined social, productive, cultural and educational systems — propose a language to foreigners who are the potential buyers of linguistic competence and cultural forms. Language, therefore becomes a sort of commercial product, the virtues of which are exalted to a sector of the public that has been identified as potentially responsive to that language due to contact with some aspect of the socioeconomic system.

The language as merchandise is often evaluated by the potential buyer in terms of how it might benefit his or her personal or social life and the pleasure he or she would feel when in contact with that culture. Language can also be viewed as a professional investment which would allow a more systematic contact with the community of its users. Also, language may provide access to additional markets by facilitating contact with other foreigners through the medium of the acquired language as a lingua franca. The metaphor of the language market may appear colorful and exotic, but, in reality, the mechanism of the diffusion of languages depends on economic competition. Industrial and cultural institutions, supported by governments, are heavily involved in the dissemination of language and culture. The more a society prospers economically, the more its language expands. The extent of the diffusion of a language is a correlation of the economic, social and cultural power of the society of its native speakers.

If we wish to apply the metaphor of the market to the Italian language, we have to ask, what values are involved and what accounts for its attractiveness? Let us use the word *ricchezza* — "richness"— to describe the main attraction of Italian. *Ricchezza* signifies an economic and cultural value associated with a specific language. By applying the metaphor of the market to L2 in the research project *Italiano 2000*, we hope to verify if, and to what extent, Italian operates within the global competition of languages (in reality a sisterly competition of cultural and socio-economic competition). What are the chances of having a non-marginal presence in this market? Furthermore, what tangible and intangible aspects form the basis for our presentation to foreigners?

3. *The cultural and economic appeal of Italian*

One aspect that seems particularly decisive is the concept of *attrattività*. What makes Italian attractive to a foreigner? Why induces him/her to study it? What are the various characteristics of attraction present in our language as diffused among foreigners?

The attraction of a language seems to depend on its ties with the entire system of its society. The stronger it is in all its components, the more a language becomes the object of attention on the part of foreigners. The appeal of Italian derives from the *sistema Italia*, that is Italy's productive system, cultural tradition, social assets, capacity to project values that transcend national borders. From this point of view, Italian, like all other languages, is sensitive to changes within these non-linguistic factors. If these factors form a compact system balanced by structural mechanisms, the negative impact of some degree of changes will have no significant impact. In regard to the Italian language, per se and its connection with the *sistema Italia*, there are three types of attractive features: a) an ancient cultural and intellectual tradition; b) contemporary economic productivity, culture and society; c) mobility and migration of Italians around the world. Our thesis is all three dimensions are dominated by another economic consideration that forces us to reassess the way Italian becomes diffused by among foreigners.

3.1 *The intellectual tradition*

The Italian intellectual, literary, artistic and musical tradition establishes its own distinct cultural identity. It is immediately perceived by foreigners as representing a homogeneous and attractive entity. It goes without saying that this heritage is held in extraordinarily high esteem by foreigners. If we dedicate so little space to this fact, it is only because we prefer to analyze more recent factors determining the presence of Italian in the world market of languages.

3.2 *The image of contemporary Italian society*

A highly productive system has made Italy one of the most industrialized countries in the world. In terms of international economic and cultural stature, what is more important is Italy's specialization in products of extraordinary aesthetic quality such as design and fashion. Other strong features are in Italian achievements in sports such as soccer and car racing. Phenomena such as these, have given the Italian language a great deal of international appeal and help reinforce Italy's place within an international system of economic competition by producing enormous wealth. Well-crafted Italian made exports, furthermore, project an image of Italian society as being innovative and creative yet rooted in tradition.

3.3 *Migration*

Due to immigration, foreigners can observe a version of Italian even though dialects are most often spoken by the majority of immigrants. At this time, we do not wish to summarize the linguistic history of Italian emigration abroad, but would rather consider it as a component of the identity of

Italian language and culture within the language market. The appeal of Italian to foreigners has gone through — and continues to goes through — the evolution of identity systems of immigrant communities which can be vehicles for transmitting our language as well as representing our society abroad.

4. *The status of Italian in the world*

4.1 *Indications and partial signs of change in the condition of Italian in the world*

What has sustained the research project known as *Italiano 2000* is a collection of indexes and partial data that, though inextricably interrelated, sheds light on the origins of the profound changes in the condition of Italian L2. Over the last few years, a considerable number of foreigners, mostly adults, have studied Italian. This is demonstrated by research carried out by Ignazio Baldelli at the end of the 70's as commissioned by the Ministry of Foreign Affairs (Ignazio Baldelli, *La lingua italiana nel mondo. Indagine sulle motivazioni allo studio dell'italiano*. Roma. Istituto per l'Enciclopedia Italiana, 1987)

Baldelli's study is the most extensive research done on the study of Italian abroad. We used it as a point of reference in our study due to its abundance of information on the subject; however, the conclusions Baldelli reached are quite different from those of today due to a series of changes that began in the late 70's. Ten years later came an extensive governmental research project regarding incentives for studying Italian. The data are well known. My personal observation is that at that time we were all caught by surprise, not only for the abundance of data but also by the fact that such vast and systematic research was funded and carried out by our political institutions. This conference brought together political figures, teachers, industry and labor union leaders as well as representatives of cultural institutions. This was the first post-war opportunity to examine the status of the Italian language abroad and what strategies should be adapted to manage it. It should be remembered that in the field of linguistic research, there were only a few previous conveyances such as the one organized by the *Società di Linguistica Italiana* in 1970 (see, Mario Medici et al. *L'insegnamento dell'italiano in Italia e all'estero*. Roma, Bulzoni, 1971).

Baldelli's research revealed that a considerable number of people — over two million — were studying Italian that year. This number was so impressive that it changed the attitudes of our political leaders towards the Italian language which up to that point, was considered of only interest to academics. At the end of the 70s, Italian appeared to be sought after and studied perhaps not as much as English or French, but enough to place it among the top languages with international diffusion. Our point of view is that Baldelli's research was pivotal in marking the end of an era and beginning a new period in which strategies for future language promotion would begin. New global reality changed the relationship among languages with international diffusion.

5. *Italiano 2000*

5.1 *The results of Italiano 2000*

The first quantitative data to which we want to call attention is the increase in the number of students attending Italian courses offered by the Italian Cultural Institute (IIC) in 2000 by comparing this figures with the data from 1995. According to *Italiano 2000*, in 1995 there were 33,065 students enrolled in Italian courses, while, in 2000 the number was, 45, 699, a difference of 12,634 (38.2%)

[Chart No. 1: Students enrolled in IIC courses]

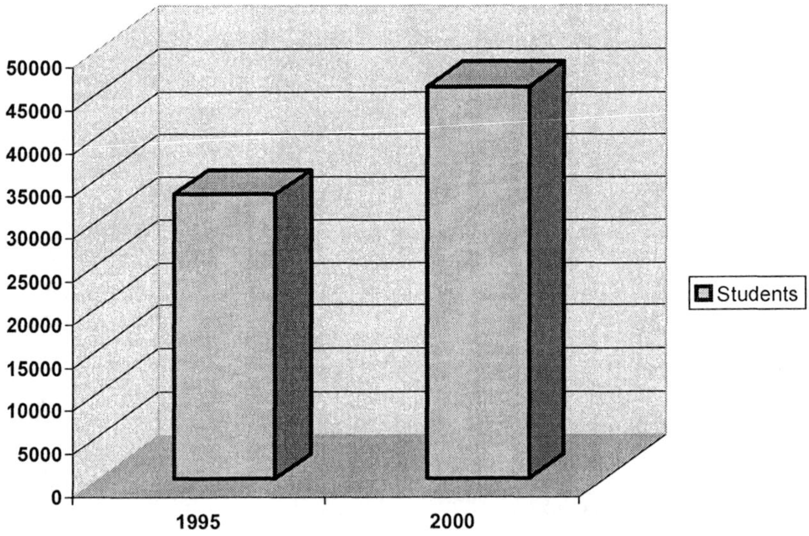

This is significant, because it means that the *sistema Italia* (language-culture-society) associated with the IIC became an increasingly attractive feature of the language. We have to ask if the IIC compares with other cultural organizations that offer Italian courses such as Italian private schools and *Società Dante Alighieri*. Data provided by the *Società Dante Alighieri* (1999) show an increase in their enrollment as well. More Italian private schools are also being established in many countries. In the United States of America, a recent survey (Lebano 1999) shows that Italian is the fourth language taught at the college level with an increase of 12.6% between 1995 to 1998. The survey also contains additional data of interest: the majority of students studying Italian are not descendants of Italian immigrants, but are mostly non-Italian in origin: (61% vs 39%)

5.2 *A first hypothesis*

The results of Italiano 2000 lead us to believe that the late 90's were marked by an radical increase in demand for Italian as a language of instruction. The cause of its increasing popularity can be explained by the way foreigners relate to the *sistema Italia* which, taken together with cultural programs offered by the ICI, form a new image of Italy. We could say that the *sistema Italia* has been successful in the sense that the traditional appeal of our language combined with new socio-economic and cultural factors have become stronger determinants when foreigners select a language for professional advancement.

5.3 *North America*

The data for North America provided by Italian 2000 shows increased enrollment in five out of seven IIC programs. Thus, there is a trend toward an increase of Italian as a subject of learning in the overall network of cultural and educational agencies.

6. *The dissemination of Italian in the world: not only the Italian Cultural Institutes*

Italiano 2000, as noted above, has drawn exclusively from data provided by the Italian Cultural Institutes worldwide. This is due to the fact that the IIC, being created and funded by the Ministry of Foreign Affairs, function best as observers of the Italian language worldwide because their specific goal is to promote Italian culture abroad. To this end, they have developed rapport with local residents by providing educational services such as libraries and media centers and by organizing cultural events such as conferences, exhibits, and retrospectives, etc. and offering Italian classes in collaboration with local universities and organizations.

Italian Cultural Institutes are excellent places to observe fluctuations in the appeal of Italian language and culture. It is necessary to underscore that the diffusion of Italian languages in any given country should not be the responsibility of the IIC exclusively. In fact, there are relatively few IIC operating in the world: 90 in 59 countries. Their headquarters are located in state capitals or in major metropolitan areas. For instance, there are only seven IIC in the USA; some of which don't even offer language classes, since they feel it is not a top priority. Also IIC language classes are often geared to adults. They have not taken into account the interest of other age groups such as children, adolescents and the elderly. For these groups, there may be other institutions such as public and private elementary and secondary schools, consulates, university courses, adult education classes, private schools, Chambers of Commerce, and various immigrant aid societies. North America is a part of the world where the situation of Italian is very complicated. Unfortunately, no criteria describe all the dynamics that affect the demand for Italian at various levels. The available research is incomplete; referring either to a specific category, such as university courses (Lebano, 1999) or to quantitative data such as the surveys made annually by the *Direzione Generale per gli Italiani all'estero* and *le Politiche Migratori* which collects data limited to individuals who participate in linguistic or cultural activities sponsored by DL 297/94 article 636. However, all research carried out by various organizations point to a steady trend of increased interest in studying Italian.

The same trend is found in responses to questionnaires distributed by *Italiano 2000* to various cultural and educational agencies such as consulates, public and private schools, university departments and cultural associations. Observing these data, we are struck by evidence which show the fickleness of the public regarding Italian L2: out of the tens of thousands of children who studied Italian in classes financed by the Italian government through the above mentioned legislation (DL297/94, article 636), few continue to study Italian into adulthood. We should point out that the offerings in Italian stops at the first level. Once a student has reached a minimum level of proficiency, the interest for Italian somehow dissipates. In order to explain this phenomena, more sophisticated research is needed regarding institutions engaged in teaching Italian. Not only quantitative, but also qualitative data should be analyzed, so that interventions can be made to correct problems in situations where the presence of Italian is deemed critical.

7. The placing of Italian in the market language: contraction and expansion

It seems feasible to propose an interpretation of the complex and sometimes contradictory processes pertaining to Italian L2 even if we must limit our analysis to more macroscopic data without reverting to the proposed model of the language market, which is, in fact, a metaphor for an international system of competition among economic and cultural models as well as individual and collective values. From the point of view of the language market, the number of students studying Italian worldwide can not be compared with those enrolled in English, French and German. This classification, however, is not static. The supremacy of English depends heavily on its value in everyday communication and in commercial interactions. Though English is a language of great cultural importance, its appeal does not depend merely on this. This means that the value of using it as a primary language in interlinguistic exchanges depends on the variety of functions its users attribute to it. The simplification a language undergoes as it spreads globally, is accelerated by non-native speakers. The outcome, even in competition with other languages, is neither simple nor predictable. As a result of internal restructuring, we can't rule out the eventuality of change occurring in the classification of the most popular international languages, such as English, due to the influence of non-native speakers. Languages evolve in the course of use, even their syntax as they interact with values determining which language to use in interlingusitic exchange.

In certain geographical areas, Italian competes with a few other languages. French, German and Spanish are preferred over Italian as a subject of study if we only view the situation in general terms; but on closer scrutiny, Italian appears to be the preferred language in certain locales. The competitiveness of Italian in these instances depends on issues such as economic-commercial applications, and the degree to which Italian fits the linguistic/cultural/social models emulated by a specific social group. If we accept the idea of competition within the language market, we will find many variables, and so whatever seems to be a negative phenomenon regarding the study of Italian per se will be found to be common to language study as a whole. As this suggests, Italian is affected by whatever positive or negative variables are present across the board in the entire language market. It seems plausible, therefore, to go back to the increase in the number of foreign students of Italian from 1995 to 2000. This increase in enrollment is a result not only of the *sistema Italia*, but also of the world language market characterized, on one hand, by a tendency toward standardization and globalization, and on the other, by changes in local preferences. We live in a time when foreign language learning is expanding so vigorously that it could be viewed as an aspect of economic growth. Terms such as 'language industry,' imply that there is a need for technological elaboration, scientific research and innovation in this field. Paradoxically, the commitment made by France and England to popularize their languages abroad has had a negative effect. In an ever-expanding world market of languages, in which Italian has demonstrated an increase in enrollment, it is unimportant whether Italian is first, second or third L2 as long as it is included. Having said this, neither do we intend to diminish the role that efforts to promote the diffusion of Italian have had in the last ten years; nor do we want to justify a lack of promotion by claiming that all marketing done in this area benefits Italian indirectly. Instead, we prefer to highlight two initiatives which seem to contribute to an understanding of the expansion of our language.

8. *From Italiano 2000 to the Osservatorio linguistico permanente dell'italiano diffuso fra stranieri. (Geodata Programma 2000)*

As we noted above, the dual objectives of the *Osservatorio* is to create a map of *Italiano L2* and to assess its health by locating indicators of its presence other than language courses and cultural activities. Some indictors currently under investigation by the *Osservatorio*, are lexical units, or exoticisms, Italian words or phrases that have entered the linguistic and social spheres of other languages. It is necessary to distinguish between phrases already present in standard lexicons of various languages from exoticisms found in public spaces usually in urban environments. We refer to the appearance of Italian phrases in contexts such as billboards, posters and other forms of advertising. The presence of such texts in public spaces signifies that not only is an immigrant community taking root in certain locales but also, thanks to the *sistema Italia*, Italian is being accepted by certain socio-economic sectors.

The *Osservatorio* study concentrates on these exoticisms by utilizing technology to collect and process linguistic data. This approach requires competence in linguistics, computer science, statistics and geography. The objective is to obtain computer-generated geo-linguistic maps representing a specific locality by collating evidence about the intensity of an Italian presence abroad. The methodology used for this study uses three types of instruments: photographic archiving of texts; accurate pin-pointing of locations; linguistic analysis of the texts themselves. All data collected as well as linguistical and geographical analysis are collated by computer. Each photograph of a text is identified on a map by a indicating the place where the text was found. This is done with a PDA (a hand-held Palm Pilot-type of computer) containing geographical maps. When the text has been collected, information needed for classification and linguistic analysis as well as the location parameters are entered into a database. Then, photographs, maps and other data are transmitted from the PDA to a more powerful computer in order to allow quantitative and qualitative analysis to take place. *Geodata Programa 2000* allows researchers to calculate the frequency of recurrence of exoticisms within a given public space so the phrase can be analyzed from both semiotic and linguistic points of view. The result is a geo-linguistical map of a city or a neighborhood marked by clusters of dots each of which indicates a place where the exoticism was found. Each dot is also linked to information regarding the semiotic, textual and linguistic analysis of the collected data.

What follows is a description of the database card utilized for the classification of the photo and the texts[6]:

> In the card, each photographic image represented by a geographical dot is classified by a number code describing the date and time the photograph was taken, what the photograph depicts, the type of camera used and the name of the photographer. At the time the text is collected, an analysis of the phrase contained in the photograph is made with the intent of identifying its semiotic and textual function. Each text is, in fact, classified on the basis of localization, domain, context and placement.

Localization is defined as the public space in which the survey has been carried out and where texts have been located. This category is divided into urban (big, medium or small urban areas); and suburban (industrial, commercial, artiginal or rural). Urban and suburban neighborhoods are classified as residential, luxurious or ethnic.

Domains are spheres of action and areas of specific interest into which social life can be divided. Such subdivision, though, is arbitrary since the number of domains is indeterminate and a specific context could refer to one or more domain, yet this is relevant to linguistical analysis. For this reason, four types of domains have been identified: private, public, educational, professional, which are subdivided into referential contexts. When classifying a text by domain, three interrelated factors must be taken into account: the author of the text, the intended audience of the text and the purpose for which the text was created. For instance, if someone displays a poster in a bar containing Italian lexical units advertising certain beverages, this text would classified as being in a public domain, because the message is intended to influence customers in general about which beverage to order. Instead, a help-wanted sign displayed in the same bar would belong to the professional domain, because it is addressed to a specific group of individuals in their roles as potential employees.

Contexts are the sub-categories of every domain, intended as centers of interest around which the communicative interaction is developed. Every domain contains a potentially endless list of contexts.

Placement, a subcategory of context, defines the specific areas in which the communication takes place: bar, school, store, restaurant, gym, city hall, police station, etc. By position we mean the semiotic function of a text base given its placement and degree of visibility. The semiotic function of a text varies if it is placed in a open area which allows it to be seen by a large group of people. On the other hand, the same text could be displayed in a closed indoor space likely to be seen only by limited number of people such as residents of an apartment building. Generic texts fit a broader definition such as bulletin boards, menus, flyers, posters, ads, announcements, local ordinances, etc. On this basis of classification made contextually at the time of photographic documentation, global characteristics can be identified which provide indications mainly about its semiotic function.

The third aspect of the investigation consists in a strictly linguistic analysis of the text itself. This analysis does not take place at the time of the survey, but only afterwards, when the collected data are downloaded from the PDA to a computer. Once the text is transcribed and its lexical components identified, these become classified according to language, transliterated (if written in a non-Roman alphabet) and translated. The classification of the lexical component proceeds according to structural characteristics: grammatical categories such as parts of speech (e.g., subject, verb, adverb, etc.); gender; case. Should the lexical unit belong to the grammatical category of verb, for example, it will then be further classified in terms of mood, tense and personal pronoun. Every lexical unit must be classified on the basis of usage: whether or not it forms part of the language's basic vocabulary in common usage or is esoteric, literary technical, obsolete, or dialect. (8)

This method of investigation is completed by verifying the presence of each exoticism contained in the lexicographical sources of languages spoken in the country where the text was found. This type of study does not limit itself to gathering expressions containing exoticisms, but by analyzing them within a larger framework of cognitive data which can provide a great deal of information about the status of the diffusion of particular language through an analysis of the social environment as a nexus. In the case of Italian, the analysis of exoticisms in various social contexts can shed light on the extent of the diffusion of Italian spoken abroad. Exoticisms also enable us to trace the presence of a given culture within particular socio-economic environments and/or the presence of immigrants within a community. For instance the lexical unit cappuccino among a list of beverages on a restaurant menu, does not necessarily indicate the presence of Italian immigrants in the local community, but it is certainly signifies the acceptance of certain aspects of Italian culture such as cuisine and culinary products in that locality.

Conclusions

The study made by the *Osservatorio* regarding the spread of Italian abroad by collating exoticisms provides quantitative and qualitative data that may further define the status of our language and its dynamic beyond national borders. The situation may appear to be characterized by complex and possibly confusing variables, but understanding data regarding the status of Italian abroad is fundamental for anyone interested in promoting Italian abroad through programs tailored specifically to local situations. For this reason, the *Osservatorio* aspires to be a center of scientific research for the collection and dissemination of data among various organizations involved in the diffusion of Italian, such as public and private institutions and the broad spectrum of the cultural industry, in general.

Translated by Gioacchino Balducci, Stony Brook University and Carolyn Balducci, University of Michigan

[1] The two authors are responsible of the following parts: Monica Barni is the author of paragraphs 6, 8, 9; Massimo Vedovelli is the author of all other paragraphs.

[2] French (-3%) German (-7%) and (0%) for Spanish.

[3] Italiano 2000 questionnaires were sent to all the administrative and cultural representatives of the Italy abroad. Italiano 2000, for reasons explained in De Mauro et al, 2002, chose to deal only with the data by the Italian Cultural Institutes. We refer to data present in questionnaires coming from North America, which do not concern the IIC.

[4] The students of language and Italian culture classes were 84,328 in 1999-2000 and 89,330 in 2000-2001 in North America (Source: DGIT of the Ministry of Foreign Affairs).

[5] The study of the Osservatorio does not limit itself to Italian language abroad. It has uses the same methodology to describe the linguistic space by mapping of the presence of immigrant languages in Italy.

[6] Other contributors to the database card are Carla Bagna (research assistant, Osservatorio) and Sabrina Machetti (doctoral candidate in Linguistics and Didactics of Italian for Foreigners at the Università per Stranieri in Siena. For the realization of the computer our consultants are the Etruria Telematica Co. Coordination between the team of linguists and the computers experts was facilitated by Giampiero Ciacci, Engineer, at the Centro Informatico of the University for Foreigners in Siena.

[7] In researching Italian language exoticisms abroad, transliteration and translation are not necessary. For a definition of the concept of *marca d'uso* see De Mauro (1980 and 1999).

Bibliography

Baldelli, Ignazio, ed. *La lingua italiana nel mondo. Indagine sulle motivazioni allo studio dell'italiano nel mondo.* Roma: Istituto della Enciclopedia Italiana, 1987.

Baker Philip and John Eversley. *Multilingual Capital.* London: Battlebridge Publications, 2000.

Bernardini, Carlo and Tullio De Mauro. *Contare e raccontare. Dialogo sulle due culture.* Roma: Laterza, 2003.

Calvet, Louis-Jean. *Le marché aux langues.* Paris: Plon, 2000.

De Mauro, Tullio. *Grande Dizionario Italiano dell'Uso.* Torino:UTET, 1999.

De Mauro, Tullio and Massimo Vedovelli, Monica Barni, Lorenzo Miraglia. *Italiano 2000. Indagine sulle motivazioni e sui pubblici dell'italiano nel mondo.* Roma: Bulzoni, 2003.

Lebano, Edoardo. *Survey on the Italian language in the U.S.A.* Welland, Ontario (CA): Soleil, 1999.

Medici, Mario and Raffaele Simone, edd. *L'insegnamento dell'italiano in Italia e all'estero*. Roma: Bulzoni, 1971.

Società Dante Alighieri. *Vivere l'italiano: il futuro della lingua. Bozza del rapporto dell'indagine svolta il collaborazione con il CNEL, presentato il 30 marzo 1999*, Roma.

Section IV

✦

The Shapes of a Culture

How the "Italian" is Woven with the "American" in my Life and Art

B. Amore
LIFELINE-filo della vita
The Carving Studio and Sculpture Center

"Many Immigrants had brought on board balls of yarn, leaving one end of the line with someone on land. As the ship slowly cleared the dock, the balls unwound amid the farewell shouts of the women, the fluttering of handkerchiefs, and the infants held high. After the yarn ran out, the long strips remained airborne, sustained by the wind long after those on land and those at sea had lost sight of each other."

Luciano de Crescenzo

Tanti immigranti hanno portato a bordo gomitoli di lana, lasciando un'estremita' del filo con qualcuno a terra. Mentre che la nave partì lentamente dal molo, i gomitoli si sfilarano fra i gridi d'addio delle donne, i battiti dei fazzoletti, ed i bambini in braccio mantenuti in alto. Dopo che la lana si esaurì, le strisce lunghe rimanevano in aria, sostenute dal vento finche' non si persero di vista sia a quelli di terra sia a quelli di mare.

Luciano De Crescenzo

Home was always in another place. We were in America: The "true home" was Italy. Arriving as a student when I was nineteen years old was like a homecoming. Entering the Bay of Naples at dawn wrapped in a blanket on the top deck of the Cristoforo Colombo was reliving the experience of my mother discovering Italy when she was five, a sense in me of discovering the "heart place." Italy was the heart place where dreams sprang from, where life was nurtured.

My grandmother's stories were the first I heard. They were all about Italy, her play was there in the *Giardino* as a child, her strict grandfather who made her sit silent at the dinner table, trips in the carriage with her father from Lapio in the mountains to *Via Carracciolo* in Naples. Her childhood was my place of beginning. I lived in these places in the inner life of my own earliest years.

Italian was the first language with which she walked me to sleep upon arrival from the hospital. I grew up by the ocean always knowing that there was "another shore" — the other shore being Italy. There was the ever present sensation of suspension between the two, a floating sense of feeling, a floating sense of language, an easy movement from the dialect to English to dialect. I was never encouraged to speak Italian. It was always there, within and without the household, conversations in cars with friends, on the street, in other houses. If I spoke Italian, it had to be "pure" Italian, not the dialect! Since dialect was what I mostly heard, that was very confusing to me.

Like the barge being guided by the tug on the river, ethnicity is a force influencing my life. It is the subtle and not so subtle undertone which colors everything I do. I took it in with my mother's *salsa*. There was no thought to it, it was part of the ground of existence. When I need comfort, a rich red sauce over pasta still IS the mother! I can't understand my own soul without understanding my Italian roots

My world was centrally Italian when I was young. Everyone who was not Italian was American. That included Irish, English, French, Jewish — all manner of "other" who were not Italian. There was nothing derogatory said about any other nationality. In fact, we were encouraged to accept everyone but I was not American, I was Italian! It took me until my mid-twenties, post Bachelor of Arts, to realize that there were Italian Americans; that in fact, I was not only Italian, I was also American.

Being Italian, there is always a sense of history. A moment is never only that moment. It stretches back in time to other related happenings which are attached to it like sticky spidery strands, barely visible, missing if you blink, blowing in a breeze of memory which in actuality can begin to feel like a forged chain binding one to the past. The past seemed more important than the future. There was, for me, growing up, always the sense of people looking back rather than forward.

This was partially what prompted a year of study in Italy at nineteen, at The University of Rome in the *Facoltà di Lettere e Filosofia*: a year when the university was on strike most of the time, a year of exploring museums and ruins, but more importantly a year of living in the village of my maternal grandmother, of watching a cow slaughtered on the cobbled street, of following a life sized Christ carried on the shoulders of village men in procession, of participating in the viewing of the "Misteri" at Easter on their yearly tour of the village, attending mass in the churches of my great grandparents, listening to the high pitched nasal sing song chanting of the women as they stood before the rush seated chairs on smooth marble floors. These direct, authentic experiences, led me back to the town I inhabited as a child in my inner spaces and connected me, in the present, to my grandmother's experiences in the past.

My sense of my Italian heritage is a point of departure for many aspects of my creative expression in art and writing. The clearest example of this is a recently completed multi media six room exhibit for the Ellis Island Immigration Museum called *"LIFELINE — filo della vita."* I sometimes call it a visual novel which sets the destinies of two families from Italy's *Mezzogiorno* in the historical context of emigration from Italy and assimilation in America in the one hundred years of the 20th Century. The exhibit is traveling in the US and Italy and will also be published as a book.

LIFELINE includes ancestral objects and family writing dating back to 1802, as well as sculptures, installations, text, video and photographic panels. It celebrates many layers of the life weaving which transcend seven generations and explores the complex tidal wave of change which engulfs immigrants and their descendants.

It is a story told in a non traditional way, across the boundaries of class, gender, race, and identity crises that span two countries. The entire installation is like a huge shrine with smaller sub chapels. I grew up in an Italian Catholic milieu where the magic of the liturgy was always present; the gold, the glow, the mystery of bread and wine being transformed. That is also the essence of making art, to transform material so that it has a possibility of expressing the ineffable. *LIFELINE* takes popular devotional forms, triptychs and altars, and elevates the everyday to the status of the sacred. It speaks of ordinary lives which were lived with extraordinary courage. We are used to thinking of history as major occurrences. The Story of Humanity is, more often, a compendium of daily life events, small memories.

The pick ax of my grandfather, elegant in form and still bearing the scars of his labor becomes the central element in a reliquary dedicated to the two Anthonys — *Antonio*, the pick and shovel guy who dug the foundations of Harvard University and his son, Tony, who was able to pursue the dream of an education but not the full dream of his life. The sense of the sacred was part and parcel of my Italian American youth; not only in church, but also within the family. Certain memories were sacred. When my grandmother spoke of her father or mother, she spoke as if they were Saints. There was always a reverence for the ancestors, for history.

LIFELINE is a complex narrative utilizing text and visual stimuli. The narrative is processed along the red thread of memory, the life line, the death line, stretching back to the past and into the future. It is a powerful metaphor for immigration. As in De Crescenzo's poem, the lines of connection to the ancestors persist whether we are aware of them or not. Their sufferings of dislocation and the requisite accommodation continue to mark our lives across generations, perhaps a bit less than they marked the second generation, but marking us just the same.

The story is often told through objects. Many families have lost their talismanic objects. My grandmother kept so many that they have become the material of art. The objects themselves are key elements. There is a physical relationship to each one which is indexically connected to the ancestors. The hand fashioned brass ravioli cutter, the *vecchia caffettiera napoletana*, the bound bundles of fabric and coarse linen sheets woven in the 1800's all stand for a whole way of life, an entire culture. The scholar, Pellegrino D'Acierno, felt that both the red thread of *LIFELINE* and these material remnants functioned as transitional objects in an immigrant life, akin to a baby's thumb or favorite blanket, offering the comfort of familiarity. Looking up through seven glass layers of objects in a three meter high "reliquary," one has the sense of an archaeological dig, like looking up and through history. Viewers often spoke of rediscovering their own family history through experiencing *LIFELINE*. In this way the narrative functions as collective memory. The narrative itself becomes a sort of homeland.

In a sense, LIFELINE was a collaboration with my past, with everything I had been taught in my Italian American family. My hands were always worker's hands, like my paternal grandfather's. I remember watching his hands building a granite wall when I was about four years old — wanting to help, thinking I could hold the grey cobbles but being pushed away because I was a girl. Still, the work ethic came from family example. Becoming a stone sculptor is not unrelated to these early experiences of a strong sense of the material world.

In the exhibit, there is an installation of life sized black trentino marble figures swathed in fabric. They are kin to the Italian village women carrying jugs of water and baskets of produce on their heads. In America, there were different burdens, not all so easily definable. The tall strong, stone women carry bundles on their heads. They are the bundles of their history. The stones are wrapped with fabric: fabric which was so much a part of my childhood, of my mother's life and my grandmother's and great grandmother's existence. They used fabric to make beautiful clothes but were often trapped in their traditional roles. The tearing of the fabric into strips brings me right back to my childhood, to hearing my grandmother tear fabric. Here we experience the torn fabric of the immigrant's life in a revisioning of history. I use fabric to bind things together — pieces of experience — to make it whole. Sometimes, images and fabric are layered as if the "truths" are floating under an opaque surface, difficult to see clearly.

I often speak of collaborating with my grandmother, using her objects, her memories, the unanswered questions of her life which reverberate in mine. My heritage, her collections, have become part of my artistic expression. There was a deep transmission from her to me, in the religious sense, of the passing on of a lineage. My search into family had as much to do with what was not said, what was not divulged. It is interesting how one can hold the "facts" of lives lived, but not really know the truth. There will always be unanswered questions which provoke more questioning, more imagining, more writing, more art.

Memory "fixes" things, like a photographic fix. The flow gets stopped and we take that image-feeling and it becomes "hardened" in a sense but this is an illusion because reality can never really be "fixed." It is moving and changing all the time and even what we "remember" is only like a glint of light off a faceted surface. If we "remember" to remember this, memory takes on a different hue and we can recognize with a "grain of salt" that what we recall is really only a very partial "truth" of a moment in time, but it is "our truth" and it is a point of departure.

In a sense, to create *LIFELINE*, and any writing, I have to take apart the "truth" as I know it, take the carved box of memory where stories lie secreted, and open the lid, exposing the brittle pages and faded writing to a different sort of light which occasionally brings transparency to the page, so it can be "seen through," so I can peer into the history which has been given me and either find the deeper history, or make up something which resembles more a deeply intuited or felt truth which makes more sense than the story which was written by my great grandfather or my grandmother.

I inherited a *Libro di Memorie* a diary from 1802, memories and experiences of my great-great-grandfather and my great-grandfather. On the cover are these words, "*Quando io parto da questo mondo, che il signore mi chiama, qui sono memorie e tutti i ricivi e pesi dei nostri fondi e altre notizie, forse per ridere. Addio.*" I've been translating many of these entries written in an old cursive script that even my friends in Naples have a hard time reading. It is entering a profoundly intimate and moving world, where *Don Lorenzo's* voice whispers from a distance of nearly two hundred years: relating his experiences of joy in his daughter's marriage, grief at her death two months later replete with detailed descriptions of all of the attendant circumstances, wedding rituals, medical practices, burials, learning that snow is measured in *palmi di neve* and that lightning can course through a house and set a good woolen mattress on fire, reading of him using the weights and measures to pay taxes and holding the very same weights and measures in my hands.

There seems a responsibility in the wealth of inheritance of objects and stories, a sense of duty, a sense of *destino*. The stories and the objects seem to have chosen me. It is both a burden and a joy, which I seem to have no choice in accepting if I am to be truly who I am. A sense of *destino* is ever-present. *Nonni* always talked of *destino*, inescapable. When something was inexplicable, it became *destino*.

Concetta, my grandmother, never wrote in the diary. Only men wrote in the diary even though all of the women in her family were educated and could read and write in the last half of the 19th century, no small accomplishment in the southern provinces at that time where illiteracy superceded 70%. Her writings happened at school, at American International College which she attended for two years from 1911-1913 as one of 10 Italian immigrant women in higher education at that time.

In her themes, speaking in another's voice, is where I feel that her own feelings are most truly expressed. Not in her photographs, where for the most part, she is quite composed. There is only one photograph of her, a side view, taken in a kitchen in Italy, circa 1924, where the bold pose is relaxed. She sits, fuller bodied than her norm, with an apron on, leaning into the support of the chair's back, staring loosely into the space in front of her. In this picture, there are no pat answers. Her life has decomposed. She is separated from her husband, a scoundrel. She is mother of a seven year old child and head of the household comprised of her father and sister. Having returned to Italy for two years, perhaps with the intention of remaining, she looks devastatingly unhappy in the tiny village of her youth. She leaves for America soon after and does not see Italy again until 1956, a distance of 34 years. She is always Italian in her demeanor and mores, but no longer fits into the Italy of her origin. She speaks English perfectly, but is never "American." She is always between the two.

My paternal grandfather left Italy in 1909 and never returned. The Italy of his childhood was so harsh, so self-defeating, so poor, so pained, that he never looked back. He also never became an American citizen. His wife did renounce her Italian citizenship, yet returned many times. His children returned and two of them married Italians so the present generation of cousins has a lively relationship back and forth across the ocean which used to take two weeks to cross and now takes eight hours. My grandmother's *Giardino* is still in my name.

LIFELINE, and my present writing, both poetry and prose, are an intricate intermingling of myriad layers of understanding, perception, questioning. Because the stories which were told did not "explain it all," despite their insistence that they were "telling the truth," there remains the necessity of searching back within oneself to see what can be seen. There is a song which my father used to sing called "The bear went over the mountain to see what he could see." And so I inherited the mountain. Perhaps it was *Lapio* or *Montefalcione*, the primal Irpinian mountain towns of my family's origin. I find myself on a continual journey of inquiry. Although some of the paths may be familiar as related to me by my parents or grandmother, I am traveling with a different pair of eyes. They traveled down the mountain to America and I am traveling up the mountain with a sack of questions about the reality they related and conveyed as well as the gaps in the story. It is actually through making the work that I discover myself and my roots. They reveal themselves unexpectedly through dark, densely packed soil which I am excavating in the seemingly slowest of ways, digging by hand, a small bit at a time, until a fragment is unearthed almost without my knowing, but the light catches it and shows me the way forward.

CIRCLE OF BODIES

We stand on the sidewalk
A circle of bodies, arms entwined
Flesh finding flesh
Blood finding blood

Brother to sister to brother to sister
Unbroken line inbred with
mother's breath

Cement gives way to softly tilled earth
before early summer planting
We sink ankle deep into grainy darkness
turned to light
by our father's hand

Like a field stretching wider than we see
The ground of our parents and grandparents
draws our white feet
Sucking into the spaces between our
toes — rooting us in mysteries

How alike our hands, lined, firm
Veins - blue green rivers of the ancestors
Gnarled connectors
watering familiar
soil.

B. Amore

STONES FLOAT

One stone for each Paisano
who left the village

Like beads on a rosary
strung in a long line
from Lapio to Avellino
to Naples to Marseilles to
the promised land

Lapio itself named for stone
Irpinian hill town looking across the
valley to Chiusano
also made of stone

Vegetation so scarce
goats could hardly
find enough to
eat

The stones of the Village cried
as they were dismantled one
by one and taken in
sacks to L'America

Eroded by time
eroded by circumstance
The town shrank to accommodate
its reduced form

Harvest of wheat threshed
on age-old stone circles
Now thrown in soft patterns under
donkey's hoofs by the few
women who remain

Faces creased, hands hardened to an
even deeper bronze

The same donkey turns the milling
stone which crushes rich
olives bleeding golden oil

Stones weep their loss
Remembering the stout
short fingered hands
who set them, nestled one by one,
into the structure of home

Stones sink into bags
of rags picked by tired nimble
fingers of southern women

Jagged, sometimes tearing through,
dropping a heavy frozen piece of
foreign soil onto an even
more foreign land

Fixed into low stone walls built
by Italians in Brooklyn
Containing a postage stamp
garden of Memory

The city by the water
Connected to the town in
the mountains by the chain of
broken stone rosaries
Called into dark night
after dark domed
night

B. Amore

ITALIANITÀ: REVIEWING THE SPATIAL SEMIOTICS OF LITTLE ITALIES

Jerome Krase
Brooklyn College, C.U.N.Y.

No consideration of culture and literature about Italian Americans and/or that produced by they themselves (which may not be mutually exclusive categories) can avoid a symbolic excursion to and through the urban landscape(s) of Little Italy. This is especially true if we wish to provide particular attention to the role of *Italianità* in the cinema of North America. Little Italy is (can be conceived as) a concrete entity composed of buildings and people. More importantly, and more powerfully, it is an ideal ethnic enclave (a symbolic model) that can be visualized as a product and a source of economic, social and cultural capital. Naively, the authentic residents of these places, ignorant of powerful societal structural forces that affect if not control their existence, adapt to and modify their home territories in urban neighborhoods. During the course of their lives they become part of the scene as though they were unpaid, and unknowing, actors on a streetscape stage. Even more abstractly, people and their spaces become symbols. In the process of presenting, and then re-presenting themselves they also lose their autonomy. The idealized ethnic enclave symbolizes its imagined inhabitants and stands for them independent of their residence in it. Reproductions of the places they create are also commodified. As a consequence, the expropriated cultural capital of the Italian American vernacular can marketed, for example; as "safely sinister" as in *The Bronx Tale* (1993), written and directed by Italian Americans Jazz Palminteri and Robert De Niro respectively, exhibited as "old world charm" as was Carroll Gardens, Brooklyn in *Moonstruck* (1987), written and directed by non-Italian Americans John Patrick Shanley and Norman Jewison. Little Italy is almost always shown as the "way it used to (but no longer can) be" as in "Variations on the Theme of the Old Neighborhood" of *The Godfather* (1972), written by Mario Puzo and directed by Francis Ford Coppola, and *Do the Right Thing* (1989), written and directed by Spike Lee. We must never forget when thinking about being Italian or Italian American, as dramaturgy, or merely as performance in everyday life, that the scenery can be as confirming or disconfirming as the script.

Mine is not the only work that emphasizes the importance of understanding the essential semiotic/symbolic character of *Italianità. In Italian Signs, American Streets: the Evolution of Italian American Narrative*, the noted Italian Americanist, Fred L.Gardaphé, as a writer, naturally pays most of his attention to the written and spoken word, as opposed to my own interest in the still and moving image, while relating that:

> For the purposes of this study, I will define an Italian sign as one signifying *Italianità*, or the qualities associated with Italian culture. The most obvious signs will be the lexical units that appear in the Italian language or dialectal variants. Beyond language, there are two cultural codes that govern public behavior: *omertà*, the code of silence that governs what is spoken and not spoken about in public, and *bella figura*, the code of proper presence or social behavior that governs an individual's public presence. These codes were carried to America through the oral traditions of southern Italian culture, and so it is important to first consider the folkloric basis of Italian American culture. (20)

My own contribution to Italian and Italian American Studies is to bring closer attention to the spatial and visual components of the complex, as yet undeconstructed, notion of *Italianità* in Italy, America, and elsewhere. For example, I have written extensively on the way by which the visually contradictory notions of both *omertà* and *bella figura* are visually available as social performance and in vernacular architecture. (1993) A recent autobiographically framed anthropological exposition by Loretta Baldassar about her *Visits Home* in Italy from Australia supports my assumption that acting about spaces and places is an important component of *Italianità*. I am reminded here by her geographic and symbolic journey that spaces have geographical, and places symbolic, meanings attached to them.

> The Lombard migrants I had connections with (through my mother's family) mainly lived in the rural countryside, south-west of Perth. I grew up in the city where my father was a member of a Veneto social club called Laguna, a reference to the lagoon of Venice, principal city in the Veneto region. I attended Laguna whenever my family went, at least once a week, generally on Sundays. About the time I started high school,

> going to Laguna became something of a chore. My non-Italian friends from school were spending their weekends together, and none of them appeared to have to frequent a place like Laguna with their parents. Because Laguna represented "being Italian" to my father, my resistance alarmed him, and his reaction was to enforce my presence there. This became a source of conflict.
>
> My father interpreted my lack of interest in Laguna as a rejection of *Italianità*. By *Italianità* I mean a set of values and beliefs an individual associates with being Italian. According to my father, everything I did was "Australian." In our household, "being Australian" was set up in contention with being "Italian." Indeed, all identities are defined in opposition; there are many and varied theories to define ethnic group identity, but one point they all include is that notion that ethnicity only has salience in contexts of interaction between groups that are perceived to be different. (23-24)

At the conclusion of his analysis of being Italian in Toronto (*Eh, Paesan!*) Nicholas DeMaria Harney gives us both a transnational sensibility to the mutability of Italianness/*Italianità* and, inadvertently, its connection to spaces and places. The extensive quotation that follows below is necessary as it demonstrates a certain, important, logic of ethnic identification typical in both the Social Science and Humanities literature on generations of Italian immigrants.

> At the beginning of the 1980s a transformation occurred in the way Italianness and the Italian community were imagined. New meanings entered the swirl of competing images to create further layers and greater complexity with the construction of Italianness. The images of Italians and Italianness were recast. A people that were once seen as peasant simpletons became entrepreneurs of rustic design and eternal wisdom, or innovators in fashion and industrial design. The portrait of Italians as organized criminals changed to one of Italians as hard-working, prescient, and insightful business people. As a result the children of Italian immigrants confronted new meanings with which to construct their Italianness, and the altered generational meanings of work, education, and gender began to contribute to misunderstandings between age cohorts.
>
> In the fall of 1994 the Eyetalian helped organize a career and culture day at the Columbus Centre in conjunction with the Canadian Italian

> Federation of Students. After a series of informative career sessions and artistic performances the ended with a panel discussion of the question, "Beyond Baggio: do Italians have a reason to get excited about anything but world cup soccer?" The 1982 spontaneous outpouring of communal pride had occurred again throughout the World Cup games in 1994, but hadn't happened on other occasions. Was there anything else? For some in the second generation of Italian Canadians there is an impatience with the caution of their parents. For many more, suburban life offers few opportunities to express themselves. Furthermore, stereotypes still linger. The charm of Mediterranean exotica in "Little Italies" around the city creates opportunities for Italian Canadians to reap financial rewards by marketing their "Italian" authenticity, their "practical knowledge," and the "cultural vitality" to the Canadian public, but it also limits and restricts those who wish to break out into different fields and new directions.
>
> Nevertheless, as members of the second generation talked to me about their ethnic identity, many seemed overtaken by an optimistic mood. The were confident of their numeric strength, as though they had absorbed Anderson's (1983) notion of the imagined community and were comfortable negotiating between Canadian cultural expectations and *Italianità*. Many felt strongly that the moment has arrived for Italian Canadians to assert themselves in the emerging transnational era. (172-73)

For my final digression I wish to offer a contradictory notion of ethnicity, in this case *latinidad*, expressed by Mike Davis in his most resent *Magical Urbanism: Latinos Reinvent the U.S. City*. After discussing some of what I would call the range of signs and symbols, semiotics if you will, of various Latino groups in American cities, he concludes:

> Yet, if there is no reducible essence to *latinidad* — even in languages or religion — it does not necessarily follow that there is no substance. In playing with the Rubik's Cube of ethnicity, it is important to resist the temptation of prematurely resolving its contradictions. "Hispanic/ Latino" is not merely an artificial, racialized box like "Asian-American," invented by the majority society to uncomfortably contain individuals of the most emphatically disparate national origins who may subsequently develop some loosely shared identity as a reaction-formation to this labeling. Nor is it simply a marketing ploy — like right-wing Coors brewery's opportunistic promotion of the 1980s as the "Decade

> of the Hispanic" — that exploits superficial national similarities in language, cuisine and fashion. To be Latino in the United States is rather to participate in a unique process of cultural syncretism that may become a transformative template for the whole society. *Latinidad*, Flores emphasizes, has nothing to do with "post-modern aesthetic indeterminacy, ... it is *practice* rather than representation of Latino identity. And it is on this terrain that Latinos wage their cultural politics as a social movement. As in Octavio Paz's famous definition of *mexicanidad*, to be Latino is "not an essence but a history." (15)

As a pre-postmodernist, I might add that each of these arguments can also be made for Italian Americans and for *Italianità*, but a fuller exposition of this must be left for a future paper. Suffice it to say that the preceding contributions by Fred Gardaphé, Loretta Baldassar, Nichoals Harney, and Mike Davis clearly indicate the necessity of exploring the role played by space and place in ethnicity and ethnic identity of all self or otherwise identified social groups.

We now will briefly explore the related concepts of Italian Ethnicity and Italian Ethnic Identity through a Visual Sociological study of two geographically different venues — Italian American neighborhoods in the United States and neighborhoods in Rome, Italy. By studying the Vernacular Landscape (Jackson, 1984) via the methods of Visual Sociology (Grady, 1996 and Harper, 1988, Rieger, 1996), and the theoretical perspectives of Urbanization of Capital (Harvey, 1989) and Spatial Semeiotics (Gottdiener, 1994) the question: "What does it mean for a place of a space to 'Look Italian?'" is addressed. For data, the discourse draws from my extensive collection of visual studies in both the United States and Italy of the "Public Realms," or spaces accessible to all (Lofland, 1998). Here are featured my observations and photographic research on the "New Immigrants to Rome" which in many ways symbolically represent the ethnic and otherwise demographic changes which have occurred in America's Little Italies. Note that if the meanings of the spaces change, as a consequence they become different places and the in turn the meanings of what is Italian an Italian American are at least challenged. A few photographs of Rome, Italy, and corresponding "representational" photographs of Little Italies in America are presented at the end of the text. I ask that the reader consider the images as visual text to be read about the contested meanings of Italianness;

a symbolic competition which reflects the battle for the dominance of the spaces themselves.

It is argued that the urban landscapes of both Italian America and Italy are affected by "natural" and migration-driven demographic forces, as well as the powerful processes of globalization, de-industrialization, and privatization. As I have argued elsewhere (Krase, 1999), "Contemporary urban sociologists appear to be suffering from parallax vision. One eye sees the 'natural' spatial form and function of the city as a biological analogy as did Parks and Burgess (Gubert and Tomasi, 1994). The other eye sees these same urban places and spaces as the reproductions of power, and circuits of capital, *a la* Castells (1977), Harvey (1989), and Lefebvre (1991)." I must emphasize that my research into ethnicity and space has not been merely a theoretical exercise. It has important practical applications to the present and future problems of Italian cities which are unprepared to deal with the rapidity of ethnic and racial change engendered by globalization and the development of a European Union (Krase, 1997). This history-in-the-making can be easily compared to the centuries old processes of invasion and succession which have characterized major cities in the United States.

What is Visual Sociology?

For the less-informed Visual Sociology is merely using a camera as an adjunct to the "regular" process of research. Douglas Harper explains that the growing field is divided into "Visual Methods," which includes any project where researchers 'take' photographs in order to study social worlds." And "Visual Studies" in which researchers "analyze images that are produced by the culture" and where "sociologists typically explore the semiotics, or sign systems, of different visual communication systems." It is this aspect which also lends itself most easily to the practice of Spatial Semiotics. (1988) John Grady goes further and offers a three part, "Pragmatic Definition" (1996). 1. "Seeing": how sight and vision helps construct social organization and meaning." 2. "Communicating with Icons," how images and imagery can both inform and be used to manage social relations. And, 3. "Doing Sociology Visually" "... how the techniques of producing and decoding images can be used to empirically investigate social organization, cultural meaning and psychological processes." (14). Finally,

Jon Rieger noted that among many other advantages in research, such as freezing a complex scene or enabling unobtrusive measurement, "Photography is well-suited to the study of social change because of its capacity to record a scene with far greater speed and completeness than could ever be accomplished by a human observer taking notes" (1996: 6). Given the rapidly changing scenes, which in some cases whiz by contemporary urban sociologists, the value of visual methods and techniques is obvious. Because Italian settlements change slowly they are excellent sites for studying the changing world around them.

What is Vernacular Landscape?

For Bernard Rudofsky the "vernacular" is "nonpedigreed," "anonymous," "spontaneous," and "indigenous" (1964: 1). John Brinkerhoff Jackson adds that studying vernacular landscapes can teach us about ourselves, and how we relate to the world around us. They lie below the symbols of permanent power expressed in the "Political Landscape." They are also flexible, without overall plan and contain spaces which are organized and used in their traditional way. Much of it is "countrified; home made using local techniques, local materials, with the local environment in mind. Vernacular landscapes are part of the life of communities which are governed by custom and held together by personal relationship. For him and his students "vernacular landscape cannot be comprehended unless we perceive it as an organization of space; unless we ask ourselves who owns the spaces, how they were created and how they change" (1984: 6).

American or Italian administrators and planners of multiethnic cities could benefit greatly from an understanding of immigrant and ethnic vernacular urban landscapes. For Dolores Hayden, ethnic urban landscapes consist of ethnic vernacular buildings, ethnic spatial patterns, ethnic vernacular arts traditions, and "territorial histories" which are "the history of bounded space, with some enforcement of the boundary, used as a way of defining political and economic power. It is the political and temporal complement of the cognitive map; it is an account of both inclusion and exclusion" (7).

In a related vein, Harvey argued that: "Different classes construct their sense of territory and community in radically different ways. This elemental fact is often overlooked by those theorists who presume a *priori* that there is some ideal-typical and universal tendency for all human beings to construct a human community of roughly similar sort, no matter what the political or economic circumstances" (1989: 265). For the powerless "the main way to dominate space is through continuous appropriation. Exchange values are scarce, and so the pursuit of use values for daily survival is central to social action. This means frequent material and interpersonal transactions and the formation of very small scale communities. Within the community space, use values get shared through some mix of mutual aid and mutual predation, creating tight but often highly conflictual interpersonal social bonding in both private and public spaces. The result is an often intense attachment to place and "turf" and an exact sense of boundaries because it is only through active appropriation that control over space is assured" (265-66). Furthermore, Anthony Giddens "structuration theory" also cautions that in order to understand urban regions, cities, and neighborhoods one needs not only an understanding of theory but local history, resources, ideas of local leadership (1984). The Visual Sociology of ordinary neighborhoods demonstrates "Human Agency" by the "deliberate efforts of human beings, thinking and acting, alone or in concert" to create their own vernacular landscapes.

Semiotics, Ecology, and Spatial Semiotics

Visual Sociology and Vernacular Landscapes are connected via Spatial Semiotics. Mark Gottdiener writes that "the study of culture which links symbols to objects is called semeiotics" and "spatial semeiotics studies the metropolis as a meaningful environment" (1994: 15-16). "Seeing" the uses and/or meanings of space require sensitivity and understanding of the particular culture which creates, maintains, and uses the re-signified space. In other words even the most powerless of urban dwellers is a social "agent" and therefore participates in the local reproduction of regional, national, and global societal relations.

The question for pre and post-modern urbanologists has not been "Who or what is where in the city?" but "How and why" they got there. Researchers look at the same objects but the meanings of those objects seem to vary by the ideology of the viewer. The purely descriptive models of Classical Urban Ecology come from a biological analogy. In the city, equilibrium is expressed through the interaction of human nature with geographical and spatial factors producing "natural" areas. Political economists on the contrary see these natural areas, and ecological zones as the result of "uneven development," and perhaps even planned cycles of decay and renewal. Symbolically and ecologically, James Dickinson sees in the landscape of the "zone of social pathology" more than a simple process of dereliction — the view shared by both the Chicago School and Marxists geographers. Looking at ruined neighborhoods he posits that, "These decaying zones become factories producing the ruins that will be become the monuments of tomorrow. Here then, are the liminal zones where new meanings and values are negotiated for old structures" (1996: 82. See also Vergara, 1995).

Harvey's "Grid of Spatial Practices" from Lefebvre's *The Production of Space* (262) is a powerful connection tool for connecting the new and old urban sociologies. As a paraphrase I would say that in the arena of social conflict and struggle, commanding and producing spaces, reproduces and enhances power.

Down left hand side of the grid we find:

1. *Material social practices* refer to the physical and material flows, transfers, and interactions that occur in and across space in such a way as to assure production and social reproduction.
2. *Representations of space* encompass all of the signs and significations, codes and knowledge, that allow such material practices to be talked about and understood, no matter whether in terms of everyday common sense or through the sometimes arcane jargon of the academic disciplines that deal with spatial practices (engineering, architecture, geography, planning, social ecology, and the like).
3. *Spaces of representations* are social inventions (codes, signs, and even material constructs such as symbolic spaces, particular built environments, paintings, museums and the like) that seek to generate new meanings of possibilities for spatial practices. (Harvey: 261)

Across the top of the grid: (263-64)

1. *Accessibility and distanciation* speaks to the role of the 'friction of distance' in human affairs. Distance is both a barrier to and a defense against human interaction. It imposes transaction costs upon any system of production and reproduction (particularly those based on

any elaborate social division of labor, trade, and social differentiation of reproductive functions). Distanciation (cf. Giddens 1984: 258-9) is simply a measure of the degree to which the friction of space has been overcome to accommodate social interaction.

2. *The appropriation of space* examines the way in which space is used and occupied by individuals, classes, or other social groupings. Systematized and institutionalized appropriation may entail the production of territorially bounded forms of social solidarity.
3. *The domination of space* reflects how individuals or powerful groups dominate the organization and production of space so as to exercise a greater degree of control either over the friction of distance or over the manner in which space is appropriated by themselves or others.

According to Gottdiener (1994) the most basic concept for urban studies study is the *settlement space* which is both constructed and organized. "It is built by people who have followed some meaningful plan for the purposes of containing economic, political, and cultural activities. Within it people organize their daily actions according to meaningful aspects of the constructed space"(16). As part of national and global systems, neighborhoods are affected by a wide range of supply side forces. The connection made between Italian and Italian American vernacular landscape in later pages of this essay shows that ordinary people can affect their environment, even though they are ultimately at the mercy of larger societal forces. In recent decades we have seen some reversal in the assumedly inevitable process of central urban deterioration in the form of "Gentrification;" or the conversion of socially marginal and working-class areas of the central city to middle-class residential use which in America began in the 1960s. Sharon Zukin notes that "Gentrification thus appears as a multidimensional cultural practice that is rooted in both sides of the methodological schisms..." between neo Marxists and neo-Weberians (1987: 143). In her earlier work on *Loft Living* Zukin noted "The promotion of a historical infrastructure, for example, changes the nature of urban space. By giving value to old buildings near the downtown, preservation makes them into a scarce commodity and so creates monopoly rents. Alternatively, the uncertainty that surrounds their conservation — in the face of the predominant tendency to destroy and rebuild — can create a climate in which speculation runs rife." We might say that the promotion of ventures such, tourist or immigrant residential zones as well as, "arts infrastructures changes the nature of the urban space" (1982: 190) elaborating on her insight into "patterns of cultural and social reproduction" (1987: 131) it should be possible to see how choices of even the least "elite" members of society are also reflected in the residential and commercial landscapes of central cities in the United States and Italy.

Visual Sociology and attention to Vernacular Landscapes in the inner city allows us to see conflict, competition, and dominance at a level not usually noticed and which can easily be related to the theories and descriptions of Lefebvre and Bourdieu. Just think of how different, and perhaps more interesting, "accessibility" and "distanciation" become when we speak of racial discrimination in local housing markets, and inter-ethnic violence at the street level. What is a better introduction to the ethnic neighborhood than when Harvey speaks of spatial dominance thusly: "Successful control presumes a power to exclude unwanted elements. Fine-tuned ethnic, religious, racial, and status discriminations are frequently called into play within such a process of community construction" (266). Other productions of Symbolic Capital, defined by Bourdieu as "The collection of luxury goods attesting to the taste and distinction of the owner" (1977: 188) might help us to understand the gentrification of these very same areas during a later phase in the second circuit of capital when once run-down neighborhoods become the shabbily chic "in" places to live, such as *Greenwich Village* in New York City or *Trastevere* in Rome. Since "the most successful ideological effects are those which have no words, and ask no more than complicitous silence," so the production of symbolic capital serves ideological functions, because the mechanisms through which it contributes "to the reproduction of the established order and to the perpetuation of domination remain hidden"(Bourdieu 1977: 188).

Reviewing the Spatial Semeiotics of Little Italies (Krase, 1997)

Little Italy is a product and source of both social and cultural capital. Although ordinary people in the neighborhood are ultimately at the mercy of distant structural forces, in their naivete they continue to create and modify the local spaces allocated to them, and inevitably become part of the urban landscape. Thusly people and spaces become symbols and as a result, they come to merely represent themselves and thereby lose their autonomy. The enclave comes to symbolize its imagined inhabitants and stands for them independent of their residence in it. Localized reproductions of cultural spaces can also be easily commodified. For example, the expropriated cultural capital of the Italian American vernacular such as resistance to diversity and cultural insularity, perhaps even intolerance becomes a sales point in real estate parlance as a quaint "safe" neighborhood, with "old world charm," and romantically symbolizing the "way its used to be" in the "old neighborhood."

No model or stereotype can ever adequately represent the multiple realities of Italian, or any other, ethnic-America. There is too much in the way of permutations of generations, continuity, and change. But for many novelists, script writers, those otherwise in the Arts and Humanities, as well as Social Scientists, Little Italy does represent the idea of Italian America and how Visual Sociology helps us to understand both its structural and cultural realities. If I may suggest; the idealized ethnic urban spaces, both "Representations of Spaces" as well as "Spaces of Representation," can be summarized as follows: Oblivion, Ruination, Ethnic Theme Parks, Immigration Museums, and Anthropological Gardens.

I have argued that "semiotically speaking," models of Little Italies are as follows:

1. Oblivion. Oblivion means "the state of being forgotten." Urban Renewal, Highways, bridges, construction.
2. Ruins. The rubble of neighborhoods abandoned in anticipation of "renewal", cleared of misnamed "slums" —, and still awaiting new uses. These "liminal" zones of "in betweenness" are on their way toward oblivion.
3. Ethnic Theme Parks. Little Italies are preserved as spectacles for the appreciation of tourists.

Theme Parks usually contain (4.) Assimilation Museums, or places for the preservation and display of inanimate objects and (5.) Anthropological Gardens (Human Zoos), where the subjects of curiosity are still alive.

The primary focus in this paper are Little Italies and Italian cities as Theme Parks, or "Spectacles" for tourists. What they have in common is that they are visible commodified cultural representations of Italian America and Italy. David Harvey explains that the "organization of spectacles" can be part of "the production of an urban image" which is an "important facet of interurban competition" as "urban strategies to capture consumer dollars." (233) Although he is primarily concerned with the modern or post modern version of "display of the commodity" (271) under the constraints of " flexible accumulation," he notes that since the ancient Roman "Bread and Festivals" spectacles have existed as a means of social control (270). In short, the creation and maintenance of Spectacle is associated with a highly fragile patterning of urban investment as well as increasing social and spatial polarization of urban class antagonisms (273).

Contradictory and Complementary Explanations: Italy as an Ethnic Theme Park Spectacle

Atroshencko and Grundy provide a classic explanation for the "white villages" such as those found in *Puglia* which are a major attraction for the hundred of thousands of tourists who deluge the Adriatic coast each summer: "for centuries, the inhabitants of these villages lived almost at subsistence level. There is a notable absence of unnecessary ornamentation on the buildings. Nothing is 'fashionable' or disposable. There is no conspicuous waste. Each village keeps its integrity; it does not lose its soul. There are constant, delightful juxtapositions of strong, natural forms and ever new and varied spaces. Based on the regenerative realities of the locale, this approach to building *enabled tradition to act as an invisible hand* (my emphasis), guiding the parts toward a unified and ordered completeness. Additions 'grew' adjacent to existing structures. The builders created practical, complex and visually stunning environments without destroying the unity of the village; viewed from afar, it is elegant, sculptural form that fits naturally into the landscape (5-6).

It has practical aspects also: the whitewash protects against disease and reflects the summer heat off the walls; the hillside site provides drainage; the civic identity and cooperation necessary for the preservation and protection of the village has remained intact down the centuries. The whitewashed village is a functional organism that meets the requirements for shelter, work, quiet and social intercourse. Each element feels unique, especially the dwellings, whose scale, asymmetry and flexibility create endless combinations. These villages allow variations of the whole in order to fit individual needs. Here in these beautiful environments we see solutions to many universal problems facing the world, and they are worth emulating" (1991 :6).

Also, found in *Puglia* are conical, "beehive" roofs that is a peculiar "style" for the *Val d'Itri* area. According to Rudofsky, *trulli* are "the archaic house form of an early megalithic civilization, they are related to the Balearic *tlyots*, Sardinian *nuraghi*, and the *sesi* of *Pantelleria*. Despite the passage of a dozen nations, this type has survived almost without change since the second millenium BC" (1964:49) It is likely that the "white village" represents less of an "invisible hand" than the representation of either Spanish or Greek colonization.

There is yet another description of contemporary *trulli* which argues that although the system of *trullo* construction already existed it was preserved because of feudalism which came to the territory at the end of the 15th century. In order to maintain the vulnerability of the newly created serfs, feudal lords decreed that the shelters of peasants and shepherds had to be destroyable in only one night. "So the agglomerate of 'casedde' dry built with rustic local stone and destructible with swift manoeuvre in a short time arose" (*Alberobello*, 1982) given the end of feudalism and the invention of air-conditioning one might search for other reasons for their presentation as an important stunning element of *Alberobello's Pugliese* Ethnic Theme Park.

Over the past three decades I have observed and photographed what Lyn Lofland refers to as the "Private, Parochial, and Public Realms," of a wide range of Italian and Italian American neighborhoods. To say that they do not generally conform to the visual expectations of middle-class Anglo-American urban "ideal" would be an understatement. Here Gans reflects on the visually induced misperceptions by outsiders of the Italian West End of Boston as a "slum": "The West Enders themselves took the poor maintenance of the building exteriors, halls, and cellars in stride, and paid little attention to them. The low rents were more than made up for these deficiencies, and for the generally rundown appearance of the area. Moreover, they did not consider these conditions a reflection on their status. Having no interest in the opinions of the outside world, *they were not overly concerned about the image that the West End had in the eyes of outsiders* (my emphasis). They did not like to be called slum dwellers, of course, and resented the exaggerated descriptions of West End deterioration that appeared regularly in the Boston Press. Nor were they happy about the rooming houses that bordered the West End, or the skid row occupants who sometimes wandered into it. Unlike the middle class, however, they did not care about "the address." Consequently, the cultural differences between working and middle-class residential choice suggest that the prevailing professional housing standards which reflect only the later could not be rigidly applied to the West End" (1962: 315-16).

What Gans and other observers of inner city Italian American enclaves were not appreciative of was the vernacular aesthetic of Italian urbanism. Some social scientists did make accurate associations with the reluctance of the Italian middle class and peasants to display their relative prosperity in order to shield it from the tax scrutiny of authorities, as well as prying neighbors. However, they neglected to investigate whether exterior appearances have other cultural, economic, and social values. In the present context we must note that for centuries the rather run-down appearance of building exteriors in Italy have been part of the "charm" of the peninsula. At the extreme, visitors are attracted to Italy as a cornucopia of ruins. The built environment of much of Italy has a shabbily chic "worn" look. In recent years British and American retirees, for example, have been attracted to abandoned rural homes and villages in regions such as Tuscany. From Shakespeare to Puzo, this version of Italy has been a favorite for writers of fiction.

II. Italy, Rome. 1997 Research Narrative

Now that we have had a brief retrospective on American Little Italies and a short theoretical and historical discussion of special and ordinary Italian spaces as "spectacle," we shall turn to the contemporary Italian urban scene where there is a related problem of visual transformation. Here our focus will be on people rather than buildings. An important aspect of the city scene is the people in the picture. People become part of the space by simply being in it.

Tourism is a major international industry and the sales image of Italy is derived in large part from foreigners' mental images of the Public Realms of Italians cities and towns. These spaces contain both monumental and vernacular landscapes. We might say that, for tourists at least, Italy itself is one huge multifaceted Ethnic Theme Park. Millions of visitors flock to places like Rome every year with expectations about what the "real" Italy and "real" Italians look like. They come expecting to view an Italy which conform to their stereotypical expectations. Most get their images from popular media and think Italians should look like Marcello Mastroiani and Sophia Loren. The built icons of Rome are the Fountain of Trevi, the Spanish Steps, the Coliseum, the Vatican, the Roman Forum, and the Via Veneto.

Luckily for those who market the traditional images of Rome few visitors travel outside the historical center. Perhaps they pass thorough the central station and a few may occasionally ride on public transportation. During their sojourn they will see ethnically diverse crowds of tourists, but not much of the local population. While eating out they seldom will look beyond the dining room into restaurant kitchens. While making purchases at local stores they will not peek into the rear of shops to see the workers toiling there. In short they see only a small proportion of the Public Realm and the people who live in the city of Rome.

In recent decades what Italy and Italians look like has changed considerably. In addition to the ordinary processes of modernization of urban spaces, and the construction of new built environments, a major factor in the changing image of the Italy has been immigration. It is argued here that the past decade of immigration has already had a major impact on Italian identity. This is true not only because of the relatively large numbers of newcomers but because of their differences with indigenous Italians. These racial (physical) and ethnic (cultural) differences have produced an even great change in the "appearance" of some of Italy's well known urban landscapes. Given the projection that Italy will increasingly become multicultural as it integrates with the rest of Europe, changes in its visual identity in the 21st Century will be even more pronounced.

Research Narrative

My trip to Rome was intended to observe and capture on film the visual transformations of its well-know and the lesser known Parochial (neighborhood) and Public spaces. My first task was to identify those areas of Rome that had residential concentrations of immigrants. My next step was to observe and then document via photography how these newcomers symbolically transform the vernacular landscape. This was also my first disappointment. Based on my study of immigrant settlements in American and other cities I expected to find clearly identifiable enclaves where the majority, if not a significant plurality, of local residents were immigrants. Contrary to my expectation I learned that for Rome, this was not the case. Compared to the United States residential mobility in Italy is slow. Therefore opportunities for housing are limited. In contrast to places like New York City for example Roman neighborhoods do not completely change in a matter of a decade. I should note here that my interest was not in the mobility of the large foreign populations who are in temporary residence in Rome for business or political reasons. The area near the *Piazza del Popolo*, for example, seems to be such a multiethnic community with upscale convenience stores serving "foreign" clienteles.

Even more so in Rome, as in contrast to cities like Turin, legal and illegal immigrants participate primarily in the marginal economy. Because Rome is an administrative as opposed to an industrial city, there is little need for large scale migration and the related residential concentration near sources of industrial employment. Due to the relatively slow residential mobility and neighborhood transition immigrant populations are residentially dispersed. The classic pattern in the US central city during periods of high immigration had been the development of immigrant enclaves in urban ecological "Zones of Transition" located near the central business districts. In Rome, with few exceptions, the oldest central areas have also been the most prestigious or protected. Today, even the well-known working-class (at one time run-down) areas in central Rome are being gentrified. In the 1990s the least desirable areas for residence and commerce, near the central station, are also "in transition." Much of the upgrading of these marginal areas is probably due to the preparation for the Jubilee in 2000.

Roman Data

Some of my most valuable observations were the result of comprehensive city tours combining windshield surveys and walks by auto led by Professors Stefania Vergati and Leonardo Cannavó of the University of Rome, La Sapienza. With their expert assistance I was able to visit and photograph all the varieties of Roman housing and zones of residential development in a short period of time. After several excursions I had scanned all eighteen zones of Roman housing — high and low density, public and private, lower through upper class, and oldest to newest. These research trips also made it possible for me to select areas for more focused research. They made it possible for me to note where immigrants were most visible, and, in some other case, signs of their invisibility. (Vergati 1982 and 1994)

Not all my research was in the field with a camera. In order to better select sites for extensive observation and photographing I spoke with ordinary Romans, and informed sources at the University. The two most important published sources were the Italian *Censis* and school data collected by *Caritas*. These documents allowed me to identify those areas where at least "officially" the highest residential density of immigrants, and their counties of origin, were located. I also read selected studies on immigrants in Italian cities and scanned Roman newspapers for references to immigration issues.

According to the *Census* (Censis) of October, 1991 the population of Rome was 2,775,250, and the percentage of foreigners with permission was 3.9%. By 1998 the population grew to 2,812,473 and registered foreigners were 4.8%. Multiethnic Rome has residents from 167 different nations. *Caritas* estimates that in 1998 legal and illegal, temporary and permanent immigrants together were 6.2% of the Roman population. There were 134,578 foreign residents in Rome and an estimated 40,000 more who were unregistered. I note here in contrast that since 1900 the Borough of Brooklyn, New York has averaged a foreign born population of at least 30%.

Further information provided by *Caritas Roma* on school children demonstrated that the immigrant populations were not randomly dispersed. Foreign children (more than 2.5%) are enrolled in schools in districts (*circoscrizioni*) 1, 2, 3, 15, 18, 19, 20. The highest percentages of foreign children are found in lower grades. As one might also anticipate this concentration mirrors the census data which finds the highest concentration of immigrants in the center (1) and in descending order of concentration in districts 2, 19, 20 much less in 3, 7, 8, 9, 10, 12, 15, 17. Immigrants seem to be connected by major public transportation routes out from center to the northeast, north, northwest, and west. Of the total number of immigrants: European are 28%, African 18%, Asian 28%, and American 13.9%. It must be noted that 10% of "foreigners" are born in Italy of foreign parents. Of special value for my research was the fact that 33% of all Africans live in VII, 33% of Asians in districts 7, 9 and 10 and those from the Far East in 4, 6, 11, and 12. According to the published data immigrants from the Americas and the Far East are the most residentially concentrated.

Concern about immigrants in Italy is not limited to changes in the visible environment. The daily newspapers contained regular stories about crime and various conflicts between immigrants and authorities in many cities. I was also invited to participate in an Italian Chamber of Deputies Seminar (1998) which concerned the association of immigrants with crime in many Italian cities. In Rome, involvement in serious and quality of life (*microcrimine*) crime is also associated with immigrants. For although they make up only six percent of the total population, immigrants were arrested for 29% of robberies, 43.9%, of thefts, and 39.1% of drug arrests. At the time I was in residence, Roman enforcement authorities announced a plan to attack the problem on quality of life crimes on a zonal basis by concentrated specialized police forces in immigrant areas.

Observations

Those who study immigration in Italy well understand that the published estimates of resident foreigners, as well as information about their origins, are not very reliable. The biggest problem are underestimates of the size of the population dues to the growing number of undocumented aliens (*clandestini*). This is further complicated in places like Rome by the large number of tourists and other foreign visitors. I believe that this situation makes visual sociological research of even greater value for the understanding of multiethnic Italian spaces where foreign populations are more visibly evident on the streets than would be anticipated by official statistics.

I quickly discovered that significant expressions of immigrant concentration were not merely residential but in particular kinds of urban territory. After identifying those areas in which I expected to find immigrants I traveled to them by foot, bus and subway. This is important to note because most immigrants, when not walking, regularly use public transportation. My first findings were made in transit. Immigrants make up a larger than expected proportion of those using public transportation, especially on certain routes. Their over-representation is enhanced by the fact that Italians carry on their romance with their cars and scooters by driving to work.

Once I arrived at a designated "immigrant" zone I spent hours walking the streets, some of which I revisited some several times.

Of all the districts which I observed and photographed the most "visibly ethnic" was near the central station. There one can find concentrations of residence, work, shopping, and public transportation. It is interesting to note that in general the center of the city with its pedestrian shopping areas and thousands of tourists is multi-ethnic, but not necessarily residentially mixed. Also, in the residences near the station I believe there is a significant undercount of immigrants (probably *clandestini*), who share apartments with registered aliens and who may be sleeping in the same buildings in which they work. My street-level observations, as well as looking into private spaces behind normally closed doors, reveal a much larger immigrant world. Another problem for ethnographic researchers is that Italian residential spaces are difficult to access because they are usually set off from public spaces. Looking for indications of new immigrants around the central station I observed a Little Africa, a growing Chinatown, and a flourishing Bangladeshi jewelry trade. Both Chinatown and the jewelry markets seemed to also be light production centers; which would be consistent with undocumented alien workers in sweatshops. Local stores also displayed and sold ethnic foods, as well as other culturally appropriate services, provisions, and clothing.

One might ask "How is ethnicity visual?" Africans and Asians, because of their "different" physical appearances *vis a vis* Romans are easy to identify, as are other ethnic groups such as Slavs with light skin and light hair. These groups are apparent near the station and other international areas, even in those districts of higher class foreign residents. In the better residential districts one also gets to see "foreign" household workers. Several times people explained to me that, for example, household workers from the Philippines are "preferred." Without attempting a complete explanation in this limited space, I might say that different ethnic groups also dress differently than the local population. Many of the Slavic (Polish) working class women I observed in the center, and in markets such as the Portuguese Market in *Trastevere*, were dressed as I remembered them from my research in Poland a few years ago, and as I see them in Polish immigrant areas in the United States. In general the most obvious immigrants are those who are the most visibly different, such as Rom (Gypsy), and Moslem women.

The following are examples of situations, places, activities in which ethnic differences were most visibly notable during my research in Rome. I must caution that there are significant temporal variables; weekday, weekends, early morning and evening, as well as locational ones.

1. *Public Transportation Centers and Routes*. Due to the residential dispersal of the different immigrant populations, travel to the center (or centers) appears to be necessary in order to maintain ethnic solidarity. Foreign (non-Italian) greetings and conversations can be overheard daily on buses, trains, and at local stops. Much more intensive ethnic social interaction takes place on weekends at the central station. On summer weekends groups of Latinos picnic under the shade of bus stop shelters. Co-ethnics share food, drinks, and conversation. It would be interesting to investigate whether the bus depot islands relate to the places from which people come. The central station is also where arriving immigrants are met by co-ethnics. Most disturbing was the sight of Rom women, often pregnant or with babies, entering crowded buses and subway cars as riders moved cautiously away. I was informed that Romans associate their presence with pick pocket-ing.
2. *Centers of Telecommunication*. Large numbers of immigrants can be observed at local public telephone banks or long distance telephone service outlets. The greatest concentration was at the central station underground corridors. One may also assume that low-income immigrants, and the undocumented, lack home phones.
3. *Major Urban Arteries and Intersections*. As one travels toward the center of the city on public or private surface transportation one will observe "foreign" beggars, squeegee men, (*squigi*), and street vendors who have become fixtures of the arterial landscape. Most squeegee mean appeared to be either European (Slavic) or North African. In many places the men who work at the gas stations are also apparently "foreign;" south Asian (Indo-Pakistani).
4. *Soccer World Cup*. While I was in Rome the Italian team was competing in the World Cup. This provided the opportunity to observe expressions of Italian ethnic (national) pride. In the most multiethnic Esquilino area, foreign vendors hawked Italian flags on the streets. One

match pitted Cameroon against Italy and the African section near the central station was the site of a clash of ethnic symbols (flags).

5. *Local Social Life*. Immigrants take part in the communal social of Roman neighborhoods. For example, I observed Moslem families and children during a *festa* in the Monte Sacro *piazza*. Foreign children can also be seen in local lower schools and their mothers participate in the same ritual of picking up children for lunch at home as do Italian parents.
6. *Tourist Sites*. All around the major one can find an assortment of immigrants, as vendors, and beggars (especially Rom women and children). I was particular struck by immigrants dressed in Roman soldier costumes near the Coliseum with whom tourists could have their picture taken. They can also be found behind the scenes in downtown restaurants, and Latinos might pass as Italian waiters. One Roman native commented to me that "Egyptians" are employed as pizza makers because they look more Italian. In most cases the space in which they work, or perhaps better put "perform," is visible to patrons.
7. *Public Markets*. In local and central markets immigrants are seen in varying proportions, but always greater than then official statistics would lead one to expect in. This is especially true near the central station (*Piazza Vittorio*) and in the well-known Portuguese market. Some references have been made to a *Suk* in cities such as Naples (Amato, 1997). In Rome I did not find a market dominated by non-Italian proprietors. Increasingly however, Italian vendors sell non-Italian ethnic foods and products and in most of the markets immigrant vendors sell their wares on the periphery.
8. *Public Parks*. In most parks I saw female immigrants serving as nannies — pushing baby carriages or minding children. During the evening in marginal parklands and other open spaces foreign women appeared as prostitutes. Immigrants are also over-represented as the destitute, beggars, and the homeless who may congregate at social service centers. Although it is certainly difficult to ascertain their exact status they are frequently referred to in discussions of *micro-criminalità* (quality of life crimes). In one centrally located park area I saw several Rom women children relaxing with their young children

on the grass and having lunch. In the same area were many groups of foreign (European and North African) men lounging, eating, or sleeping. I also found evidence of overnight sleeping areas beneath bushes and in fenced-off archeological sites. Similar evidence, such as mattresses, can be found along the banks of the Tiber.

9. *Religious Centers*. Immigrants are apparent at specific houses of worship. There are several Moslem mosques and centers. Rome has a new huge central mosque that is attended by thousands of worshipers. There are several Orthodox and Slavic national churches, and a Roman Catholic, Polish- speaking church to which Poles travel from all over the city for Sunday mass. Another, *San Silvestro in Capite*, is attended by immigrants from the Philippines. Similarly there are Asian language Catholic masses and Asian (Korean and Chinese) Protestant churches which attract visually distinctive worshipers. Specific churches minister to specific immigrants, which is best expressed by signs announcing services in a variety of foreign languages. I attended mass at an "American" church "the church of Santa Susanna" which bills itself as "a home for all English Speaking Catholics in Rome."
10. *Residential Areas with Ethnic Identity*. Other than the Asian and African section (Esquilino) near the central station few areas were widely recognized as having a distinctly ethnic identity in the sense that Americans peak of ethnic neighborhoods. At one time the beach resort area, Ostia, had been a "Russian," area; especially in the off-season winter months when rents were lower. This was in the late 1980s during the time of the mass exodus of Jewish Russians who were en route to Israel or elsewhere. I learned that in recent years the Russians have moved out but that have been replaced by a smaller number of Polish renters. Lastly, I was also directed to observe a Rom settlement (perhaps "encampment") which was located in a rather run-down area of unregulated urban land at some distance northward from the center.

Summary

It is difficult to summarize in this rather brief report but I believe it can be said with confidence that immigrants (first and second generations) have been symbolically transforming the public spaces of Rome. As had their Italian immigrant counterparts to cities in the United States, immigrants to Rome have been gradually changing the vernacular landscapes by their own, merely physical, appearances as well as their activities in the spaces they use. Their presence and their "difference" also change the value of the space. As have nonwhite migrants to American city neighborhoods, in some cases they have also stigmatized places by their presence. (Krase, 1977). It is interesting to note in this regard that some better off Romans are beginning to flee the least desirable of the central zones citing classic urban dissatisfactions with changing inner city neighborhoods such as "noise," "dirt," and "crime." In contrast, at the same time that some residents move out, in other central Roman areas property values are soaring and what American urbanists would regard as 'gentrification' is taking place. This urban development paradox is not inconsistent with observations of David Harvey on "circuits of capital" (1989). It might be said that this essay is limited in scope, and perhaps value, in reference to the issue of Italian immigration. However, international crises such as those created by military conflicts in Africa, Bosnia, and Kosovo and today Iraq, have brought the problem of immigration to the forefront of Italian politics. In addition the need to control large-scale movement of illegal immigrants through Italy and into their European Union partners has made immigration to Italy a major European-wide problem. Uncontrolled immigration is not merely a problem of perception and national image.

In sum, based on my limited research efforts I would argue that Rome is much more multiethnic than Romans themselves are aware of because immigrants are found in particular kinds of spaces; especially those spaces through which Romans travel, and that they try to avoid. If I might say; it is my impression that in general Italians tend to ignore immigrants and talk as though they are not in their presence. They, immigrants, are not part of their personal Italian space. This is primarily due to the fact that until the present new immigrant populations in Rome are widely dispersed residentially, but also periodically and situationally clustered such as at the Central Station, markets, or their places of worship. Slowly but surely, the meanings of Rome's spaces are changing. One might ask when will "Chinatown," "Little India," or "Little Africa" become part of the tourist landscape and when will the meaning of "Italian" include, to Italians, the racial and national diversity which is growing before their eyes? Such questions require much further discussion and certainly greater research efforts but then can be speculated upon here. The meaning of Italy will change because it already contested as evidenced in this story from the Migration News, online about "dark-skinned" beauty Denny Mendez:

> A naturalized Italian citizen who moved to Italy from the Dominican Republic when her mother married an Italian won the Miss Italy 1996 beauty contest, prompting a number of reflections on racial tolerance in Italy, what it means to be Italian, and "Italian beauty."
>
> Two of the judges were initially suspended for saying, before the competition, that a black woman could not represent Italian beauty. According to one judge, "I would happily elect her Miss Universe. But what has she got to do with Italy? She is not Mediterranean." During the pageant, one-third of the one million Italians who called in their vote gave it to Mendez. Prime Minister Romano Prodi had commented on the Miss Italy results, "Italy is changing," he said. "We also have black soccer players, and now this too is a sign." (1996)

Those who study Italy know it has always been diverse, if not recognized officially as multicultural. For them Italy now has a new mix and perhaps a new recognition. Parallel to this reality is that of Italian America which has also increasing become more diverse and struggling with its connection to an outmoded notion of *Italianità*. Finally, I hope that this essay will lend support for the use of Visual Sociology as another tool to help in the study of a extremely important problem which will have a major impact on the future of Italy and the rest of Europe not to mention Italian and Italian American Identity.

---

*Acknowledgement is made here to Rector's Committee for Scientific Research, and the Department of Sociology, University of Rome, La Sapienza during the month of June, 1998 for support of my photographic research on the "New Immigrants to Rome," and the PSC/CUNY Travel Fund.

Works Cited

Amato, Fabio. "La città come immagine: il suq di piazza Garibaldi a Napoli e l'integrazione povera." *Africa e Mediterranea*. Bologna: Editore Pendragon, 1997: 20-23.

Anderson, Benedict. *Imagined Communities: Reflections on the Origin and Spread of Nationalism*. London: Verson Press, 1983.

Baldassar, Loretta. *Visits Home: Migration Experiences between Italy and Australia*. Melbourne: Melbourne University Press, 2001.

Bourdieu, Pierre. *Outline of a Theory of Practice*. New York: Cambridge University Press: 1977.

________. *Distinction: A Social Critique of the Judgement of Taste*. Andover: Routledge and Kegan Paul, 1984.

Campani, Giovanna. "Albanians in Italy: Asylum Seekers, Refugees, Immigrants." In *Delle Donne* op cit.: 221-241.

Castells, Manuel. *The Informational City*. Oxford: Blackwell Publishers, 1989.

Davis, Mike. *Magical Urbanism: Latinos Reinvent the U.S. City*. London: Verso, 2001.

Delle Donne, Marcella. "Difficulties of Refugees Toward Integration: The Italian Case." In Marcella Delle Donne (Ed) *Avenues to Integration: Refugees in Contemporary Europe*. Napoli: Ipermedium, 1995: 110-41.

Dickinson, James. "Entropic Zones: Buildings and Structures of the Contemporary City." *CNS* 7 (3), September, 1996: 81-95.

"Gli Studenti Stranieri nell'Area Romana" *Forum per l'intercultura Promosso* dalla Caritas Diocesana di Roma, Centro Studi & Documentazione. April, 1998.

Giddens, Anthony. *The Constitution of Society: Outline of the Theory of Structuration*. Cambridge: Polity, 1984.

Gottdiener, Mark. *The Social Production of Urban Space*. (2nd Ed.) Austin: University of Texas Press, 1994.

Grady, John. "The Scope of Visual Sociology." *Visual Sociology*. Volume 11, Number 2 (Winter) 1996: 10-24.

Gardaphé, Fred L. *Italian Signs, American Streets: the Evolution of Italian American Narrative*. Durham: Duke University Press, 1996: 20

Gubert, Renzo and Luigi Tomasi. (Eds). *Robert E. Park and The Melting Pot Theory*. Trento; Reverdito Edizione, 1994.

DeMaria Harney, Nicholas. *Eh, Paesan!: Being Italian in Toronto*. Toronto: University of Toronto Press, 1998.

Harper, Douglas. "Visual Sociology: Expanding Sociological Vision." *American Sociologist* 19 (10) 1988: 54-70.

Harvey, David. *The Urban Experience*. Baltimore: Johns Hopkins University Press, 1989.

Brinkerhoff Jackson, John. *Discovering the Vernacular Landscape*. New Haven: Yale University Press, 1984.

Krase, Jerome. "Reactions to the Stigmata of Inner City Living." *Journal of Sociology and Social Welfare*. Vol. IV, No. 7 (September) 1977: 997 1011.

_______. "Traces of Home," *Places: A Quarterly Journal of Environmental Design*. 8,4, 1993: 46-55.

_______. "Italian and Italian American Spaces" In Mary Jo Bona and Anthony Julian Tamburri (Eds) *Through the Looking Glass: Italian and Italian/American Images in the Media*. Staten Island, New York: American Italian Historical Association, 1996: 241-65.

_______. "Brooklyn's Blacks, Italians, and Jews: The Anatomy of Interethnic Conflict." In Mario A. Toscano (Ed) *Origins and Transitions*. Ipermedium: Napoli and Los Angeles, 1996: 167-83.

_______. "The Spatial Semeiotics of Little Italies and Italian Americans." In Mario Aldo Toscano (Ed) *Dialettica Locale-Globale* Napoli: Ipermedium, 1997: 75-86.

Lebrvre, Henri. *The Production of Space*. Oxford: Blackwell, 1991.

Lofland, Lyn. *The Public Realm: Exploring the City's Quintessential Social Territory*. New York: Aldine de Gruyter, 1998.

"Italy: Amnesty for Enforcement Assistance?" *Migration News*, Volume 3 Number 10, October 1996. http://migration.ucdavis.edu/mn

Rudofsky, Bernard. *Architecture Without Architects*. Albuquerque: University of New Mexico Press, 1964.

Seminario di Studio, "Modelli di Criminalità Metropolitana": il Caso di Roma. Camera Dei Deputati. Roma. June 16, 1998.

Suddivisione del Terriotorio Comunale in Venti Circoscrizione (Deliberazione N. 695 dell' 11 febbraio 1972)

Vergati, Stefania. *L'Urbanizzazione*. Palermo: Palumbo Editore, 1982.

_______. *Le Oasi Immaginarie*. Bonanno Editore, 1994

Zukin, Sharon. *Loft Living: Culture and Capital in Urban Change*. Baltimore: Johns Hopkins, 1982.

_______. "Gentrification: Culture and Capital in the Urban Core." *Annual Review of Sociology*. Volume 13, 1987: 129-47.

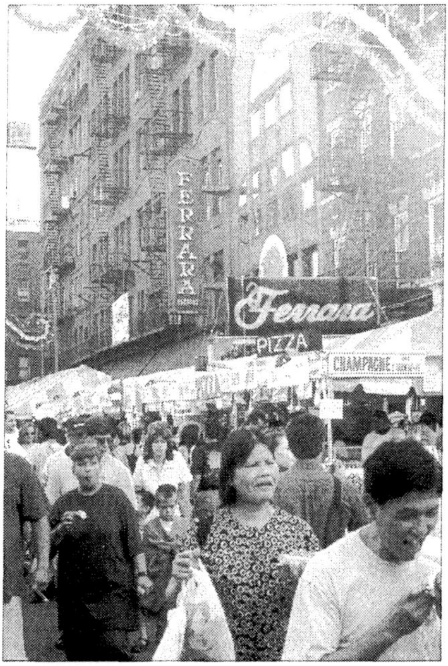

San Gennaro Festa, Mulberry Street, Little Italy, Manhattan, 1999.

Our Lady of Mount Carmel Festa, Italian Harlem, Manhattan, New York, 1997.

Gurra Café, Kosovo, Albanian Belmont Little Italy, Bronx, New York, 1999.

Tim's International Meat Market, Belmont, Little Italy, Bronx, New York, 1999.

Cinesi Italiani Alimentari, Rome, Italy, 1998 (cinesi italiani)

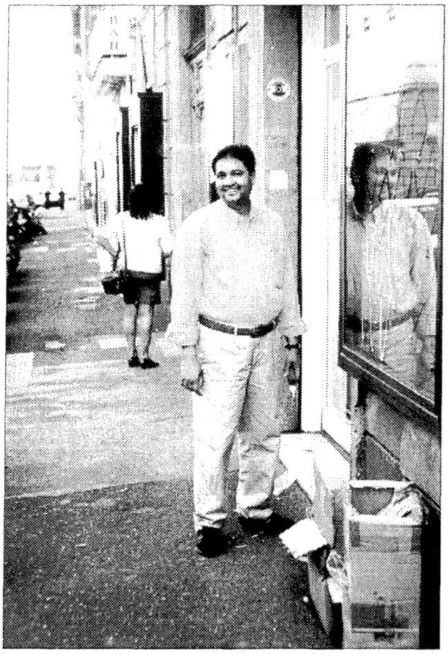

A New Roman, Rome, Italy, 1998. (Amin)

Termini Stazione Picnic Gathering, Rome, Italy, 1998.

Diversity in Esquillino, Rome, Italy, 1998.

THE OTHER PASSENGER

Antonino Mazza
Carleton University

In the Maldonado, the native villans thinned out,
and the Calabrians took root in their stead —
a people with whom no one chose to interfere,
because of their dangerously good memory for malice,
and their traitorous stabbings on the long term.
Jorge Luis Borges

I am in the middle of a landscape, in the middle of France. The year, 1972, a hot July afternoon. In the window of the compartment, streaming past, are poppy fields; small oblong pieces of pale sky farther afield, whose colour and luminosity are reflected in the faces of the other passengers.

I have boarded this train in Lyon, after a brief visit with shards of my relatives there. After a few days with cousins in a hog-shed, in Brig. After several nights spent in the company of an elderly uncle in the asphyxiating air of a greasy underground parking garage, in Turin.

I had wanted to journey back to Calabria for some time, to the land of my birth, of my childhood, with its volcano, its earth tremors, Mount Etna dancing on the water. I had set out from Ottawa, remembering the village as it had always stayed in my young memory, a village in the hills of the brain: its walnut trees and prickly pears in the lion heat, coiled black snakes on the parched earth under a pomegranate.

And then there was the mythical family. A fine tapestry of cousins, aunts, uncles, and more aunts, and great-grandparents. But the village I found had few heroes left. The family had scattered, *si sparpagghiau, figghiu meu.* I would be told this over and over, *soft as a whisper*, in my mother tongue, by my ninety-six-year-old paternal grandmother.

So, after a whole fortnight of walking up and down craggy hillsides in the sun glow, on the stones that lit up everything with the swarthy odours lost long ago; sitting with grandmother in the open air under a moon that played with her hair, grandmother who looked in a dish and read my thoughts, with those eyes of hers, half-yellow and half-grey: "*Setti pani e setti pisci lu malocchiu mi sparisci*"[1] — there was nothing more to do but copy all the addresses I could from letters she kept with her oven-dried bread, in a trunk, *nta cascia ru pani ruru*. "Be sure you go visit them all," she told me. "I know it will please your grandfather." *Cusì fa' cuntent'o nonnu*.

It didn't seem at all to matter that grandfather had been dead for sometime. So I promised her I would do it. Then, tossed all night with thoughts of breaking my oath. But, as I took my leave of her early the next morning, I sensed that I would never be held that way again. *Her lips on my cheeks were moist as if I had been kissed by dew*. And boarded the crowded northbound train.

This train is taking me to Liège. *Centre industriel: sidérurgie, metallurgie, chimie, pneumatique, verrerie*. A smoke-stacked, coal-dust ridden town in the interior of Belgium. I'm going there to visit with grandfather's other son, my father's younger and only brother, who as a consequence of years of toil in the nether world of that city has contracted the black lung disease.

Tonight, in the skeletal light in his living room I will see his skin covered in scabs, his head that has shed its hair. The dreadful sight will give me a first encounter with the eight bones that make up the human skull!

Still, I am prepared even less for the harangue that I am about to endure during this train ride across undulating Europe, with its flower beds: Lyon so much like Ottawa. Same waterways, same manicured parks, same immigrants' quarters in the shade of Gothic gargoyles. The same lacerated bodies huddled together in tiny kitchens with their broken panes, so similar to the cramped lodgings in the shadow of the Peace Tower.

The same circumspect mother and daughter entered the train compartment and sat close to the door unperturbed for the entire ride between the two towns. Then they rose and disappeared, taking their calm, oblong faces with them onto the platform where their elusive blue eyes truly belonged. And now, in the waning afternoon, my fellow travelers are two men. One, a toady medical student, is going on about vines, about his summer vacation on the family farm in Champagne. The other is middle-aged, in a suit, a historian from the University of Lyon who, graciously unwilling to exclude me from the conversation, or perhaps bored, will shortly change the subject, initiating a discussion. Though when all was said and done it was more an insulting aside on comparative demography, all directed at me; capping it all, before detraining in the gathering dusk, with a racially based exegesis of the concept of nationhood.

As for me, I was reading Rilke's *The Notebooks of Malte Laurids Brigge*, in an Italian edition, *I quaderni di Malte Laurids Brigge*, which I picked up at the Turin train station. I remember approaching the newsstand at Porta Nova, and reaching by chance for the unfamiliar book and turning to the very first page.

It began:

> "*Sept. 11, Rue Toullier [1902]*
> *And so, here is the place then where people come to live; I think rather that they die, here.*"

This sentence resonated through me, for I had harbored a similar sensation throughout my first stop-over with my relatives in that northern Italian city of Turin.

So I bought it. And went on reading it feverishly on the trains: Turin to Brig, Brig to Lyon — and now, since sunset, since with the departure of the two Frenchmen I'd been left alone once more on my journey, I'd been entranced again to the very end of the book by Rilke's version of the fable of the prodigal son.

Only then did I raise my glance.

It is night outside, in the window there is the empty compartment in a depth of liquid purple. Reflected in the glass is my crumpled face and forehead. It seemed suspended in the reckless noise of time, the French professor's voice still ringing in my ears.

— *Monsieur, êtes vous italien*? He surmised this from the language of the book I was reading.

I answered that I was born in Calabria, but that I was a Canadian citizen.

My reply must have irked him, since he rapidly retorted: — *And just how does one go about changing nationality — had I reneged my ancestry, my roots, mes racines*?

Suddenly — I could not believe it — I was defending myself. I told him that my case was hardly unusual; rather, from what I had already seen, mine could only be but one instance of the exodus and permanent resettlement of different peoples in recent years. The very reason for my traveling to his city attested to it. Indeed, all the people I had known in childhood were now strewn all over the hemisphere.

I was no renegade, I assured him. The Italy I had known had taken flight, and no longer existed but in memory. Mostly everyone I knew was living among other peoples, other languages; their citizenship surely ought to reflect it.

Something more than the marked conviction with which I talked through a pastiche of languages, almost stuttering, must have caused my traveling companion to be visibly shaken, as he became increasingly alarmed, as if what I said had unexpectedly assaulted him with images of newcomers invading, contaminating, unsettling, with their strange *coutumes*, the logocentric equilibrium of his world.

For I began to detect in what he was saying a disparagement of this foreign blood. Thus, as he spoke, my mind wandered. And I thought of my relations with whom I'd been that very morning, and the previous day, in Lyon. And again I saw the golden, unstrained olive oil in the pop bottle, and the dark red sun-dried tomatoes in the dish, and the long braid of garlic hanging on the drab wall of their kitchenette. And all those crusty, bitter and sweet tastes from the hills of Calabria that had mingled in my mouth at their dinner table in this other country came back to me now, even as the eloquent professor spoke of North Africans and Arabs, Asians and Southern Europeans, and all that squalor, and that chaos of peoples in the vagrant quarters of his city.

And now the enviable picture of refinement he made in his rosy custom-tailored suit reminded me of the card game I had played after dinner with my cousin, dealing out hands of *scupa* as we'd done in short-trousers as kids in the village — our healthy thighs and limbs straddling a stone parapet by the dirt road — my cousin having to contend with the game now as an adult with what was left of his hand. Left thumb, index and middle fingers gone. Lost at the cutting table of the garment factory where he still worked in Lyon.

Our city, said the professor. *Notre pays*, he said again. *Les étrangers*, he kept repeating. And each time the distance between our worlds and my dislike for him grew. Intensified.

And when toward the end of his lecturing me, as he got up to leave the train, the pitch of his baleful voice turned metallic, giving way to that characteristic grin seen on wax pieces, seen on the face of those who disparage the besieged in their midst, the whole affront filled me with disgust.

...[A]nd I remember that already earlier on a similar sensation was in me, even before I began to write. This too I read in Rilke.

It dawned on me, in fact, that what this man had said more or less obliquely, I had heard before, but put more explicitly. It had been in my own city, in Ottawa, and from another professor, an outspoken nationalist renowned in Canada. He had invited my undergraduate class from Carleton University to a Christmas party at his home. I remembered it was December, not two months after the October Crisis of 1970. A biting cold outside. But here, in that image of my professor's Victorian living-room that resurfaced in me now years later, in a moving train in Europe, a log blazed in the fireplace....

...And there was my professor's voice again, its metallic ring similar to the one I'd heard all afternoon. His grin, too, had drifted back onto this other professor's face. The same grin that turns asymmetrically, at once away and toward us on the periphery, as when I heard my own professor tell an anecdote as if from the summit of some regnant world within the world, from the world that officiates over our plural world. Again I saw the leer that turns all plural societies into two worlds — of insiders and outsiders — thus generating the world we know, of orphans, of strangers...

At the party, he told the young gathering an anecdote, and this in reply to a remark I made, naively, about Canadian labor unions' coldness toward recent immigrants. "*It serves them right,*" he snapped, Imagine, he went on like a polished actor, well-rehearsed — I had just returned from the States to Alberta to teach, after graduating, and on my way to class early one morning, I happen on these two obese women all draped in black who were yelling at the top of their lungs to each other in some foreign tongue across the full length of the bus I was riding, completely oblivious to the rest of us. *God forbid*, said the professor, *I thought: Why, in this last war our soldiers had died trying to defeat them in Sicily, and here they are again, the very same clans, taking over Edmonton*!

I was in my youth then, hardly out of my teens, the height of sensitivity, of fragility for an immigrant boy. And that boy with the crumpled forehead, walking out of that festive Victorian house, walking back out alone in the cold, walking back along Bronson Avenue, down Gladstone, among the immigrants' dwellings, walking home to a clapboard house on Lebreton Street, knew, even in his silence (for to say it then the new language had lacked the words), that the city where he had grown up to be what he was — and if he'd scrubbed your tires, submerged to the waist in the icy ditch of a car wash, in winter; if he'd baked your unsavory sliced white bread, his pimples sizzling, in the face of the infernal glow of the oven-door at the Morrison-Lamothe bakery, in summer — was his city just as much.

...That night, before arriving in Liège where I would no longer recognize my grandfather's youngest offspring, in the train compartment, suspended in the purple glare of a window, I saw myself truly as the other saw me. They say that to see oneself truly at one given moment even as your oppressors see you is thereby to be cleansed of the self-loathing you have internalized from them. To be certain, I wanted to remember to give it back.

I scribbled it down in braided verses, the self-deprecating image — *grinner grinning faces for me (fish purpled for the bubbled pool)* — in the margins of *The Notebooks* that still held open in my hands — *turned and see, and the cheeks (frog's skin) hang at the tremble of a bushy lip* — like the ancestral dish grandmother held poised in moonlight to fend against all the lovelessness in the world.

---

[1] English translation: "Seven loaves and seven fish, make the evil eye vanish."

'Merica: An Exhibition

Cosimo Palagiano, Cristiano Pesaresi,
*Riccardo Morri, Riccardo Russo**
University of Rome

---

1. *Introduction*

In conjunction with the Conference, *'Merica: Culture and Literature of Italians in North America*, held on January 23 to January 25, 2005, an exhibition was organized by the Department of Human Geography of the University of Rome, "La Sapienza." The aim of this exhibition was to offer a visual record of the long and difficult journey that Italian emigrants faced in order to reach America.

Some of the aspects that were highlighted included the kind of nutrition available to them during the journey and some of the hazards that their journey entailed; for example, the diseases that they frequently contracted en route. Their arrival on Ellis Island, where they were held in vast halls, was also documented, as was the subsequent quarantine that constituted a normal part of arrival in America. The life that these immigrants led once they settled in New York and other American cities was in overcrowded neighborhoods and in generally poor living conditions. Some of these elements are still a prevailing characteristic of Italian-American life. In letters written by Italian immigrants to their relatives in Italy we learn that the strongest links to their native country were their language, their religion and their cuisine. These links have remained just as powerful to this day and the well-known attachment of Italian-Americans to their mother country also forms the foundation for the close relationship that exists between Italy and the United States.

Another goal of the exhibition was to reveal parallels evident between the past immigration of Italians to the Americas and the current immigration to Italy of people from Eastern Europe, the Balkan Peninsula, Western and Eastern Asia and North Africa. A comparison of the two waves of immigration shows us that there is indeed very little difference between them in their lifestyle, health and poverty level. With respect to the occupations that these immigrants practiced, we note that Italians performed useful functions in society despite the fact that Italian films such as *Sciuscià* frequently showed them practicing humble trades such as polishing shoes. However, the present immigrants to Italy are often to be found washing car windows at intersections for a charitable pittance.

The exhibition consisted of 9 sections, which are as follows: The "Great Migration"; The Journey; The Landing: Ellis Island; Daily Life; Work in America; The Role of Movies; Emigrants' Letters; Nicola Sacco and Bartolomeo Vanzetti; New Immigrants at the Beginning of the 21st century.

Fig. 1 – *The Emigrants* (Angiolo Tommasi). National Gallery of Modern Art. Rome, Italy.

2. *The "Great Migration"*

Like many other European countries, Italy experienced a period of significant emigration that coincided with the unification of the country; that is, from the end of the nineteenth to the beginning of the twentieth century millions of Italians left their families and their familiar lives. Today most people believe that international migration meant traveling exclusively across the oceans, with a large number of Southern Italians going to North and Latin America looking for better opportunity (Brunetta, 2001). However, until the United States, Brazil and Argentina also started to attract Italian immigrants in 1885, the principal host countries were actually France, Germany, the Austro-Hungarian Empire and Switzerland. Between 1900 and the First World War this phenomenon reached its peak, with approximately 600,000 departures per year; altogether the United States received more than 3,000,000 Italian immigrants (Bonifazi, 1998).

Several concomitant events — the economic and demographic crises in the production systems of the alpine areas, the extreme subdivision of land, increasing economic pressure, the decline in the practice of traditional crafts, the hope of finding some real improvement in living conditions and opportunities for work — combined to spur this national exodus. As described by historical documentation and supplemented by photographic evidence, we experience the pathos of dramatic farewells, the oftentimes distressing arrival in the new land, the daily problems the new immigrants encountered and the struggle not to be overwhelmed by homesickness.

Close examination of the choices made by the various regional groups reveals that southern Italians generally preferred to go to North America while those from the northern regions favored Latin America. Ligurians and Piedmontese, for example constituted a significant presence in Argentina and Venetians went mainly to Brazil.

These choices were influenced by three relevant factors:

- previous immigrant flows
- information from the "new countries"
- job opportunities and their correspondence to the personal skills and experience of the prospective emigrants

The length of the projected stay abroad frequently influenced the choice of occupation, because the immigrant could decide either to leave Italy at once taking his family with him or to emigrate alone and work intensively in the new country for some months in order to maximize his income. This typical feature of migration especially relates to travel to South America and because it is reminiscent of the seasonal trips of migratory birds across the hemispheres, was whimsically referred to as "The Little Swallow One" (Migliorini, 1962), At any rate, emigration, by definition refers to a definitive move to a foreign country even when temporary mobility has preceded it as indeed it did in many cases. Thus the Italian Foreign Office calculates that of the approximately 58. 5 million people of Italian origin living abroad, a great majority of them are in North America (16.1 million, of which 15.5 million live in the United States) and Latin America (39.8 millions).

3. *The journey*

The journey to America generally lasted between thirty and forty days. The poor sanitary conditions on the ships were characterized by overcrowding, excessive proximity, and a lack of light, air and food (Di Paolo, 2001). The ships, but most especially the sleeping quarters, were so contaminated with germs as to constitute a health hazard even to the healthy passengers. Indeed, it was not unknown for passengers to die from the appalling conditions prevailing (Molinari 1988; 1996; 2002).

A brief extract from a naval hygiene treatise written by Carlo Maria Belli (who in 1905 described the hygienic-sanitary conditions faced by immigrants during transoceanic crossings) will help us to better understand the risks and hazards of the trip: "The danger of contracting diseases increases with the length of stay aboard, not only because a longer trip creates more opportunities for the direct transmission of pathologic organisms as a result of the extreme proximity of the travelers, but mostly because the journey weakens the organism, thus increasing the possibility of illness" (Belli, 1905). Hence it is not surprising to learn from a medical officer's journal that, "Temperature is not the only factor that renders the atmosphere unbreathable; other contributing factors are the vapor and carbon dioxide emitted through breathing, and the noxious airborne agents trapped on the bodies and in the clothing of the men, women and children who, as a result either of fear or laziness, do not hesitate to release urine and faeces in a corner. The cabin's stench is such that the staff often refuses to go in and wash the floor" (*Relazione sanitaria piroscafo «Republic», viaggio da Napoli a New York e ritorno*, 22 marzo – 27 aprile 1905). Data and descriptions emerging from various historical and statistical sources show the ships transporting immigrants to be "real floating hospitals" (Molinari, 2002), where viruses and infectious diseases lived and thrived (cholera, typhoid fever, chicken pox, small pox, tuberculosis, syphilis, trachoma, etc.).

In order to assist immigrants, several organizations were founded between the end of 19th century and the beginning of 20th century. Among these we find: the Congregation of the Scalabrinian Missionaries, the Humanitarian Society, the Bonomelli's Aid Organization, and the Commission for Emigration. The involvement of this last institution was particularly wide: it ranged from providing general assistance to the immigrants to the protection of women and children; from the repression of illegal immigration to the dissemination of useful and reliable news regarding migratory flows. (Di Paolo, 2001). One of the most delicate and important tasks of the Commission for Emigration was the protection of immigrants' health and the prevention of conditions that might lead to expulsion from the destination countries, for ordinary or extraordinary reasons. The specific protection adopted involved two different aspects: sanitary-immunity defense before departure and hygienic-sanitary assistance during the oceanic crossing.

4. *Disembarkation: Ellis Island*

For about six decades, from 1892 to 1954, immigrants who disembarked in the United States were subject to medical and legal evaluations, which took place at Ellis Island. Travelers arriving in New York were divided into groups of about thirty people each and transported to Ellis Island, where they were individually examined in order to ascertain their general state of health, the possible presence of diseases, disabilities, mental problems, and their suitability for admission into the United States. Only those who were particularly healthy both physically and mentally could be expected to successfully cope with the difficulties associated with the hard work and the risks of a radical change of lifestyle, a life that even under the best of circumstances remained in many ways traumatic.

Given these considerations, it is obvious that an immigrant afflicted with any of these weaknesses or disabilities, and exposed to illness or psychological stress, would be regarded as "a socially useless body for which neither the country of destination nor the country of origin would be willing to provide" (Molinari, 2002). The trepidation and uncertainty experienced by immigrants waiting to learn their fate, that is, whether they would be admitted to the Promised Land or turned away, no doubt gave rise to the well-known soubriquet for Ellis Island as the Island of Tears.

Immigrants labeled unsanitary were considered an economic burden and a threat to the national social and moral welfare. To avoid these risks, controls had to be particularly severe and in 1882 a federal decree was issued forbidding admission to disturbed and mentally ill minorities, who were to be immediately repatriated. Then, with the 1903 Act, entry to people with epilepsy and anyone who had suffered from mental problems during five years prior to arrival in the United States was forbidden. Later, with the Act of 1907, the prohibition was extended to anyone who was affected by physical and mental defects that would compromise or reduce their ability to work (Molinari, 2002).

Between 1892 and 1920 approximately 16 million people passed through Ellis Island, from 5,000 to 10,000 per day (Di Paolo, 2001). However, not all immigrants were forced to pass through Ellis Island. Those who traveled in first or second class, in fact, were examined directly on the ship and, if considered fit, were allowed to disembark in New York without further evaluation. Those immigrants who were processed at Ellis Island were in fact the third class passengers who were deemed to have been at particular risk of exposure to viruses and infectious diseases during the oceanic crossing.

The main hall of the central building was considered the most significant area on Ellis Island. The ground floor was used as storage for the luggage that the immigrants could claim only after having gone through all the stages of inspection. On the second floor was the registration room known as "the Great Hall." The central staircase, connecting the first and second floors, also divided the second floor into two sections: the eastern section, used for medical exams and evaluations and the western part, used for legal purposes. The floor above, also known as the "Balcony Floor," was the site of more meticulous medical examinations and psychological evaluations.

Ellis Island was closed on Friday, November 12, 1954. Since 1990 it has become a national monument and it houses a museum where the visitor can become acquainted with and relive its history.

5. *Daily life and work in America*

After having successfully negotiated all the formalities of admission to the country, the new immigrant had to face another even more daunting undertaking, entry into the social and work-related American life. It was not unusual during this period to find that Italians, (indeed each national group) tended to settle, at least at first, in fairly concentrated geographic spaces. The aim of this chosen segregation was to facilitate daily collaboration and solidarity, the maximizing of resources and the preservation of cultural identity.

For many years Italian neighborhoods were associated with the tenements and cold-water flats (lacking individual bathrooms) located in narrow, dark and foul alleys. Most of these tenements, on streets teeming with peddlers and hawkers, were crumbling and overcrowded with poorly dressed men and women, and children who were nearly in rags (Garroni, 2002).

The great emigration saw millions of peasants, construction workers, craftsmen, merchants and specialized workers attempt to assimilate themselves into American life and to adapt their "old world" skills to the "new world" requirements. Many of these vendors, artists and craftsmen plying their trades on American soil were deeply committed to keeping Italian customs and traditions alive abroad and they thus introduced their customs and practices into their newly-adopted cities.

Although the new Italian immigrants were unfamiliar with some of the new occupations that they found in America, they predominated in those with which they were already familiar. Thus they constituted a strong presence as masons, stonecutters, mechanics, barbers, shoemakers, seamstresses and shoeshine boys In particular, more than half of all masons who immigrated to the United States were Italian, and only Jewish immigrants coming from Russia could compete with the Italian tailors and seamstresses (Audenino, 2002). The ease with which Italian barbers found employment was also impressive, as was the great demand for Italian waiters, and above all, cooks, in the restaurant industry.

6. *The role of movies*

In the field of popular culture actors and directors made vital contributions. They were instrumental in perpetuating a real sense of cultural identity and ideally situated to pass on the incredibly rich heritage of knowledge and the values of their native country. Nevertheless, from the American perspective, the positive attributes of Italian actors and directors who had emigrated to the United States were at best considered negligible; more frequently they were associated with negative stereotypes involving ignorance, violence, crime and other forms of immoral or illegal behaviors. Still, a cursory glance at the period's actors and directors shows a significant number of Italian-Americans such as Tina Modotti, Rodolfo Valentino, Frank Capra, Frank Sinatra and Gregory La Cava. Movies and actors functioned as a privileged repository of collective memory, allowing viewers to travel in space and time, and to perceive and internalize, in a ready and practical manner, elements of cultural identity that would be otherwise difficult to discern (Brunetta, 2001). In this way, movies allowed immigrants to achieve two extraordinarily important objectives at the same time: becoming acquainted with their ancestors' land and retrieving a sense of cultural identity, often stifled by American customs.

7. *Immigrants' letters*

The steamboats and ships that crossed the ocean during the "great emigration" transported not only immigrants but also "heavy cargoes of lived and narrated tales" (Gibelli and Caffarena, 2001). Mario Soldati has powerfully defined the travel by sea that brought immigrants to new shores as "an extraordinary movement through space of a piece of the country people leave behind" (Soldati, 2000). What's more, a remarkable amount of written correspondence traveled with the men, women and children who left their country (Gibelli and Caffarena, 2001).

Letters were practically the only way to communicate at a distance and to maintain or re-establish contact with loved ones. Their often hybrid character, bordering between spoken and written language, and the simple and spontaneous sentences showed an enormous need for contact with people of one's own language and origins, in order to share anxieties and the need to communicate. Indeed, these letters functioned for the writers as an attempt to recover the abruptly interrupted ties and to preserve as much as possible the environment they left behind. We find therefore, a movement of people in one direction and a flow of letters in the opposite one.

Feelings of homesickness and painful separation were the elements that most frequently characterized immigrants' letters, and the repeated mention, for example, of home-cooked meals assumed a strong symbolic meaning of search for their origins and a recuperation of their identity. Besides these psychological and socio-cultural functions, however, we must remember the fundamentally practical and informative purpose of these letters, an extremely necessary one in order to communicate one's location to loved ones and to supply indispensable information regarding the immigrants' health status (Gibelli and Caffarena, 2001). Therefore, while home smells and tastes had the great benefit to momentarily erase distance, through immediate but highly evocative sensations, on the other hand, papers and photographs were clear evidence of health status and of a life that, although difficult, was still going on.

8. *Nicola Sacco and Bartolomeo Vanzetti*

Thousands of different human interest stories were to be found within the community of Italian immigrants to the United States. Among them there were tales of suffering and poverty, some recounting discrimination and racial prejudice. The story of two anarchist Italian immigrants, Sacco and Vanzetti, is one of these.

Nicola Sacco, shoemaker and Bartolomeo Vanzetti, street fishmonger, were accused of murder and armed robbery in South Braintree, Massachusetts in 1920. They proclaimed themselves innocent. It did not seem possible to prove their guilt on the base of the existing evidence, yet after a long trial they were condemned and executed in Boston in 1927. Thousands of people came from all over the United States to be present at their funerals.

After more than eighty years since that dramatic judicial event, public opinion throughout the world is still absorbed by it. Different political convictions, different beliefs, and perhaps some biases, circulate around the story, but two important questions endure: were those poor Italian immigrants truly guilty? Was the trial conducted in a fair manner?

It is significant to consider that this question, now forever fated to remain unanswered, has nevertheless been kept alive to the present time. Nothing can be done nowadays for Nicola Sacco and Bartolomeo Vanzetti, but the memory of what happened to them can still help present and future generations in the difficult job of building an ever fairer society without prejudice and abuse of power.

To keep the memory of that story alive, we wish to end this section by quoting from the public statement written by Vanzetti before his execution.

> "Ho questo da dire: non augurerei né a un cane né a una serpe, e neanche alla più disgraziata creatura sulla terra, di patire quello che io ho patito per cose delle quali non sono colpevole. Ma c'è qualcosa di cui sono colpevole. Io sono un radicale e lo sono veramente. E ho pagato per questo. Io sono un italiano e lo sono veramente. E ho pagato anche per questo. Ho sofferto assai più per la mia famiglia e per i miei amici che per me stesso. Ma sappiate che sono così convinto di essere nel giusto, che se voi poteste togliermi la vita due volte e poteste ridarmela altrettante, io vivrei per rifare esattamente ciò che ho fatto".
>
> Bartolomeo Vanzetti

9. *New immigrants at the beginning of 21st century*

Italian migration increased again after the Second World War and it remained a major movement until the beginning of the 1970s, when economic and industrial crises changed production processes and patterns, defining a different allocation of activities and labor.

The migratory total balance (difference between departures and returns) showed a negative result (about 314,000) for the period between 1946 and 1970. While departure towards transoceanic destinations (2,178,000) seemed to be a definitive solution, the movements of labor and their families to other destinations in Europe (4,533,000) showed a higher number of returns.

The reversal of this trend was witnessed in the 1970s, as indicated by the Italian Population Census of 1981, which showed that there was a continuous increase of returns with a concomitant decrease of departures and the first significant arrival of foreign people. These factors worked together to produce the first positive demographic balance of the migratory patterns, generating a positive difference of about 270,000 people.

But the real "explosion" of immigration occurred during the early 1990s, because of the geographic position and political role that Italy played in the European setting at the end of the century. For, as a result of the sudden lack of a political and socio-economic balance in the Balkans, and the progress made in the ongoing process of political and economic unification of Europe (i.e. the European Union), Italy became a safe haven and a gateway into Europe.

Thus, new national and ethnic groups joined the "traditional" foreign presence in Italy, which up to that point had consisted mainly of African and Eastern Asian citizens (fig. 2). The exodus of people from ex-Yugoslavia and Albania served to revive the images and stories that paralleled the Italian migratory experiences lived almost 100 years before. However, this development is often not given sufficient weight because the media has fostered an inaccurate perception of the numbers. It is important to underline that although the foreign presence has increased, it is still much lower than in other European countries, at least at this time.

The changing demographic structure of the Italian population, the community life of the different cultural, linguistic and religious groups, intercultural living and spatial segregation, the changing job markets in the context of the globalization process, these are all issues that need to be explored and scrutinized in order to gain a wider understanding of the broad situation.

These issues in all their complexity can no longer be disregarded by people like Italians, whose history has been so marked by migratory events.

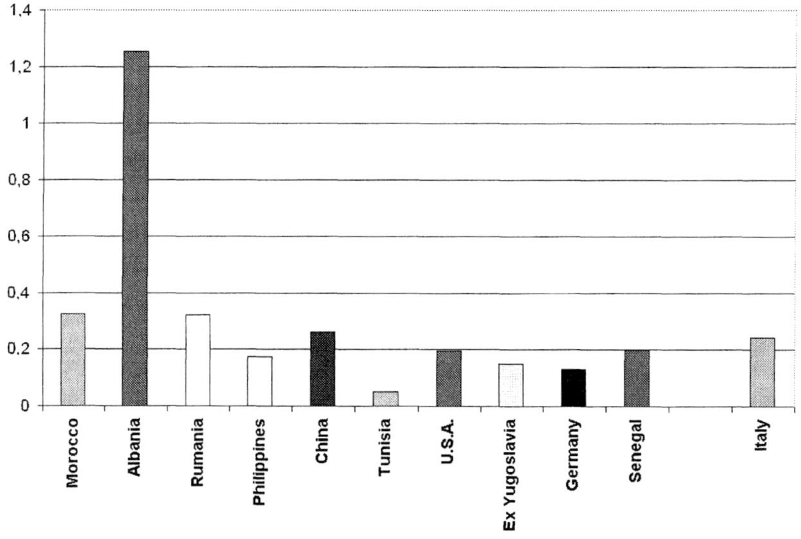

Fig. 2 - Top 10 foreign communities in Italy (1996 - 2001) shown in percentages. (1 = 100%) Source: Caritas, 1997; 2002.

* This paper has been jointly written by all authors. Prof. Cosimo Palagiano as co-ordinator has written the introduction, Cristiano Pesaresi, sections 3, 4, 5, 6, 7, Riccardo Morri, sections 2 and 9, Riccardo Russo, section 8.

Translated by Grace Russo Bullaro, C.U.N.Y., Lehman College

References

AA.VV. Images. *A Pictorial History of Italian Americans*. New York, NY: The Center for Migration Studies of New York, 1986.

AA.VV. *Migrazioni. Scenari per il XXI secolo. I – II.* Rome, Italy: Agenzia romana per la preparazione del Giubileo, 2000.

Audenino, Patrizia. "Mestieri e professioni degli emigrati". Piero Bevilacqua, Andreina De Clementi, and Emilio Franzina (eds.). *Storia dell'emigrazione italiana. Arrivi*. Rome, Italy: Donzelli, 2002, 335-354.

Belli, Carlo Maria. *Igiene navale. Manuale per i medici di bordo, ufficiali, naviganti e costruttori*. Milan, Italy: Hoepli, 1905.

Bonifazi, Corrado. *L'immigrazione straniera in Italia*, Bologna, Italy: Il Mulino, 1998.

Brunetta, GianPiero. "Emigranti nel cinema italiano e americano". Piero Bevilacqua, Andreina De Clementi, and Emilio Franzina (eds.). *Storia dell'emigrazione italiana. Partenze*. Rome, Italy: Donzelli, 2001, 489-514.

Caritas di Roma. *Immigrazione. Dossier statistico '97*. Rome, Italy: anterem, 1997.

Caritas – Migrantes. *Immigrazione. Dossier Statistico 2002*. Rome, Italy: anterem, 2002.

Commissariato Generale dell'Emigrazione (ed.). *Annuario statistico della emigrazione italiana dal 1876 al 1925*. Rome, Italy, MCMXXVI, anno V .

Corti, Paola. *L'emigrazione*. Rome, Italy: Editori Riuniti, 1999.

Di Paolo, Nino. *Emigrazione: da Ellis Island ai giorni nostri*. Salerno, Italy: Edizioni del Paguro, 2001.

Garroni, Maria Susanna. "Little Italies". Piero Bevilacqua, Andreina De Clementi, and Emilio Franzina (eds.). *Storia dell'emigrazione italiana. Arrivi*. Rome, Italy: Donzelli, 2002, 207-233.

Gibelli, Antonio and Fabio Caffarena. "Le lettere degli emigranti". Piero Bevilacqua, Andreina De Clementi, and Emilio Franzina (eds.). *Storia dell'emigrazione italiana. Partenze*. Rome, Italy: Donzelli, 2001, 563-574.

Migliorini, Elio. *Migrazioni interne e spostamenti territoriali della popolazione italiana*. Atti del Congresso Geografico Italiano. vol. 1. Trieste, Italy, 1962, 365-409.

Molinari, Augusta. *Le navi di Lazzaro. Aspetti sanitari dell'emigrazione transoceanica italiana: il viaggio per mare*, Milan, Italy: Franco Angeli, 1988.

_______. *Medicina e sanità a Genova nel primo Novecento*. Milan, Italy: Selene, 1996.

_______. "La salute". Piero Bevilacqua, Andreina De Clementi, and Emilio Franzina (eds.). *Storia dell'emigrazione italiana. Arrivi*. Rome, Italy: Donzelli, 2002, 377-395.

Pugliese, Enrico. "L'Italia tra migrazioni internazionali e migrazioni interne". AA.VV., *Migrazioni. Scenari per il XXI secolo*. Rome, Italy: Agenzia romana per la preparazione del Giubileo, 2000, II, 751-814.

Relazione sanitaria piroscafo «Republic», viaggio da Napoli a New York e ritorno (22 marzo - 27 aprile 1905). Rome, Italy: Ministero dell'Interno, DGSP, b. 984.

Russell, Francis. *La tragedia di Sacco e Vanzetti*. Italy: Mursia, 1966.

Soldati, Mario. *America primo amore*. Milan, Italy: Rizzoli, 2000.

Vezzosi, Elisabetta. "Sciopero e rivolta. Le organizzazioni operaie italiane negli Stati Uniti". Piero Bevilacqua, Andreina De Clementi, and Emilio Franzina (eds.). *Storia dell'emigrazione italiana. Arrivi*. Rome, Italy: Donzelli, 2002, 271- 282.

CONTRIBUTORS

B. Amore is an artist, educator and writer who has spent her life between Italy and America. Founder and Director Emerita of the Carving Studio and Sculpture Center in Vermont, she has won major sculpture commissions in the US and Japan. Her most recent multi-media exhibit, "Lifeline – filo della vita," is traveling in the US and Italy. The book, *An Italian American Odyssey* will be published by the Center for Migration Studies in October 2006.

Monica Barni is researcher of Philosophy of Theory of Languages at the Italian Language and Culture Faculty of the University for Foreigners of Siena, where she teaches Semiotics and Language Testing until 2002. She is Director of the Center for Certification of Italian as a Foreign Language (CILS) and coordinates a Research line in the Center of Excellence for Research "Permanent Linguistic Observatory of the Italian language among Foreigners and of Immigrant Languages in Italy" of the University for Foreigners of Siena.

William Boelhower, currently on leave from the University of Padua, Italy, is teaching Atlantic Studies at Louisiana State University, Baton Rouge. Boelhower, an editor of the journal "Atlantic Studies," has published in the areas of immigrant and ethnic literatures, has translated the work of Antonio Gramsci and Lucien Goldmann, and most recently has written on biopolitics, migrants, and globalization. He is the Vice President of the European Association MESEA.

Fulvio Caccia, a critic, poet and novelist, won the Canadian Governor General's Award in 1994 for his poetry collection Aknos. He lives presently in Paris after having lived in Canada for thirty years. He his also the author of La ligne Gothique, a novel (2004), La chasse spirituelle, poetry (2005) and La coïncidence, a novel (2005).

Francesco Durante is the author of "Italoamericana. Storia e letteratura degli italiani negli Stati Uniti" (Mondadori, 2001 and 2005). He has edited the anthology "Figli di due mondi" (Avagliano, 2002) and the collections of John Fante's "Romanzi e racconti" (Mondadori, 2003) and Domenico Rea's "Opere" (Mondadori, 2005). He has translated works by Fante, Bret Easton Ellis, Raymond Carver, William Somerset Maugham and others. He is professor of Comparative Literature in the University of Salerno.

Emilio Franzina is Professor of Contemporary History at the University of Verona with special interests in the social and regional history of Italy. In the last thirty years, he has focussed his scholarly interests on the history of emigration and the history of people of Italian origin abroad. Among his many publications on these issues it is important to note *La grande emigrazione* (Marsilio 1976), *Merica! Merica! Emigrazione e colonizzazione nelle lettere dei contadini veneti in America Latina, 1876-1902* (Fetrinelli 1979), *L'immaginario degli emigranti* (Pagus 1992), *Gli italiani al nuovo mondo. L'emigrazione italiana in America, 1492-1942* (Mondadori 1995), *Dall'Arcadia in America, 1840-1950* (Edizioni della Fondazione G.Agnelli), *La storia altrove. Casi nazionali e casi regionali nelle moderne migrazioni di massa* (Cierre 1998). T ogether w ith P . Be vilacqua e a A. De Clementi, recently he has edited *Storia dell'emigrazione italiana* (Donzelli 2001-2002).

Fred Gardaphé is Professor of Italian American studies and directs Stony Brook University's American and Italian American Studies programs. His books include *Italian Signs, American Streets: The Evolution of Italian American Narrative, Dagoes Read: Tradition and the Italian American Writer, Moustache Pete is Dead!, Leaving Little Italy, and From Wiseguys to Wise Men: The Gangster and Italian American Masculinities.* He is co-founding/co-editor of *VIA: Voices in Italian Americana* and editor of the Italian American Culture Series of SUNY Press.

Alessandro Gebbia is Associate Professor of English at the University of Rome "La Sapienza." He has written extensively on American, Canadian and English fiction, poetry and Theater History, and he is the author of a "History of Canadian Literature in English", (the first in Italy) included in *Le orme di Prospero. Le nuove letterature di lingua inglese: Africa, Caraibi, Canada*, edited by Agostino Lombardo. His latest book, *Cartografie del*

Nuovissimo Mondo. Studi di letteratura anglo-canadese, has been published by Bulzoni Editore.

Jerome Krase, Emeritus and Murray Koppelman Professor, Brooklyn College CUNY, won *Italian Americana's* 2005 Monsignor Gino Baroni Award. Books include *Self and Community in the Cit*, *Ethnicity and Machine Politics*, *Italian Americans in a Multicultural Society*, and *Race and Ethnicity in New York City*. He was President of the American Italian Historical Association, Founding Member of the American Italian Coalition of Organizations, and Director of the Center for Italian American Studies at Brooklyn College.

Martino Marazzi teaches Italian Literature at the State University of Milan and has been a Fellow of the Italian Academy at Columbia University. He is the author of *Voices of Italian America* (Fairleigh Dick-inson UP 2004), *Misteri di Little Italy* (2001), *La narrativa risorgimentale di Giovanni Ruffini* (1999), *Little America* (1997), and the curator of Giovanni Ruffini, *Lorenzo Benoni* (De Ferrari 2006), Arturo Giovannitti, *Parole e sangue* (Iannone 2005), Michael Fiaschetti, *Gioco duro* (2003), Efrem Bartoletti, *Poesie* (2001). He's currently working on an essay on the language of Italian immigrants and at the edition of the collected letters by Cavour.

Sebastiano Martelli is full professor of Italian literature at the University of Salerno. Scholar of the Eighteen century — on which he published the volume, *La floridezza di un reame. Circolazione e persistenza della cultura illuministica meridionale* (1996) — and of the Eighteenth-Nineteenth century, in the last years he devoted himself in particular to the study of the Italian Literature of emigration. On this topic, after the first volume *Letteratura contaminata. Storie, parole, immagini tra Otto-Novecento* (1994) he published several essays in Italy and abroad, among these: *Il sogno italo-americano*(1998); *Dal vecchio mondo al sogno americano. Realtà e immaginario dell'emigrazione nella Letteratura italiana* (2001). He edited for Einaudi the novel *Tiro al piccione* by Rimanelli and for Sellerio the edition *Noi gli Aria* by Bontempelli.

Antonino Mazza was awarded the 2001 Grotteria Prize *"per il pregevole impegno artistico in memoria antropologica della tradizione multietnica calabrese"* for his poetry collection *La nostra casa è in un orecchio cosmico* (Monteleone editore, 1998), and the 1992 Italo Calvino Prize, Columbia University, for his translation *Pier Paolo Pasolini Poetry (Exile Editions, 1991)*. His reissue of *The City Without Women: A Chronicle of Internment Life in Canada During World War II* (Mosaic Press, 1994), won the Brutium "Calabria" Gold Medal in Rome and inspired the National Film Board of Canada documentary film *Barbed Wire and Mandolins* (1997). He lives in Ottawa.

Riccardo Morri is Ph.D in "Geografia storica" and he is expertise in Geography at the University of Rome "La Sapienza." His main interests concern mobility and urban geography. In 2006 he has published a book on seasonal migratory flows.

Cosimo Palagiano is full professor of geography and the Head of the Department of Human Geography at the University of Rome "La Sapienza." He is member of Steering Committee of the Home of Geography of the International Geographical Union. The topics of his researches are: the Medical Geography and the History of Cartography.

Cristiano Pesaresi is attending the last year of Ph.D in "Geografia economica" and he is expertise in Geography at the University of Rome "La Sapienza." His main interests concern Medical Geography, demographic and social-economic analysis of Italian mountains and volcano risk and hazard. In the last years he has published several papers on these subjects.

Riccardo Russo is Ph.D in "Applicazioni territoriali della geografia" and he is expertise in Geography at the University of Rome "La Sapienza." He is particularly interested in the problems of the developing Countries and in the use of audio and video recording in geographical research.

Marcello Saija is Full Professor of History of Political Institutions and Director of the Department of International and European Studies at the Faculty of Political Sciences, University of Messina, where he teaches

History of International Relations. His main interests refer to institutions, Italian political system, history of emigration and the Balkans in the 20th century. He had visiting professor at the New York State University at Stony Brook.

Cosma Siani teaches English Language and Translation at the University of Cassino. He contributes to the Italian book-review monthly *L'Indice dei libri del mese*, and among other books has authored *Libri all'*Indice *e altri*, a collection of reviews (2001), and *Le lingue dell'altrove. Storia testi e bibliografia di Joseph Tusiani* (2004).

Frank Sturino is an Associate Professor of History and Coordinator of the History and Canadian Studies Programs, Atkinson School of Arts and Letters, York University, Toronto, Canada. He was coordinator of the Mariano Elia Chair in Italian-Canadian Studies, York University 1983-1993. Sturino has written several articles on Italian immigration to North America, including chapter on "Italians in Canada" in the *Encyclopedia of Canada's Peoples*, University of Toronto, 1999. His major book is *Forging the Chain: A Case Study of Italian Immigration to North America, 1880-1930*, (Multicultural History Society of Ontario, 1990) and his latest book is *The Lucky Immigrant: The Public Life of Fortunato Rao*, edited with Nicholas Harney (Toronto, 2001).

Rudy Vecoli is now Professor Emeritus of History, having retired after 38 years of teaching and serving as director of the Immigration History Research Center. The Rudolph J. Vecoli Chair in Immigration History has been established at the University of Minnesota; Donna Gabaccia, the first occupant, succeeded Vecoli as director of the IHRC. Vecoli is busy writing a biography of Captain Celso Cesare Moreno, nineteenth century soldier of fortune, whose career spanned the Pacific and Atlantic oceans.

Massimo Vedovelli is full professor of Language and Didactics at the Italian Language and Culture Faculty of the University for Foreigners of Siena, where he also taught Semiotics until 2004. He has been the Director of the Center for Certification of Italian as a Foreign Language (CILS) and Director of the Center of Excellence for Research "Permanent Linguistic

Observatory of the Italian language in circulation among Foreigners and of Immigrant Languages in Italy." He has been Rector of the University for Foreigners of Siena since November 1, 2004.

Pasquale Verdicchio teaches at the University of California, San Diego. His books include *Devils in Paradise: Essays on Post-emigrant Cultures* (Guernica: 1998) and *Bound by Distance: Rethinking Nationalism through the Italian Diaspora* (Fairleigh Dickinson, 1997). He is a translator of Pasolini, Porta, Merini, Caproni, Zanzotto and Gramsci.

Robert Viscusi, Broeklundian Professor and Executive Officer of the Wolfe Institute for the Humanities at Brooklyn College has published *Buried Caesars, and Other Secrets of Italian American Writing* (SUNY PRess, 2006); the novel *Astoria* (Guernica Editions 1995; American Book Award 1996); a collection of poems, *A New Geography of Time* (Guernica 2004); and the long poem *An Oration upon the Most Recent Death of Chirstopher Columbus* (VIA Folios 1993).